STAN
THE MAN
Musial

TO JOE ZAZYCZNY

ANOTHER PENNSYLVANIA
POLE.

9-3-94   Thad Cooke

Born to Be a Ballplayer

Jerry Lansche

TAYLOR PUBLISHING COMPANY
Dallas, Texas

Published by Taylor Publishing Company
                1550 West Mockingbird Lane
                Dallas, TX 75235

Library of Congress Cataloging-in-Publication Data

Lansche, Jerry, 1951–
    Stan the Man Musial : Born to Be a Ballplayer / by Jerry Lansche :
        p.   cm.
    Includes bibliographical references.
    ISBN 0-87833-846-2
    1. Musial, Stan, 1920–   2. Baseball players—United States—
Biography.   I. Title.
GV865.M8L36   1994
796.357′09—dc20
    [B]   93–45459
                                                                           CIP

Printed in the United States of America

10   9   8   7   6   5   4   3   2   1

For my father,
Charles Kenneth Lansche

Acknowledgments

◆─────────────────────

Most people don't bother to read the author's Acknowledgments, and that's a shame. For non-fiction writers, this is the only place in the book where we can cut loose, kick back, and say whatever we want. It's where the author thanks everybody from his first-grade teacher to the guy who kept his computer serviced. (And come to think of it, I *would* like to thank Kevin Dean, my Computer Technician For Life, for building the VIP IBM-compatible computer on which this book was written and getting the blamed thing back up and running early one Sunday morning when the hard drive crashed on me. Mechanical aptitude: never had it, never will.)

My sincere gratitude must go to Jim Donovan, my editor at Taylor Publishing, for his belief in this book and the two or three we tried to write before it. This was the second time I've worked with Jim and despite the fact that he edited out a couple thousand of the best words ever written this side of the Gettysburg Address, it's been a pleasure being associated with him and the good folks at Taylor Publishing.

My heartfelt appreciation goes, once again, to Robert Franklin, for a leg up; to Frederick Ivor-Campbell, one of the nicest guys I know and about as knowledgeable as they come on the subject of baseball; Paul Adomites; Bill Deane; Brian Ellis; Clint Gentry for some timely inspiration; Steve Gietschier; John Holway; Lorena Jones; Shawna Kelly; Herman Krabbenhoft; Grace Laffey; Paul Mathews; Mark Rucker; Ruth Tallman; John Thorn; Jack Whitson; Creative Multimedia Corporation; the Society for American Baseball Research (SABR); WordPerfect Corporation of Orem, Utah; and to George Durnell and the staff at the St. Louis County Library for their frequent assistance repairing the only decent microfilm copier machine when it frequently broke down.

Additional huzzahs go to my lovely bride of more than a decade, Sonia, for all the many things she did that gave me some extra time to work on this book. And finally, thanks to my nine-year-old son, Hunter, a left-handed dead pull hitter, for bragging about me at school and just generally being the neat kid he is.

Contents

16 pages of photographs follow page 116.

STAN
THE MAN
Musial

Introduction

Here stands baseball's perfect warrior.
Here stands baseball's perfect knight.

BASEBALL COMMISSIONER FORD FRICK

◆

How good was Stan Musial?
He was good enough to take your
breath away.

DODGER BROADCASTER VIN SCULLY

Branch Rickey, quoted in the October 12, 1963, issue of *The Sporting News,* said, "That preliminary move Stanley uses at the plate is a fraud. When the ball leaves the pitcher's hand, that is the time you take a picture of a batsman to determine the correctness of his form. Now the ball has been pitched and Stanley takes his true position. He is no longer in a crouch and his bat is full back and so steady a coin wouldn't fall off the end of it. Then the proper stride and the level swing. There is no hitch. He is ideal in form as well as courage."

Hundreds of National and American League hurlers from 1941 through 1963 would attest to the truth of Rickey's description. Hundreds of them stood on the mound, looking in at Stan Musial, many thinking, wrongly, that no batter who looked that silly at the plate could possibly hit the ball. Roger Kahn, writing in 1957, echoed Rickey's opinion. "He stands there," said Kahn, "stooped but graceful, stirring his bat in a low and languid arc. Then, in the instant before the pitcher throws the ball, Musial cocks the bat and crouching severely, twists away from his adversary so that he is staring out of the corners of his eyes. Curled, poised, waiting, Musial is

1

suddenly a cobra coiled for a deadly strike. Even now no one professes to know how to pitch to him. No one likes to try. His bat has shattered each theory as quickly as it was put to test."

More than thirty years after Musial last swung a bat in the major leagues, many baseball fans can still conjure up a picture of the Cardinal legend stepping into the batter's box, planting his left foot on the back line, his right foot twelve inches in front of his left, then loosening up with a few preliminary swings and that distinctive hula-like wiggle. Stan would crouch and come set, peering out over his right shoulder, holding the bat a good two feet from his body. The pitcher would go into his windup, Musial would dip his right knee, and at that moment, in the words of Ted Lyons, he looked like "a small boy looking around a corner to see if the cops are coming."

There was no wasted energy, only a lightning-fast, flat swing that would often result in a line drive somewhere. Eyesight, coordination, instinct, timing, and speed, all God-given talents, combined with Musial's keen judgment and sharp mind to make him the bane of major-league pitchers and the pride of baseball for over twenty years.

In 1986, writing in *The Bill James Historical Baseball Abstract,* Bill James said:

> The image of Musial seems to be fading quickly. Maybe I'm wrong, but it doesn't seem to me that you hear much about him anymore, compared to such comparable stars as Mantle, Williams, Mays and DiMaggio, and to the extent that you do hear of him it doesn't seem that the image is very sharp, that anybody really knows what it was that made him different. He was never colorful, never much of an interview. He makes a better statue. What he was was a ballplayer. He hustled. You look at his career totals of doubles and triples, and they'll remind you of something that was accepted while he was active, and has been largely forgotten since: Stan Musial was one player who always left the batter's box on a dead run.

This book began in June 1992 when my editor at Taylor, Jim Donovan, asked if I'd like to do an autobiography of Honus Wagner, the Hall of Fame shortstop of the Pittsburgh Pirates. Although we eventually abandoned the project, my initial research on Wagner got me thinking about another ballplayer who was similar in many respects, Stan Musial. Like Wagner, who took the field and played superstar baseball day after day better than anyone before or since at his position, Musial's reputation has diminished in recent years because he was so uncontroversial. He was a gentle, God-fearing human being who engendered the admiration of fans everywhere and the affection of people who'd never seen a baseball game in their lives. First of all, the only scandalous events in Stan's career were the two or three salary holdouts to which he treated himself. Secondly, sports coverage was different in Musial's day from what it is now. Sportswriters weren't hanging on a ballplayer's every word back then the way they do now when some two-bit superstar who couldn't hold Stan's glove imparts a precious pearl of wisdom like, "Well, I just tried to stay within myself." Until late in his career, Musial hardly ever got quoted in the newspapers. One of the byproducts of the intense and pervading press coverage afforded the modern ballplayer is that the sheer volume of it tends to makes us forget about the superstars of yesterday.

Stan Musial wasn't a womanizer like the Babe or a mama's boy like Larrupin' Lou. He didn't run out from under his hat like the Say Hey Kid, he didn't marry anybody famous like Joltin' Joe or Leo the Lip, and he never spit at sportswriters like Teddy Ballgame. No backflips like the Wizard, and as near as I could tell from my research, he never had a 900 number like Jose Canseco. (I am rather certain about this.)

Bill James concluded a comparison of Williams and Musial by saying this:

> I think he [Williams] was the second-greatest left-fielder who ever lived. That's not criticism. But if I had to choose between the two of them, I'd take Musial in left field, Musial on the basepaths, Musial in the clubhouse, and Williams only with the wood in his hand. And Stan Musial could hit a little, too.

Could he ever.

When Musial retired, he held almost every conceivable Cardinal record, some fifty major-league and National League marks, seven All-Star Game records, and one World Series record. He was selected to *The Sporting News'* All-Star Major League team twelve times, named the magazine's Player of the Year twice, was the first recipient of *TSN's* Player of the Decade, and owned three National League Most Valuable Player awards. In addition to the many honors he received during his long and distinguished playing career, Stan was feared by major-league pitchers, envied by big-league hitters, and had earned the respect of the baseball world, the adoration of baseball fans, and the friendship of everyone he met.

Here, then, is the career of Cardinal legend Stan the Man Musial, baseball's perfect warrior, baseball's perfect knight.

◇ 1 ◇

Life in Donora

---

*He was baseball hungry. He wanted to play
ball. He would rather play ball than eat.*

MUSIAL FAMILY FRIEND JOE BARBAO

The town of Donora lies twenty-eight
miles south of Pittsburgh, in western Pennsylvania's heavily industrial Monongahela Valley. The frame houses of the town are a dirty gray, covered
with decades of smoke and ash from blast furnaces, galvanizing mills, and
a zinc plant built in 1915. The hills and surrounding countryside are bare,
the vegetation having been killed by sulphur and chemical fumes many
years ago. (In 1948, those deadly fumes filled the valley with a killing fog
for nearly a week. Twenty-one people died and almost everyone in Donora
suffered debilitating effects to some degree. Musial's father would be one of
the smog's victims.)

Most of Donora's inhabitants were immigrants from Germany, Poland,
Czechoslovakia, and Russia. Mary Lancos, one of nine children born in
New York City to parents of Czech descent, came to this small town in
Pennsylvania and by the age of eight was working as a house cleaner. As
a teenager, she rowed her coal-mining father across the Monongahela River
so he could work deep within the bowels of the earth for ninety cents a
day. In 1910, Mary went to work sorting nails at the American Steel and
Wire Company, where she met a shy, wiry Pole named Lukasz Musial.

Lukasz, four years Mary's senior, was born on a farm near Warsaw, had little education, and spoke broken English. He worked in the shipping department, earning eleven dollars every two weeks for handling back-breaking hundred-pound bales of wire. Less than two years later, when Mary was seventeen, she and Lukasz were wed.

Then came the children. First Ida, then Helen, Victoria, and Rose. All girls. Having a man child was important to Lukasz and he was more than a little relieved when Mary gave him his first son on November 21, 1920. Little Stanislaus was immediately nicknamed Stashu. Lukasz was so proud of his first son that he promised his friends the boy wouldn't be baptized until he had another. Two years later, when Ed was born, young Stanislaus toddled along to his own baptism. Stan and Ed were born near the center of town, on Sixth Street, but in 1928, the family moved to Grandma Lancos' house at 1139 Marelda Avenue, a five-room house which held nine people. Mary bought food in bulk: fifty pounds of potatoes, a hundred pounds of flour, twenty-five pounds of sugar, and fifteen pounds of coffee every two weeks. Bread, baked ten loaves at a time, lasted just two days.

Because routine household tasks were the duty of female children in an Old World house, Stan and Ed did few of the chores, leaving them more free time to play in the backyard. "My real favorite sport then was tumbling," said Stan later. "Each week my father took me to the Polish Falcons. The club wasn't far from the house. He took me there and we did tumbling together. One thing I learned was how to fall. I've always known how to take a slide and take a tumble."

At seven, Stan got his first baseball and bat, and he and Ed and their friends would spend endless hours catching and hitting the battered ball. Musial wanted to be a major-league ballplayer the first time he picked up the ball and bat. Because he was a left-hander, he fantasized that he was Lefty Grove. (In his teens, he would switch his idolatry to another southpaw, Carl Hubbell.) Stan's father worked all day and, bone-weary when he arrived home at night, was too tired for children's games, so Stan and brother Ed played catch with their neighbor, thirty-year-old Joe Barbao. Barbao was a former minor-league pitcher and outfielder who still played semi-pro ball and worked as a short-shifter in the zinc mill—a job so brutal no one worked more than three hours a day because of the intense heat. Joe often spent the evening hours talking baseball to the Musial brothers; with this one-on-one tutoring, Musial soon became proficient enough to play pick-up games with the older boys at Palmer Park.

When Stan was fourteen, he joined the Heslep All-Stars, a junior city-league team. His first newspaper clipping shows that he struck out fourteen batters and walked two in a five-hour 24–2 win over Cement City. More indicative of the youngster's future, however, was his work with the bat: a single and three doubles, the hit which would prove to be the Musial signature.

Barbao managed the Donora Zincs, a semi-pro club. At fifteen, Musial was the team's bat boy until one day the Zincs were playing hard-hitting Monessen. When Donora's starting hurler was cuffed around early on, Barbao, who had pitched the day before, asked Stan if he'd like to try his hand on the mound. Weighing just 140 pounds, the young southpaw worked six innings and struck out thirteen batters, all adults. The Zincs, playing their home games at Americo Park, finished the year in first place, and Musial learned a valuable lesson. The left-field fence was considerably closer to the plate than right field, the natural target for a left-handed hitter, and Stan taught himself to reach out and punch the ball past the third baseman.

In 1936, the sixteen-year-old lost his first outing, to Fairhope, 7–5, mainly because his teammates made four errors behind him. "Musial is too small for steady playing now," said the Donora *Herald*. "He has a world of stuff and a brainy head, but overwork can harm a young player very easily."

Stan spent another full year with the Zincs and played a number of games for the Eugene V. Debs American Legion Post of Donora as well. When coach Michael "Ki" Duda revived the baseball program at Donora High School, located on the corner of Fourth Street and Waddell Avenue, a half mile from Musial's house, Stashu, in his first outing on the mound, set a school record with seventeen strikeouts in a seven-inning victory over nearby Monessen. Years later, Stan would still remember another game he worked because of a mighty home run. "We were playing Monongahela City at Legion Field, the Donora high school park," recalled Musial. "My brother, Ed, a ninth-grader who was playing the outfield for us, walked to fill the bases in a late inning of the game we were losing. I was up next. The Mon City pitcher, a right-hander named Jack McGinty, threw me a fast ball low and inside. Unlike most young players, I was a good low-ball hitter. I hit the ball so far, about 450 feet against the distant right field fence on one bounce, that I had circled the bases before the ball was touched by the retrieving fielder."

Despite the prodigious home run, Musial, only a fair student, was offered a basketball scholarship from the University of Pittsburgh. It was an opportunity his father and the athletic director at Donora High School, James K. Russell, very much wanted him to take. Tall and slender, Musial was probably more athletically suited to basketball, but baseball was his first love, and he was still sixteen years old when Andrew J. French, the business manager of the St. Louis Cardinals' Monessen farm club, invited him to work out with his Class D Penn State League club. French turned the youngster over to Monessen manager Ollie Vanek when he reported, and Vanek fitted Stan with a uniform. Club officials watched Musial play, and French filed a scouting report with the Cardinal front office on June 5, 1937, which said:

> ARM? Good. FIELDING? Good. SPEED? Fast. Good curve ball. Green kid. PROSPECT NOW? No. PROSPECT LATER? Yes. AGGRESSIVE? Yes. HABITS? Good. HEALTH? Good.

During the summer of 1937, Stan played baseball and busied himself pumping gasoline for twenty-five dollars a week. Both French and Vanek visited Donora that summer, trying to talk Stan's father into letting the boy sign a professional contract. In late August, French made one last-ditch effort to convince Lukasz to give his son a shot at a major-league career. Lukasz, who knew little about baseball but a great deal about life, realized the odds against his son were enormous, and once again refused. Stan knew who wore the pants in the family and didn't dare argue, but he couldn't hold back his tears. At this point, his strong-willed mother stepped in.

"Lukasz," asked Mary, "why did you come to America?"

"Why?" replied Musial's father, caught by surprise at his wife's question and unsure where she was heading with her logic. "Because it's a free country, that's why."

In perhaps her finest hour, Mary Musial nodded and said, "That's right, Lukasz. And in America a boy is free not to go to college, too."

Magnificently hoist on his own petard, Lukasz faltered. "All right, Stashu," he sighed, "if you want baseball enough to pass up college, then I'll sign."

Stan and his parents signed the contract, which was not filed with the baseball commissioner's office until June of the following year. The elder Musial, unhappy with his son's decision, was unhappier still in the winter of 1937–38 when the Donora High School basketball team, helped in part by Stanislaus, had its best year ever. Lukasz could see the prospect of Stashu's college education evaporating before his eyes. But for the first time in his life, the younger Musial had something more important than either baseball or college on his mind.

One of Stan's teammates on the basketball team, Dick Ercius, had introduced him to Lillian Labash, an attractive blonde who knew Musial from watching him play baseball and basketball. Dick was dating one of the Labash sisters and had asked Stan to take Lillian to a dance after one of the games. The shy Musial agreed. Young Stanislaus and Lil, two months older than Musial but a year ahead of him in high school, began dating.

By now, Stan was being pressured from all sides to accept the basketball scholarship. Coach Russell spoke to Lil privately and asked her to urge Musial not to play pro ball in 1938, but Lillian told him firmly the decision was not hers to make. Musial's gym teacher at Donora, Charles H. "Jerry" Wunderlich, applied the most severe pressure of all when he took Stan to meet his old college coach at the University of Pittsburgh, Dr. H.C. Carlson, the man who would formally tender the offer of a basketball scholarship. Carlson told Musial he would probably throw his arm out in the low minors, a frequent occurrence, and wind up back in Donora working at the mill. Stan's baseball coach, Ki Duda, had perhaps the best perspective of all. He realized Musial would never be able to concentrate on college while he still had the desire to play baseball. But the advice that provided the final impetus to Stan's Hall of Fame career came from a most unlikely source: Miss Helen Kloz, the Donora High School librarian. Musial respected Miss Kloz and when he asked what she would do, she swallowed hard and said, "Stan, I've never known a boy who wanted something more than you do. College is a wise course for a man to follow, but you've got to want it enough, almost as much as you want baseball. If you're going to try baseball, the younger you start, the better. You can't afford to lose your head, but you can afford to follow your heart."

Shortly after his conversation with Miss Kloz, Musial ran into the sports editor of the Donora *Herald*, Johnny Bunardzya. Johnny asked him if he'd like to ride down to Pittsburgh and see his favorite team, the Pittsburgh Pirates, play the New York Giants. (Bunardzya, unaware that Stan had already signed a contract with the Cardinals, was trying to interest him in a contract with his home-state team.) Although he lived just twenty-eight miles from the Steel City, Musial had never been to a Bucs game. He eagerly jumped at the opportunity, playing hooky from school in the bargain. After a few innings, the brash young man turned to Bunardzya and said, "John, I think I can hit big-league pitching."

By this time, Stan was somewhat disillusioned with the Cardinal franchise, which had been ordered by Commissioner Kenesaw Mountain Landis to release ninety-one farmhands because the Redbirds had violated baseball law by controlling two or more clubs in the same minor league. When Irv Weiss, a Donora businessman, offered to drive Musial to Pittsburgh to work out with the Pirates, Stan, who had yet to be told by the Cardinals where he was to report, began hoping he might be one of the players to be released. Weiss and Musial, armed with letters of interest from the Cleveland Indians and New York Yankees, made the journey several weeks later. Pittsburgh manager Pie Traynor, after watching the youngster throw to his regulars, took Musial aside and said the Pirates would be glad to offer him a minor-league contract. Stan told Traynor about the contract he had already signed, but said he was certain the Cardinals had forgotten about him. "I doubt that, son," replied Traynor. "You'll be hearing from them one of these days. If they do release you, let us know."

Traynor shook Musial's hand and wished him luck. A few days later, a telegram arrived from the Cardinal front office, ordering him to report to Williamson, West Virginia. A telegram was a big event in the Musial household. Stan's hands shook when he opened the envelope. There it was, the news he'd been waiting for: Musial was slated to play in the Class D Mountain States League. They wanted him to leave immediately.

◇2◇

Bush Leaguer

---

*I hit at Musial when he was a left-handed
pitcher in the Cardinal farm system. I don't
think anybody knew what a great hitter he
was going to be, because of that odd batting
stance he had.*

—ENOS SLAUGHTER

Riding the 240 miles from Donora to Williamson in the spring of 1938, Musial got more homesick with each revolution of the bus tires. Located on the border between Kentucky and West Virginia, Williamson had a population of just nine thousand people and was an even smaller mining town than Donora. When Stan stepped off the bus the next morning he was greeted by E.S. "Lefty" Hamilton, the general manager of the club, and taken to meet Nat Hickey, the man who would become his first professional manager. Hickey, who also played center field for the club, was a fiery man with a vocabulary to match. A few days later, when Hickey gave his newest recruit his first start, Stan quickly found out that life was different in pro ball, even at the minor-league level. The first time he tried to pick a runner off first, the umpire jumped out from behind the plate and yelled, "Balk!" Musial had trouble finding the strike zone, but on the few occasions he did, his infielders ran for their lives as Huntington knocked the cover off the ball. After a couple of innings, Stan was back on the bench.

Stan made sixty-five dollars a month, lived in a five-dollar-a-week rooming house, and bought five-dollar meal tickets at local restaurants. While not exactly living the life of Riley, he still managed to send a little money home to his parents each month. Musial didn't set the world on fire in his first year at Williamson, but he did post a 6–6 record with a 4.66 earned run average for a mediocre club. Like most young left-handers, he was uncommonly wild, walking eighty batters while striking out just fifty-seven in 110 innings pitched. At the plate, Stan batted .258 and pinch-hit occasionally, showing a hint of power with three doubles and a home run included in his sixteen hits. Wid Mathews, one of Branch Rickey's scouts, filed a report on Musial which stated, "Arm good. Good fast ball, good curve. Poise. Good hitter. A real prospect."

By the time Stan returned to Donora that winter, he had learned many of the basics of the game. The Cardinal farm system has always been instructional in nature and Musial had spent hours working on his hitting, sacrificing, and the proper way to run the bases. These features of the game came easily to Stan, a natural athlete. The "thinking man's" aspects such as backing up bases, hitting the cutoff man, and signs, required a little more effort.

Stan finished high school in the spring of 1939, becoming the first member of his family to graduate. Along the way he helped coach the Donora baseball team, and also pitched for the Zincs. He reported back to Williamson in 1939 for seventy-five dollars a month. Although he was still filled with doubt, Musial knew he could always fall back on a job at Lillian's father's grocery store in Donora. Williamson's new manager, Harrison Wickel, was just the opposite of Nat Hickey, quiet, reserved, and soft-spoken. Stan rented an apartment with three other teammates and developed shoulder trouble, the result of an old basketball injury. After some time off, he returned to the mound, but was erratic.

On July 15, 1939, Wickel penned a report on Musial to the Cardinal front office:

> This boy is quite a problem. He is by far the wildest pitcher I have ever seen. He hasn't pitched a complete game here in ages and he must average at least ten walks a game. He has fair stuff and at times he has a good fast ball and pretty good curve. He will strike out just as many as he will walk, but I certainly can't depend on him, and most of the games he has won we have given him a dozen or more runs, or [reliever Wayne] Bruce has been called in to finish his work.

I recommend his release because I don't believe he will ever be able to find the plate. I don't think he has enough stuff to get by. I've noticed that when he does get the ball over, he is hit rather freely, and I am led to believe that his wildness is his effectiveness. The opposition never gets anything good to hit. The only place he can pitch is Class D, where the player strikes at almost anything a pitcher tosses up there. I am at a loss to say definitely what to do with him. He has the best of habits and is a fine boy.

But Stan picked up later in the year. His three successive low-hit victories helped boost Williamson into the Mountain States League playoffs. The team was knocked out of any further post-season competition by Bluefield, but Musial finished the year with a 9–2 record and lowered his ERA to 4.30, an improvement of a third of a run a game. In ninety-two innings, Stan had surrendered just seventy-one hits and fanned eighty-six, and while Wickel had exaggerated somewhat when he said Musial had allowed "at least ten walks a game," Stan had given up eighty-five free passes in thirteen appearances, an average of over eight bases on balls for every nine innings pitched. At that pace, the youngster was going to have to have an awful lot of 9–2 seasons to get a shot at the major leagues. More germane to Musial's future was his hitting. Williamson carried just fourteen players and when one of the outfielders had been injured late in the year, Stan was inserted into the lineup on days he wasn't pitching. In seventy-one at-bats, he collected twenty-five hits, including three doubles, three triples, and a home run, for a .352 mark and a .521 slugging average.

When Musial returned to Donora that fall, he and Lillian surprised everyone when they eloped on his nineteenth birthday.

In 1940, after an off-season of working in his father-in-law's grocery store, Musial was eager to play a full season. He was ordered to report to Columbus, Georgia, the Cardinals' minor-league camp for Class B and C clubs. But Stan wasn't yet competent enough and he was transferred to Daytona Beach, Florida, in the Class D Florida State League. At Daytona Beach, two important events occurred in the young couple's lives: making a hundred dollars a month now, Musial sent for Lil, who was expecting their first child; and Stan met Dickie Kerr and his wife Pep. A former major-league hurler, Kerr had won thirteen games in his rookie year for the 1919 Chicago White Sox, then went on to capture two victories in the 1919 World Series. When the news broke the following September that the Sox had thrown the Series to Cincinnati, Dickie's two wins loomed large and he became a national hero. He was, quite possibly, the most popular man in Chicago in 1920 and 1921, seasons in which he won twenty-one and nineteen games, respectively. In the spring of 1922, White Sox owner Charles A. Comiskey—the tight-fisted owner who wielded baseball's reserve clause like his own personal club and was blamed by many as the reason Joe Jackson, Chick Gandil, and the others went for the gambler's money and fixed the Series—refused him a pay increase. Kerr played semi-pro ball for the next three years. By the time he returned to the pros in 1925, his talent was gone.

Musial learned quite a lot from Kerr, now Daytona Beach's manager. On April 10, Stan's former manager, Harrison Wickel, filed a report with the Cardinal front office that said, "Pitched only one game while I was here. I still think he will never reach the majors as a pitcher, but he might as an outfielder." Two weeks later, Branch Rickey's scout Wid Mathews confirmed Wickel's letter when he wrote, "Good fast ball, curve fair. Nice poise, big boy. He can hit and may be too good a hitter to keep out of the game."

"Good form and curve," wrote Springfield manager Ollie Vanek on May 1, scouting the young pitcher for his own club. "Fast ball a bit doubtful. Also a good hitter. May make an outfielder."

Unknown to him, Stan's future in the Cardinal organization was undergoing a metamorphosis. Meanwhile, the young southpaw, playing the outfield between starts, was pitching his heart out. (Once, letting the competition get the better of him, Musial was ejected from a game for arguing a call at first base, the only time in his professional career he was thumbed by an umpire.) He and Lillian were staying in a small hotel in Daytona Beach. Because none of Lil's family lived nearby, the Kerrs, out of kindness, took the young couple into their home just before their son, named Richard out of gratitude, was born. The night after Dick's birth, Stan celebrated by beating Gainesville in twelve innings, 3–2. In Musial's next start, Daytona Beach moved into first place in the Florida State League when Stan again went twelve innings, downing Sanford, 3–2. But a few days later, August 11, his future underwent a drastic change.

Daytona Beach's best pitcher, Jack Creel, started the game against Orlando. Musial was playing center field. An Orlando batter slammed a low line drive to center, and just as Stan dived to catch the ball, his spikes caught on the outfield grass and he crashed hard on the point of his left shoulder. Musial knew he had been injured seriously, but X-rays of the huge knot on his shoulder showed nothing the next morning. All Stan had was a bad bruise, for which he took heat treatments. In his next scheduled start, he pitched and beat Ocala, 4–3. When the Florida State League All-Star Game was held at Sanford on August 30, Kerr declined to use Stan as his pitcher, putting him into the game in center field instead. A week later,

Daytona Beach clinched the pennant, but the club was downed in the playoffs by Orlando in four games. Musial, making just his second start since the injury, contributed to the defeat when he was knocked out in a 12–5 laugher. Publicly, Kerr blamed Stan's ineffectiveness on the dual duty of pitching and playing the outfield. Privately, he suspected Musial's arm was dead. Stan was still good enough to hit, however: in the final game of the playoffs, he tripled and scored Daytona Beach's only run as Jack Creel suffered a heartbreaking 2–1 loss.

Musial had pitched well enough to post an 18–5 record for Kerr and lead the league with a .783 winning percentage. In 223 innings, Stan had allowed just 179 hits, struck out a very respectable 176 batters, and compiled an even more respectable 2.62 earned run average. But he was still wild, having surrendered 145 bases on balls. That the scouting reports touted Musial's hitting was obvious: Stan had come to the plate 405 times and belted out 126 hits, among them seventeen doubles, ten triples, and one home run. He had scored fifty-five runs, driven in another seventy, and hit .311.

Stan and Lil spent the winter in Daytona. Musial worked in the sporting goods department of the local Montgomery Ward store, making twenty-five dollars a week. When 1941 rolled around, he left for spring training at Class AA Hollywood, Florida. Daytona Beach sports editor Bernard Kahn wrote a complimentary column on Stan in which he said, "Musial runs like silk hose, throws like a bullet and hits like, well, like hell." Stan was assigned to Class AA Columbus, Ohio, and told Kahn, "Naturally, I want to play with Columbus, but the Cardinals will probably farm me out to Asheville or some other B team. I don't want to play any more D ball, but if I have to, I want to play it right here in Daytona Beach. I'd play in an E league if they told me to. I like baseball too much to ever give it up."

But Musial's pitching arm was weak, a fact noticed almost immediately by Columbus skipper Burt Shotton. "At least, I know you're not throwing hard enough to pitch here," said Shotton. "I think you can make it as a hitter. I'm going to send you to another camp with the recommendation that you be tried as an outfielder."

Stan was sent to Albany, Georgia, where the Cardinals' Class D teams trained, then on to Columbus, Georgia, where he joined a player pool made up of Class A, B, and C teams. The Cardinals, barnstorming their way back to St. Louis, stopped for a game against Columbus, and when they scored six runs in the first, manager Clay Hopper told Stan to go in and pitch. Musial protested weakly that he was an outfielder, but took the mound and retired the side without any further damage. In the second, Terry Moore hit a long home run with a man on base and Johnny Mize followed a few moments later by blasting one even further. Stan worked three more score-less innings, but even he could see the handwriting on the wall. A few days later, working against the Phillies, Musial surrendered seven runs on four hits, six walks, and two wild pitches and came to the realization that he was through as a pitcher. In three years as a minor-league hurler, Musial had appeared in sixty-one games, worked 425 innings, surren-dered 364 hits and 310 bases on balls, and struck out 328 batters. His won-loss record was a sparkling 33–13 and his minor-league earned run average was 3.52.

Washed up as a pitcher, Musial's only avenue to the major leagues now lay in his hitting ability.

When it came time to assign the damaged-goods outfielder to a club for the balance of the 1941 season, no one in Class A or B was interested. Musial's career might have ended right there, but Ollie Vanek, manager of Class C Springfield, spoke up and said he'd take a chance. Vanek put Stan in right field and batted him cleanup, but the young pitcher-turned-outfielder failed to turn any heads in his debut when he singled once in four times at bat. Worse than his lack of hitting, Musial showed immediately that he had trouble playing White City Park's less than professionally manicured outfield. In his first three games, Stan collected just two hits in thirteen times to the plate, but against St. Joseph, Missouri, with Cardinal General Manager Branch Rickey in the stands, Musial singled, tripled, and blasted his first home run of the year. Rickey, the man who would ultimately decide Stan's fate, was suitably impressed. So was Vanek. "The way you're going," he told Musial, "I wouldn't be surprised to see you reach the major leagues in a couple of years."

Musial was batting .430 for the young season when, at Springfield one evening, he crushed three home runs against Stockton. Lillian was at the game, but nine-month-old Dickie had needed his diapers changed fre-quently during the contest and Lil had wound up missing each of Stan's blows.

By now, Musial's arm was growing stronger. Baserunners who had heard through the minor-league grapevine that the arm was dead were often surprised to find themselves being thumbed out when they tried to take an extra base. In late July, Stan and Vanek were fishing when a reporter from the Springfield newspaper told Musial he had been ordered to report to Rochester, New York, of the International League. This was big news: Rochester was just one rung below the major leagues. In eighty-seven games for Springfield, Musial had hit a league-leading .379 with 132 hits in

348 at-bats. Among Stan's safeties were twenty-seven doubles, ten triples, and twenty-six home runs, the most of any hitter in the league. Musial scored an even hundred runs, drove in ninety-four, and stole sixteen bases.

When Stan joined the fourth-place Rochester Red Wings, his new manager, Tony Kaufmann, inserted him into the lineup immediately, playing right field. Sportswriter J. Roy Stockton would later assert that Musial hit a home run in his first at-bat, but Stan remembers correctly that he contributed just an infield single in four trips to the plate. A few nights later, when Musial played his first game in front of the home crowd, he rapped out two singles, a double, and a home run. "The kid is an iceberg," said Kaufmann. "If you tapped him, you'd find ice water in his veins. Yankee Stadium or cow pasture—just another place to play ball, to him."

The Red Wings won sixteen of their last twenty games and wrapped up a playoff spot with a doubleheader sweep of Buffalo on the final Sunday of the season. Musial collected six hits in the twin bill and three more the following night as Rochester clinched fourth place, 4–2, but the Red Wings were defeated in the playoffs by Newark, three games to two. In the final contest, during which Stan singled and doubled as Rochester lost, 9–6, it was announced that the Cardinals had purchased the contracts of pitcher Hank Gornicki, third baseman George "Whitey" Kurowski, and Musial. The news that he might be spending some time with the parent club in 1942 was going to make the winter unbearably long for the hard-hitting minor-leaguer who, in fifty-four games with Rochester, had driven in twenty-one runs, scored forty-three, and batted .326.

Stan called Lillian and told her he was taking the night coach back to Pittsburgh that Saturday. The next morning, after attending Mass, a bone-weary Musial was taking a nap when Lil awakened him. "There's a wire from Rochester for you. I think they want you to report to St. Louis." Flabbergasted, Musial and Lil decided that because the major-league season had just two weeks to go, Stan would make the trip to St. Louis alone. Lillian spent the afternoon feverishly washing and ironing her husband's wardrobe so he could make the train to St. Louis.

On September 17, two months shy of his twenty-first birthday, Stan Musial reported to the Cardinals. With him were Erv Dusak, Whitey Kurowski, and Walt Sessi. Equipment manager Butch Yatkeman led the quartet to the back of the clubhouse in Sportsman's Park, where rookies and batting practice pitchers dressed. But Stan, who had started the season as a hundred-dollar-a-month Class D pitcher and was now drawing four hundred a month in the majors, wasn't complaining. When Yatkeman handed out uniforms, Musial drew number six, the only number he would ever wear at the major-league level.

Fate had dealt Stan Musial a shot at the big leagues with less than 150 games behind him as a full-time outfielder. Only time would tell if he could capitalize on the opportunity.

◇ 3 ◇

The Big Leagues

Stan was a good kid. He was quiet and shy when he first came up, too, and if you'd seen him back then with that unorthodox stance of his, you'd say to yourself, this kid's never gonna make it. We soon learned otherwise, didn't we?

TERRY MOORE

S t. Louis, Missouri, lies on the Mississippi River, just south of its confluence with the Missouri, a leading railroad center and one of the nation's busiest inland ports. Untouched by the Civil War, St. Louis grew rapidly and by 1900 was a major manufacturing center. Much of the city's south side, known as the "scrubby Dutch" to long-time residents, has a German atmosphere, and the west-central region is a fiercely proud Italian district known as The Hill. By the time Stan Musial pulled into Union Station in September 1941, the St. Louis Cardinals had been pennant winners in 1885–88, 1926, 1928, 1930–31, and 1934, and World Series victors in 1885–86, 1926, 1931, and 1934. The club this young and apprehensive minor-league ballplayer joined was engaged in a fierce battle with the Brooklyn Dodgers for the 1941 National League pennant, a struggle the Redbirds and Dodgers would repeat many times over the next decade.

A few blocks north of Sportsman's Park was the place Musial would call his St. Louis home for the next several years, the Fairgrounds Hotel. If you were a major-league ballplayer in the 1940s, you might quickly get your fill of living out of a suitcase. The Fairgrounds was about par for the course, but a few of the hotels were better than others. For years, National League ballplayers looked forward to road trips into Cincinnati, where the Netherland Plaza featured the only air-conditioned lobby on the circuit. Boston's Kenmore Hotel featured the best littleneck clams in the world, but the Bellevue Stratford in Philadelphia had European waiters and world-class service.

Cardinal reserve catcher Del Wilber would remember these road trips fondly years later. "One of the best road trips with the St. Louis Cardinals," recalled Del, "was playing in Chicago, playing day games at Wrigley Field. When the ball game was over we'd get on the bus and go to the Dearborn Street Station and we'd catch the Wabash Cannonball. It was classy. There was a big domed lounge car that we'd use and the fans would be there to meet us at the Delmar Street Station in St. Louis. We would play a day game here in St. Louis and about six o'clock we'd be on the New York Central as it pulled out. We'd leave St. Louis, go across the river, head back to the dining car and get something to eat. Then first thing you know you'd be in Indianapolis and you'd wake up the next morning and be in Albany, New York; then down the Hudson River to New York City."

Others didn't remember the playing conditions with such nostalgia. Duke Snider said, "You'd sleep with the window open and the city dirt would float in and darken your pillow. The Schenley Hotel in Pittsburgh was the worst in that department." Terry Moore recalled that coming off the trains was tough. "We'd finish a doubleheader in St. Louis," said Terry, "and it would be about 110 degrees in the shade. Then we'd get on the train, and it'd be so darn hot we'd have to go into the dining car because that was the only one that they'd cool off with ice. Then we'd try to go to bed and we'd roll and toss and sweat and everything else."

Dodger outfielder Billy Herman encapsulized a road trip this way. "Here's how you went from Chicago to St. Louis to Cincinnati," said Herman. "I'm talking about July and August, when it's always ninety or more degrees in those towns. You got on a train at midnight, and maybe that train has been sitting in the yards all day long, under a broiling sun. It feels like 150 degrees in that steel car. You get into St. Louis at six thirty in the morning, grab your own bag, fight to get a cab, and go to the hotel. By the time you get to the hotel, it's seven thirty, and you have an afternoon ball game to play. So you hurry into the dining room and it's hot in there, no air conditioning, and you eat and run upstairs to try and get a few hours' rest. Then you go to the ball park, where it's about 110 degrees. You finish the ball game around five or five thirty and go into the clubhouse. It's around 120 degrees in there. You take your shower, but there's no way you can dry off. The sweat just keeps running off of you. You go out to the street and try to find a cab back to the hotel. You get back to the hotel and go up to your room and you lose your breath, it's so hot in there. But the dining room isn't much better, so you order room service and stay right there and eat. Then you go to bed and try to sleep, but you can't, you're sweating so much. So you get up and pull the sheet off the bed and soak it with cold water and go back and roll up in a wet sheet. But it dries out after an hour or two, and you have to get up and soak it again. This goes on for four days in St. Louis, and you go on to Cincinnati and it's the same thing."

The stars of the 1941 Cardinals were outfielders Enos Slaughter and Terry Moore, first baseman Johnny Mize, shortstop Marty Marion, catcher Walker Cooper, and pitchers Mort Cooper (Walker's brother) and Max Lanier.

The Southern-born Slaughter, described by Marty Marion as "a good ballplayer, not a great, great player, but a real good one," and by Musial and dozens of others as "the greatest hustler of all time," was a big favorite in St. Louis and consistently one of the best outfielders in the National League. The story is told that when "Country" was in the minor leagues, he trotted in from right field one day and slowed to a walk around the pitcher's mound. When he finally arrived at the dugout, his manager asked if he was too tired to continue to play. From then on, Enos Slaughter never walked when he could run. He ran out each grounder, ran down every fly ball, and even sprinted to first when he drew a base on balls. Hall of Fame manager Bucky Harris said he was "the finest example of what it means to do your level best I've ever seen. His name should be in school textbooks along with this country's most revered heroes. He never quits. He never will. He won't even let down." For years after his retirement, Enos grumbled about not being in the Hall himself until the baseball writers finally silenced him with induction in 1985.

To Enos' right in the Cardinal outfield was another Southerner, Terry Moore, one of the best defensive center fielders the game has ever known. The Cardinal team captain, Moore was a timely hitter with an accurate arm, ham-sized hands, and the ability to play ground-ball singles like an infielder. "Tee" was so well-liked and respected that Harry Walker named his son after him.

On the Cardinal infield were Johnny Mize, Marty Marion, and Walker Cooper. Mize, a soft-spoken, unassuming hulk of a man who carried a big stick, had been with the club since 1936. Burly and slow-moving, the 215-pound first baseman had been nicknamed "the Cat" because of his graceful batting style. Marion, at six feet, two inches and 170 pounds, was tall for shortstops of his day and it wasn't hard to see why he was nicknamed "Slats." Musial was in awe of his fielding ability. "Marion was one of the best defensive shortstops of all time," Stan would say years later. "He was a long, lanky fellow with great range, a good pair of hands and a good accurate arm. Even from deep short, he could throw a perfect strike to first base. He could come in on a ball, go behind second, do everything with the glove." Described by announcer Red Barber as "movin' easy as a bank of fog," Marion had a quick wit and often referred to himself jokingly as the guts of the team. "I was pretty good," Slats would chuckle, "especially with men on base. The players used to laugh and say, 'We'd rather see Marty up there with a man on third than Musial.'" Occasionally, Marion's easygoing nature and playful sense of humor got him in trouble. Facing off one day against Brooklyn's Whit Wyatt, a fierce and sometimes dirty competitor, Marion took his time smoothing out the dirt around home plate and digging a hole with his back foot. When he finally settled in the plate, Marion looked out to the pitcher's mound to see Wyatt glaring in. "You ready?" yelled the Dodger hurler, who promptly knocked the Cardinal shortstop down with his first pitch. Marion got up, laughing, and Wyatt's next pitch hit him right in the rib cage. "Jesus Christ, Whit!" he yelled, exasperated. "Don't laugh when I'm on the mound," Wyatt answered.

Behind the plate for St. Louis was Walker Cooper, as heavy as Mize and an inch taller. The club prankster, Cooper delighted in cutting neckties in half, crushing others' straw hats, giving hotfoots, and putting lighted cigarettes in the back pockets of his fellow ballplayers. But Walker's particular favorite was waiting until one of his teammates was comfortably en-sconced in a hotel lobby chair, then setting his newspaper on fire. This last trick was especially popular with hotel managers when the Redbirds were on the road. According to Dodger outfielder Duke Snider, Cooper had an idiosyncrasy not shared by any other major-league catcher, before or since: instead of carrying the usual padding in his mitt, a sponge or handkerchief, Walker used a woman's falsie.

The Cardinal pitching staff was anchored by Lon Warneke, Max Lanier, and Cooper's older brother, Mort. If Walker was happy-go-lucky, his brother was just the opposite, especially on the pitcher's mound. Mort had a good fastball and was always around the strike zone, rarely walking anyone and working a complete game with ninety to a hundred pitches. The right-handed Cooper chewed aspirin on the mound because of pain from bone chips in the elbow of his pitching arm. His no-nonsense approach to his job kept his fielders on their toes, always alert. Max Lanier, the club's ace left-hander, was possessed of a pretty fair fastball himself, but his real pride and joy was a stunning, overhand curveball he enjoyed throwing to right-handed hitters. In one respect, at least, Lanier was somewhat of an enigma: he pitched very well against contending clubs, but seemed to let down when he faced the second-division teams. Lon Warneke had one of the most colorful nicknames in baseball history: the Arkansas Humming Bird. Warneke had come to St. Louis from the Cubs in 1937 and had averaged fifteen wins a season ever since. A guitar-picking hillbilly, Warneke would rack up seventeen wins in 1941, fourth-best in the National League.

Piloting the club was William Harrison "Billy" Southworth, a forty-eight-year-old former major-league outfielder whose deep voice belied his youthful nickname. Southworth had first been named the St. Louis skipper in 1929, but his harsh methods (and sub-.500 record) had earned him a quick trip back to managing in the minor leagues eighty-eight games into the season. Given a second chance with the Cardinals in 1940, Billy had taken over a sixth-place team and guided it to a third-place finish.

The Redbirds had gotten off to a hot start, but the Dodgers, on the strength of an eight-game winning streak, fought their way back into the race. By June 3, the National League lead had changed hands seven times over the previous nine days. On June 22, the Redbirds led Brooklyn by three games. On July 6, the situation was reversed: the Dodgers led St. Louis by three games. The spirited race heated up again later in the month when the Redbirds swept a two-game series at Ebbets Field and moved to within a game of the Dodgers. Back and forth it went, Brooklyn and St. Louis swapping the league lead five times in the middle of August. The Cardinals were a game back when the Dodgers arrived at Sportsman's Park for the first of three games on September 11. Brooklyn had to win two of the three contests to hold their lead.

St. Louis manager Billy Southworth tapped Ernie White for the opener and Brooklyn's Leo Durocher went with foul-mouthed Freddie Fitzsimmons. Fitzsimmons would pivot all the way around to center field before delivering the ball and he kept the Cardinal batters loose all day, taunting, cursing, throwing at their feet. Dolph Camilli's three-run homer and a sacrifice fly gave Brooklyn a 4–2 lead, but the Redbirds tied the score in the seventh. That's where matters stood when Joe Medwick led off the Dodgers' eleventh with a line drive single. After a base on balls, the dangerous Camilli came to the plate. Everyone in the park expected a bunt and Camilli obliged, pushing the ball straight at first baseman Johnny Mize. Mize, in his haste to get off a throw to third, slipped, fell, and kicked the ball toward home plate for an error. With the bases loaded, Dixie Walker ended the suspense with a ground single through the left side and Brooklyn had held on to first place. The Redbirds took the next contest, 4–3, and it all came down to the rubber game of the series on September 13, Whit Wyatt vs. Mort Cooper. Cooper had a no-hitter through seven innings, but the Dodgers took a 1–0 lead when Dixie Walker doubled and scored in the eighth. That was all the Bums needed for a thrilling 1–0 victory. The Dodgers left St. Louis with a two-game lead and fourteen games to play.

Brooklyn won the next day, but the Redbirds took two from the Giants and narrowed the gap to a game and a half. On September 15, the Dodger front office began accepting applications for World Series tickets and while the Cards were idle, the Bums beat Cincinnati. On the sixteenth, Brooklyn lost to the Reds, but the best St. Louis could do was play ten innings to a tie with the Giants. The next day, Musial reported to the Cardinals just in time for the doubleheader with the Braves at Sportsman's Park. Howie Pollet won the first game easily, 6–1, and Billy Southworth decided that game two of the twin bill would be Musial's major-league debut. If the pressure of trying to break into an outfield that included Enos Slaughter, Terry Moore, and Johnny Hopp bothered Stan, he didn't show it. He knew, after all, that he was only playing to give the regulars a much-needed day off.

Stan shagged flies in the outfield between games and made his first evaluation of the ball yard which would be his home for the next twenty-three years. Sportsman's Park, the residence of the American League St. Louis Browns since 1902 and the Cardinals since 1920, would be the home field for both clubs until the Browns departed St. Louis for Baltimore after the 1953 season. Pavilions extended from both sides of the infield down to the foul poles and although the dimensions varied throughout the years, the distance from home plate down the left-field line was usually 351 feet; to the right-field line 310 feet; and to dead-center field, 422 feet. The fences were eleven-and-a-half feet high, but the right-field pavilion featured a thirty-three-foot-high screen off which Musial would slam many a two-base hit. (The Browns put the screen up in 1929, the day after the Detroit Tigers had hit eight home runs in four games.) When Musial joined the Cardinals, blacks were segregated from whites in the seating arrangements, allowed only to buy tickets for the bleachers and pavilion section. Management would not abolish the practice until 1944, the last major-league team to do so.

Cardinal third baseman Jimmy Brown singled in the first, but Gene Moore made an eye-popping catch of Johnny Hopp's long fly ball at the wall in right-center and easily doubled off Brown. When Musial left the on-deck circle to face knuckleballer Jim Tobin, many of the nearly eight thousand fans reached for their programs to check who the slender, six-foot-tall right fielder with the friendly, open face was. Stan had never seen a major-league knuckleball before and he was nervous. When he stepped into the batter's box, Musial planted his feet, took one practice swing, crouched, and peered over his right shoulder at Tobin. When Stan swung his hips, the crowd couldn't help but titter at his unusual batting stance. Off-stride in his first major-league at-bat, Musial popped harmlessly to third baseman Sibby Sisti and the inning was over. Red-faced and embarrassed, the rookie tossed his bat aside and trotted out to right field as his new teammates, in the time-honored tradition of baseball, razzed him unmercifully from the dugout. Fans all over the park ordered their first beer of the day, gulped down a bite of hot dog, or lighted a cigarette. Some chuckled, remarking how feeble the busher looked. On the Cardinal bench, manager Billy Southworth arched his eyebrows at catcher Walker Cooper.

In the third, with two out and two on, the rookie from Rochester came to the plate again. Boston catcher Ray Berres conferred with Tobin about how to pitch to the newcomer. The first delivery was wide of the strike zone. Umpire Bill "Beans" Reardon shrugged his shoulders for ball one. Tobin came to the plate again and Musial timed the pitch just right, smacking the ball off the wall in right-center field. When Stan cruised into second base with his first major-league hit, a two-run double, a big, broad grin lighted up his face. A few of his teammates applauded politely. Most made a big show of ignoring him. Musial finished the game with a two-for-four performance, and it was his two-run double which provided the winning margin in the Cardinal 3–2 victory.

The Associated Press report of the game listed the newest Cardinal outfielder as "Steve," a mistake it wouldn't repeat.

The next day, Stan garnered a single in four times at bat in his second big-league game, but the Redbirds lost to the Braves, 4–1, leaving St. Louis one game back with nine to play. The Dodgers were idle on Friday, September 19, but were looking forward to doubleheaders with the ineffectual Phillies on Saturday and Sunday and a single game on Monday. That evening, the Redbirds downed the Cubs, 3–1, and closed to within a half game and two percentage points of the Dodgers. Musial scored the

Cardinals' first run and was three-for-three with two singles, a double, and a run batted in. But the game took a toll: Redbird slugger Johnny Mize tore ligaments in his right arm and was lost for the remainder of the season.

Although he was given a new contract to manage the Cardinals for 1942, September 20 was the worst day of the season for Billy Southworth. In Philadelphia, Whit Wyatt and Kirby Higbe pitched the Dodgers to a doubleheader win over the Phillies, while in St. Louis Chicago's rookie catcher, Bob Scheffing, blasted a ninth-inning grand-slam as the Cubs wheeled their way to a 7–3 win over the Cardinals. Musial was retired in a pinch-hitting appearance. The next afternoon, the rookie was six-for-ten as the Birds downed the Cubbies twice. Musial had already roughed up Claude Passeau and Ken Raffensberger for three hits in the opener, made two great catches, stolen a base, and thrown a runner out at the plate, but the score was tied at five-all in the ninth. Gus Mancuso was an easy out and after Raffensberger dusted Stan off, the Cardinal rookie singled for his fourth hit of the game. Estel Crabtree grounded out on a bang-bang play as Musial advanced to second. Two men out now, and Cubs manager Jimmie Wilson ordered an intentional walk to Frank Crespi in order for Raffensberger to work to Coaker Triplett. Triplett topped one of Raffensberger's forkballs to the left side of the mound. Raffensberger got to the ball and threw to first, but Triplett had just streaked across the bag. Musial rounded third and saw that catcher Clyde McCullough, backing up the play, was about to argue the call with first base umpire Lee Ballanfant. Home plate wasn't covered and Stan just kept going, scoring the winning run on a ball that hadn't traveled more than twenty feet. "That kid," said Billy Southworth to one of his coaches when Musial returned to the dugout, "was born to play baseball."

Musial continued hitting in the nightcap, going two-for-five as the Birds pounded out an easy 7–0 victory. At Philadelphia, the Dodgers split, and Brooklyn's lead was down to a single game. The race wasn't over just yet. St. Louis *Globe-Democrat* sportswriter Bob Burnes, in his column, "The Bench Warmer," said of Stan: "Musial is really the answer to someone's prayer. His terrific hitting since joining the club last week has insured at least two triumphs. He can just about do everything. The only thing that one could still want to know is whether or not he can cook."

When the Cardinals left town that evening, Stan took a seat in the Pullman car next to Terry Moore. Relating his whirlwind journey to the majors that season, he offhandedly mentioned the home runs Moore and Mize had hit off him in spring training. Recollection came slowly to Moore's face and he called over to Mize. "Hey, John, you won't believe this. Musial is the left-hander who threw us those long home-run balls at Columbus this spring!" Neither Moore nor Mize ever let Stan forget that pair of homers.

At Pittsburgh on Tuesday, September 23, Musial was given a "day" by his family and friends from hometown Donora. Stan was the first person from his neck of the woods to make the major leagues since outfielder Bob Coulson joined the Reds in 1908. Pirate lefty Ken Heintzelman shut down Stan and the rest of the Redbirds, 4–0, in the opener of a twin bill. The Cards rebounded in the nightcap, ripping Rip Sewell, 9–0, in a game which featured two RBIs and three hits for Musial, one of which was his first major-league home run. For the round-tripper, Stan received a case of Wheaties cereal, a common advertising gimmick of the time. On Wednesday, September 24, the Redbirds made it two straight over the Pirates, but the Dodgers wouldn't falter, coming from behind to beat the Braves. The next afternoon, Musial was two-for-four with a run scored, but the Cards lost to Pittsburgh, 3–1, while Whit Wyatt blanked the Braves to clinch the pennant for the Dodgers. The Cardinal locker room was as quiet as the grave.

Four days later, the Redbirds closed out their season with a 3–1 win over the Cubs, Musial scoring the last run of the year. St. Louis had finished the season with ninety-seven victories, good enough to win a pennant in most years. "We gave it all we had," said Southworth. "I guess it just wasn't our year. My congratulations go to the Dodgers, who have just won the greatest pennant race in history."

Musial had good reason to wish the year was just getting underway. In his first twelve major-league games, he had collected twenty hits and batted .426. (In an odd twist, at each level Stan had hit for a higher average than the batting champions of the Western Association, International League, and National League, but hadn't appeared in enough games in any league to qualify for the batting title.) Including his minor-league statistics, Musial had played 153 games, rapped out 224 hits, including forty-one doubles, fourteen triples, and thirty home runs, for a .364 average, scored 151 runs, and batted in 122. Years later, Johnny Mize vilified Branch Rickey for not bringing the youngster up sooner. "We might have gone ahead and won the pennant," fumed Mize. "I'll tell you what the talk used to be about Rickey: stay in the pennant race until the last week of the season, and then get beat. I heard some talk to the effect that that was what he preferred. That way he drew the crowds all year and then later on the players couldn't come in for the big raise for winning the pennant and maybe the World Series. I don't know if it's true or not, but that was the talk."

What Mize couldn't have known was that Rickey was less interested in Musial than in Erv Dusak, a husky right-handed power hitter with good speed, good defense, and an arm considerably stronger than Stan's. (Dusak, as it developed, had trouble hitting the curveball, and never realized his minor-league potential.)

When Musial returned to his hometown of Donora that fall, the Donora Zinc Works Association honored him with a banquet at which he was presented with a watch and trophy by his old friend Joe Barbao. Honus Wagner, a native Pennsylvanian, was in attendance, and as Stan would recount many years later in his autobiography, "Even in my most fanciful dreams, I never would have dared imagine that I would play long enough and hit well enough to break many of old Honus' National League records."

◇ **4** ◇

Rookie

---

*I think the success of our ballclub back in
the '40s—other than havin' Musial in the
lineup every day—was due to the fact that
nobody thought of himself as a star.*

Max Lanier

On December 7, 1941, the Japanese
attacked Pearl Harbor in Hawaii, and a peace-loving America found itself at
war. Four days later, lacking any official direction, Commissioner Kenesaw
Mountain Landis asserted that baseball would be played in 1942, subject
to any wartime restrictions. Landis' stance was as much for the good of the
game as it was political: intensely anti-Roosevelt, the judge was attempting
to pre-empt what he feared might be an unfavorable decision by the President. As it developed, he had nothing to worry about. On January 15, 1942,
Roosevelt wrote what has come to be known as the "Green Light" letter,
granting permission for baseball to continue throughout the war. When
asked if the World Series would be played, Landis replied vehemently, "The
World Series is a national institution and those fellows fighting out there in
the stench and dirt want it just as much as we do."

The symbols of patriotism were everywhere. New Cardinal programs
featured the Statue of Liberty. In 1942, Redbird broadcaster France Laux

auctioned Cardinal gloves for war bonds. In October, Cardinal skipper Billy Southworth and Yankee manager Joe McCarthy would broadcast World Series reports to U.S. troops in England and Ireland, courtesy of the BBC. Late in 1943, when Major Greg "Pappy" Boyington, marine air ace of the "Black Sheep" fighter squadron fame, vowed that his men would shoot down a Japanese Zero for every baseball cap received from the winner of the 1943 World Series, the Cardinals (although vanquished) sent along twenty hats. By February 1944, Boyington's men had downed an additional forty-four Japanese fighters.

Less than a week after the Japanese sneak attack, Branch Rickey made his last important St. Louis deal, sending slugger Johnny Mize to the Giants for pitcher Bill Lohrman, first baseman Johnny McCarthy, catcher Ken O'Dea, and $50,000. Mize had become a thorn in the side of the Cardinal front office every year when it came time to talk contract, and with first-base duties now being split with the flashy-fielding rookie, Ray Sanders, and Johnny Hopp, Rickey felt safe trading Mize's big bat.

A pre-war father, the draft-deferred Musial left Lil and Dickie in Donora and headed to spring training. Because of his meteoric climb from Class C to the majors in 1941, Stan was the most talked about rookie in the major leagues, but as he would often do in later years, Musial started slowly in the Grapefruit League. He wasn't hitting and his throwing arm was weak, but Billy Southworth wouldn't give up on him. After benching the youngster for a couple days, Southworth put him back into the lineup facing a right-handed pitcher, a good percentage move. Stan responded by slamming line drives all over the ballpark, and when a left-handed reliever entered the contest in the late innings, the Cardinal manager left his prize rookie in the game. Musial came up with two men on base and his RBI triple gave the Cards another exhibition victory.

"That's why I can't quit on him," said Southworth. "He's that kind of a boy. Slump, maybe, we all have 'em. Pressure, yes, it's been terrific. Everybody wants to know where's that guy Musial they've been hearing so much about. The kid naturally thinks he ought to hit a home run every time up. But he was born to play baseball and he'll make it."

Years later, Cincinnati hurler Bucky Walters would recall the first time he saw Musial in the Cardinal lineup. Walters figured that Stan, like most bushers, would be a sucker for the high inside pitch. "Well, the next time I pitched against the Cardinals," said Bucky, "I waited for Musial to come up. I put one inside. I thought I'd got in there pretty good and tight. Boy, he hit a screaming line drive down the right-field line. I'll bet he put blisters on that ball. Well, I thought, there goes that theory. You could see that this fellow was going to make a lot of money in the big leagues and it wasn't going to be for stealing bases."

When the club traveled north, manager Billy Southworth consoled a dejected Musial over his failure to produce in Florida. "Don't worry, Stan," he said, "You're my left fielder. You can do it."

The day before the season began, Branch Rickey called Musial to his office. Rickey tore up Stan's old contract, which called for four hundred dollars a month, and gave the youngster some added incentive with a new pact for seven hundred dollars a month. Musial called Lillian that night and told her to pack her bags. She and little Dick were moving to St. Louis and would be spending the season at the Fairgrounds Hotel with Stan.

The following day, in the season opener, Musial tripled and singled off Claude Passeau, but the Cubs outlasted big Mort Cooper, 5–4. Stan homered and rapped a pair of singles the next afternoon, but a couple of days later at Pittsburgh, with his parents in the stands, he was lifted for Coaker Triplett, a right-handed-hitting pinch-hitter, as lefty Ken Heintzelman shut out the Redbirds. Musial was a rookie, after all, and this wouldn't be the only time he'd leave for a pinch-batter in 1942.

In May, the Dodgers won eleven of twelve games and made a shambles of the early going in the pennant race. The Cardinals, shut out in five of their first two dozen games, were generally ineffectual and lucky to be 15–15, but when the Dodgers arrived at Sportsman's Park, the Redbird players came out of their slump and swept the three-game series. St. Louis still trailed Brooklyn by six lengths when June opened with the Cardinals downing Chicago, 3–0, on a shaky, but effective, ten-hit performance by Howie Pollet. Pollet, called "the smartest young pitcher I ever saw" by Sam Breadon in the spring, was described by Musial as "an artist, a class pitcher, a stylist with pitching rhythm and a student of the game. His fast ball moved and he had the great straight change and slow curve."

In mid-month, Billy Southworth made Johnny Hopp his everyday first baseman, shifted Jimmy Brown to second, a move which relegated Frank "Creepy" Crespi to the bench, and handed the third-base job to Whitey Kurowski.

When Kurowski was an eight-year-old boy in Reading, Pennsylvania, he had fallen off a fence and gashed his right arm badly. Whitey's father was a mill hand who, with ten children in the family, lacked the resources to obtain adequate medical treatment for the boy and young George contracted osteomyelitis. Much of his ulna rotted away and had to be cut out, leaving George with some three inches of bone missing from his right arm between his wrist and forearm. (This condition would later exempt the Cardinal third

31

baseman from military service.) Red Schoendienst would later call Kurowski "one of the most underrated ballplayers I've played with," and Musial likened him to a sleeping giant when he said, "Whenever a pitcher knocked him down or threw at him, he invariably hit the next pitch out of the ball park. He really would wake up when aroused."

With their new infield and an outfield of Musial, Terry Moore, and the ever-hustling Enos Slaughter, St. Louis was set.

The Cardinals had won seven straight and trailed the Dodgers by four and a half games when they met Brooklyn at Ebbets Field on June 18. Four losses in the five-game set left St. Louis seven and a half lengths back and seemed to end all pennant hopes. The Associated Press had already written the Redbirds off: "The ambitions of the Cardinals to make it a two-club race for the National League pennant were all but totally wrecked here today."

At the All-Star break, St. Louis trailed Brooklyn by eight and a half games. If the Cardinal players would have just conceded the pennant, the AP's prediction might have come true. When team owner Sam Breadon sold the high-salaried Lon Warneke to the Cubs for the waiver price, most St. Louisans felt the front office had given up for the year. Breadon disagreed, saying he had dispatched Warneke to make room on the pitching staff for youngsters like right-hander Johnny Beazley. (During spring training, New York sportswriter Harry Grayson had called the cocky Beazley "another Dizzy Dean" because of his confidence, control, good fastball, and dazzling curve.) The next afternoon, Beazley posted his first shutout of the season, downing the Giants, 9–0, for his ninth victory of the year.

By the time the Dodgers came to town for back-to-back doubleheaders on July 18 and 19, the Cardinals had closed to within seven games of the lead. In the first twin bill, the Bums jumped out to an early 4–1 lead only to watch as the Redbirds scored seven times in the middle innings and went on to a 7–4 victory. Musial's single sent home the two go-ahead runs and fractured the finger of Brookyn's premier reliever, Hugh Casey, who would see no action for the next three weeks. Curt Davis, in his first relief appearance of the year, retired the last eight Cardinal batters as Brooklyn eked out a 4–3 win in the nightcap. On the nineteenth, before the largest crowd of the year at Sportsman's Park, the Redbirds mounted a 7–0 lead in the first game of the twin bill, then held on for an 8–5 win. But the Cardinals suffered a serious blow in the contest when Mort Cooper strained a ligament, an ailment which team physician Dr. Robert F. Hyland said would sideline him for a week to ten days. Matters were looking bleak when Brooklyn scored twice in the first inning of the nightcap, but the

Cards enjoyed their second five-run inning of the day in the third to take a 6–2 lead. The scrappy Dodgers tallied four runs in the fifth to tie the score at six-all. That's where matters stood until the eleventh, when Enos Slaughter hit a long drive to center. Pete Reiser dashed back, and at the moment he caught Slaughter's line drive, crashed into the center field wall, then slumped onto the outfield grass. The Dodger outfielder said later, "It was like a hand grenade had gone off inside my head."

Reiser somehow relayed the ball to the infield, but shortstop Pee Wee Reese's throw to the plate was too late. Slaughter had an inside-the-park home run and the Cards had a 7–6 win, narrowing Brooklyn's hold on first place to five games. Reiser was expected to be out for at least two weeks, but Durocher and Dodger management hurried him back into the lineup three days later in a pinch-hitting appearance. Less than a week later, he returned to full-time duty, but suffered from dizzy spells, double vision, and severe headaches for the balance of the season. At the time of the injury, Reiser was leading the National League with a .350 batting average, but from that day to the end of the year, he hit just .244 and was never again the same ballplayer.

The Dodgers, at 71–29, reached their high-water mark of the season on August 5, when they opened up a ten-game lead over St. Louis. Dodger general manager Larry MacPhail visited the clubhouse after their 1–0 win over the Phillies that day and said, "I'm telling you boys, the Cardinals are going to beat you if you're not careful. You guys are getting lackadaisical, you think you have it clinched, and before you know it, they are going to beat you out."

The tide turned for the Cardinals three days later at Pittsburgh. St. Louis tied the score in the ninth when Musial tripled and faked a steal of home. Bucs hurler Luke Hamlin, distracted by Stan's base-running antics, committed a balk, and Stan trotted home with the tying run. The game went sixteen innings and ended in a tie when darkness called a halt to the proceedings. That same day, Brooklyn hurler Whit Wyatt lost for the first time in four years to the lowly Boston Braves in a game which featured one beanball brawl after another. The Dodgers were getting a richly deserved reputation for playing dirty ball.

"If I had a ball club as good as Durocher's," said Boston manager Casey Stengel, "I wouldn't throw at a ball club as bad as mine. We're going to battle those guys all the harder from now on, and I've talked to [Pittsburgh manager Frank] Frisch, [Chicago manager Jimmie] Wilson and other managers who feel the same. Sure, Brooklyn has got a big lead, but they're not in yet. In case you guys didn't notice, St. Louis is winning steadily. Why,

I've never seen anything like 'em. They don't steal many bases but they sure put the pressure on your infielders and outfielders, making 'em handle the ball faster than they can, to keep 'em from taking an extra base."

Jimmie Wilson echoed Stengel's sentiments. "The Cardinals knock you out of the way on the bases just for fun," said Wilson, "yet we don't have any trouble with any team except Brooklyn. Seven teams can't be wrong. When a guy starts hitting you in the clinches, you've got to protect yourself. Well, we're not asking for it, but from here on in, it's every man for himself. The funny part about the whole business, when you come right down to it, is they don't have to do things like that to win."

During one game at Wrigley Field, Durocher could be heard clearly, shouting from the Brooklyn bench to "stick it in his ear" with each new Chicago batter. Durocher's unsportsmanlike conduct enraged Hi Bithorn, the opposing pitcher. Bithorn went into his windup, raised his leg, and was called for a balk when he fired the ball into the Brooklyn dugout, straight at Leo the Lip's head.

The Redbirds, who would lose two games in a row just once in the second half of the season, reeled off an eight-game winning streak in mid-August, helped along, oddly, by a song. Team trainer Dr. Harrison J. Weaver played the mandolin, Musial the slide whistle, and Harry Walker would put "Pass the Biscuits, Mirandy" on the record player. Spike Jones' novelty song became a sort of victory march for the Cardinals and it worked, perhaps the most unusual good-luck amulet in baseball history.

Riding a six-game winning streak of their own, the Dodgers arrived in St. Louis for a four-game series beginning on August 24. At the time, no one thought the Cardinals had more than a distant chance at winning the pennant even though the Redbirds had reduced their deficit to seven and a half games. Billy Southworth noted, "The Dodgers haven't had their slump yet. We have had ours. So have all the other clubs in the league. I've been around a long time and never saw even the best team fail to hit some kind of a slump sooner or later."

Prophetic. On the twenty-fourth, the Cards drubbed Brooklyn, 7–1, while Musial raised his average to .319, fourth-best in the National League. The next evening, in front of the largest night crowd in St. Louis history, superstitious Mort Cooper took the mound against Whit Wyatt. Cooper had a thing about the number thirteen. His uniform number was thirteen, he was born in 1913, his wife was born on June 13, and his son on September 13. Earlier in the season, Mort had been stuck on thirteen wins and had twice lost a shot at number fourteen, so to change his luck, he began changing uniforms and uniform numbers to match the victory he was seeking. Wearing Gus Mancuso's number fourteen, he hurled a two-hit shutout over Cincinnati's Paul Derringer. Four days later, he donned brother Walker's number fifteen and downed the Cubs. On August 25, he wore Ken O'Dea's number sixteen.

Through twelve innings, the game was deadlocked in a scoreless tie. In Cooper's unlucky thirteenth, the Dodgers took a 1–0 lead, but in the bottom of the frame, Enos Slaughter drew a walk, and back-to-back singles by Musial and Walker Cooper pulled the Cards into a 1–1 tie. Cooper's hit brought an avalanche of seat cushions and straw hats floating down onto the field and sent Whit Wyatt to the showers in favor of reliever Larry French, who had worked five innings the night before. When Whitey Kurowski led off the bottom of the fourteenth with a bunt single, Brooklyn manager Leo Durocher motioned to the bullpen for rookie reliever Les Webber. Marty Marion reached base safely when first baseman Dolph Camilli gloved his attempted sacrifice bunt but threw too late to second to force Kurowski. One out later, Jimmy Brown walked, loading the bases. Terry Moore's infield hit sent Marion home and gave the Redbirds a hard-fought 2–1 victory. French suffered his second loss in two nights and third of the season, all at the hands of the Cardinals. The Redbirds had now won fourteen of their last sixteen games and the Brooklyn lead was down to five and a half.

The next day, the contest was tied at 1–1 when Jimmy Brown drew a base on balls in the tenth and pulled into second on Terry Moore's single. Enos Slaughter hit an easy one-hopper back to Brooklyn hurler Max Macon, who spun around for the play at third, but Brown, off with the pitch, was already sliding into the bag. Macon retired Slaughter at first, but when Coaker Triplett hit a slow dribbler to the left side of the infield, the Brooklyn hurler skidded and fell to the grass, attempting to field the hit. Brown crossed the plate and the Redbirds had another extra-inning 2–1 victory. Former Cardinal Curt Davis beat Max Lanier in the series finale, leaving the Birds five and a half back with thirty games remaining in the season. Only two of those contests were head-to-head with the Dodgers, in Brooklyn, no less, but Billy Southworth refused to be pessimistic. "We'll keep after them and if we keep hustling on every play, we can pass them. And once we do, they'll never catch us. Never mind what Brooklyn does. It's what we do that counts."

By the first of September, St. Louis trailed the Dodgers by just three and a half games. On September 5, aided by Musial's only hit of the day, an RBI triple which broke a 2–2 deadlock, Johnny Beazley improved his record to 18–5 with a 5–3 win over the Reds. The next afternoon, while

Brooklyn lost to the Giants, the Redbirds fashioned a come-from-behind victory at Cincinnati. Cardinal speed paid off in the sixth when Musial caught the Reds napping and scored all the way from first on a two-out pop fly single by Ken O'Dea. Whitey Kurowski's RBI single in the ninth gave St. Louis a 3–2 decision. With twenty-four wins in their last twenty-eight outings, the Redbirds were now just three games out. The race tightened up even more the next day when the Dodgers split a doubleheader with the Giants at the Polo Grounds. At Crosley Field, Cardinal hurler Mort Cooper won his sixth game in a row and number nineteen on the season, wearing teammate Harry Gumbert's uniform, as the Redbirds pasted Cincinnati, 10–2, and moved two and a half games back of Brooklyn. On September 9, Musial was involved in a weird pre-game mishap which affected the outcome of the St. Louis contest with New York. Carl Hubbell had just begun warming up on the mound when Stan unleashed a wild throw to the infield. The ball hit Hubbell squarely behind the right ear and he was unable to pitch. Hal Schumacher hurriedly warmed up, but was still jittery when the game began and surrendered three quick runs in the first as the Redbirds went on to post a 5–1 win.

When the Redbirds visited Ebbets Field on September 11 for their final series of the year against the Dodgers, they had won twenty-seven of their last thirty-two outings. The once formidable Brooklyn lead had dwindled to just two games, the Bums' slimmest margin since May 9. Tension in both clubhouses was thick enough to cut with a knife. On September 11, hoping to become the major league's first twenty-game winner, Mort Cooper, wearing Coaker Triplett's uniform and number twenty, faced Whit Wyatt. For five innings, both hurlers were near letter-perfect. Each team had one hit, but neither baserunner had advanced to second base. In the sixth, Cooper singled to center, was sacrificed to second by Jimmy Brown, and scored on Enos Slaughter's base hit off first baseman Dolph Camilli's glove. That was all Mort needed as he went the distance for a 3–0 win, surrendering just three harmless singles. The Cardinals were now one game back.

The following afternoon, Max Macon and Max Lanier squared off in the National League's biggest game of the year. With Walker Cooper on base in the second, Macon tried to fluff a slow curve past Whitey Kurowski, but got the delivery a little too close to the strike zone. The Cardinal third baseman slammed the pitch into the lower left-field seats, barely fair, for a 2–0 lead. When Billy Herman took the last pitch of the game down the middle for a called strike three, the Redbirds had a 2–1 win and Brooklyn, after 144 days atop the National League, was now tied with St. Louis for first place. Both teams had identical 94–46 records. A little over five weeks earlier, the Dodgers had held a seemingly insurmountable ten-game lead. Flushed with success, Sam Breadon declared, "I think we're in," and ordered tickets printed for the World Series.

The Cardinals left for Philadelphia. When the players detrained at Broad Street Station, pitcher Johnny Beazley got into a heated argument with a redcap who insisted on carrying his bag. The redcap swore at Beazley, who retaliated by throwing his suitcase. When the porter pulled a knife, the Cardinal pitcher threw up his arm in self-defense and was cut on the right thumb. The wound was deep and bled profusely, and Beazley's teammates wondered if he would be able to pitch the next day. On Sunday, September 13, Brooklyn dropped a doubleheader to Cincinnati while St. Louis split a pair with the Phillies. Beazley's injury was less serious than it first appeared, but he nevertheless lost the first game of the twin bill, 2–1. The Redbirds came from behind to win the nightcap, 3–2, on a tie-breaking home run by Terry Moore. With two weeks to go, St. Louis now enjoyed sole possession of first place and a one-game lead.

On September 14, Musial drove in the lead run in a 6–3 win over the Phillies. The following evening, it was Stan's two-run double which kept the Redbirds in a game which eventually went fourteen innings before Murry Dickson captured a 3–2 victory over Philadelphia. A day later, Musial batted in a pair of runs and scored another as St. Louis downed Boston, 6–2, while the Cardinal front office began accepting applications for World Series tickets. Reserved tickets were going for $17.50.

On the seventeenth, the Cards were trailing Boston, 4–1, when they rallied for five runs in the ninth and another come-from-behind win. Southworth lifted Musial (batting .314 at the time) for pinch-hitter Coaker Triplett in the final frame, and Triplett came through with his second pinch-hit of the season, driving in the winning run. Coupled with Brooklyn's loss to the Pirates, the Cardinals had given themselves a little breathing room as they boosted their lead to three games over the Dodgers. On the next-to-last Sunday of the season, Mort Cooper out-duelled Lon Warneke in the first game of a doubleheader at Chicago for the Cardinals one hundredth win of the season, while at Brooklyn, the Dodgers swept a twin bill from Philadelphia and picked up a half-game in the standings.

The Cardinals returned home to down the Pirates, 2–1, in the opener of a two-game series at Sportsman's Park. On September 22, the Redbirds were trailing by a run in the bottom of the fifth inning when Musial came to the plate with the bases loaded to face Rip Sewell, the pitcher who had yielded his first major-league home run. Sewell's first delivery to Musial was high, the second a hanging slider. Stan timed the pitch perfectly and drove it over the right-field pavilion for a long home run as the Cardinals breezed to a 9–3 victory. It was their 102nd of the year and a new St. Louis record. The next afternoon, Musial rapped three hits, scored a run, and drove in two more, pacing the Redbirds to a 4–2 win over Cincinnati, and on September 24, Stan repeated his three-hit performance while Mort Cooper blanked the Braves.

A St. Louis victory or a Dodger defeat would end the pennant race, but none of the Cardinals was celebrating just yet. "We're not saying a thing," insisted Terry Moore. "That twenty-one-game winning streak the Cubs had in 1935 taught me a lesson. We didn't go into any tailspin, they just overhauled us. So the thing is to say nothing, but do plenty, until you're really in."

The Redbirds were idle on September 25, but Brooklyn staved off elimination with a 6–5 win over the Braves. St. Louis was rained out on the twenty-sixth while the Dodgers crushed Philadelphia, 8–3, and even though the Redbirds had won nine of their last ten, they arrived at the last day of the season with just a game-and-a-half lead over Brooklyn. The Dodgers were playing at Philadelphia and the Cardinals were entertaining Chicago in a twin bill at Sportsman's Park. A win by Brooklyn and a sweep by the Cubs would leave the two clubs in a deadlock for the pennant, necessitating a playoff. The Bums won their contest, 4–3, but the Redbirds rolled over Chicago, 9–2, in the opening game of the doubleheader. When Musial pulled down Clyde McCullough's long fly ball in the left-field corner for the final out, the Redbirds had clinched the pennant with their 105th win of the year, the first time since 1934 that a National League race had gone down to the last day of the season.

The Cardinal locker room was a madhouse. Trainer Doc Weaver put the "Notre Dame Victory March" on the phonograph while manager Billy Southworth was hoisted on the shoulders of Max Lanier and Harry Walker. Dozens of reporters interviewed happy Cardinal players and at least one photographer snapped a shot of Southworth kissing pitcher Ernie White. Southworth was proud of his charges. "We won this one the hard way," he exulted, "and no one won it for us. We went out and won it ourselves and we'll go out and beat the Yankees the same way. One thing this young club isn't afraid of is reputations. All are great kids. They hustled and worked together and it would be difficult and unfair to point to any one or two, saying they contributed most to victory."

The Cardinals had won forty-three of their final fifty-one games, a blazing .843 pace, in what was arguably the greatest stretch drive in baseball history. St. Louis finished with 106 victories, most in the National League since the 1909 Pirates, but more importantly, the Cardinals had downed the Dodgers five out of six times in the crucial head-to-head contests in August and September. Durocher had driven his club to twenty-five wins in their last forty-two games, but the effort fell short as Brooklyn became the third team in the twentieth century to post one hundred victories and still lose the title.

Years later, Musial said, "The best team I ever played for was the 1942 St. Louis Cardinals . . . We didn't make many mistakes in 1942. We had good pitching and a lot of speed. We were hard line drive hitters. And we were daring. But the best thing we had was that spirit among us. We just felt like we were unbeatable. We played together, and we spent a lot of time together. We had a great spirit on that team."

Terry Moore agreed, without equivocation, "I think the '42 Cardinal club was the best I was with. If the war hadn't come along, I feel we could have won maybe six or seven pennants in a row." Harry Walker felt the same. "The best club I ever played for? The 1942 Cardinals. They were super. Oh, the pitching we had, and the hitting and fielding, too. All through the 1940s we had great teams, but that '42 club was something special."

St. Louis had captured the 1942 pennant with a rather modest year offensively. No Cardinal hit more than fifteen home runs and, save for Slaughter with ninety-eight RBIs, none of the Redbirds had accounted for over seventy-five RBIs. Only Slaughter (.318) and Musial (.315) hit for better than a .300 average. Despite this seemingly bland offense, St. Louis had led the National League in runs scored (755), doubles (282), triples (69), and batting average (.268), and even though the Redbirds had slugged a mere sixty home runs, the club topped the National League with a .379 slugging average.

Pitching was where the 1942 Cardinal club shone. As a team, the Redbirds led the National League in strikeouts (651), shutouts (18), and earned run average (2.55). Mort Cooper posted a 22–7 record and topped all National League hurlers with a glittering 1.78 ERA and ten shutouts, the most for any National League pitcher from 1942 through 1960. (Cooper's excellent showing would earn him the league's Most Valuable Player award, only the sixth time a pitcher had taken the honor.) Twenty-four-year-old Johnny Beazley trailed only Cooper in wins and earned run average, compiling a 21–6 mark with a 2.13 ERA in his rookie season. Max Lanier split sixteen decisions as a starter, but posted five additional wins in relief to go with two saves and a 2.98 earned run average. Right-hander Howie Krist, who finished at 13–3 with a 2.51 ERA, was 5–1 as a spot starter, 8–2 in relief, and saved a game.

Musial had compiled some respectable numbers in his rookie season, finishing with eighty-seven runs scored, seventy-two RBIs, thirty-two doubles, ten triples, and ten home runs. The weak arm, an albatross around his neck in spring training, had improved as the year wore on, as many a surprised National League base-runner had discovered. By August, many of the naysayers who had tagged the young Polish boy as a ninety-day wonder were beginning to admit he might not be a flash in the pan after all. Baseball insiders such as Casey Stengel hadn't been fooled by Stan's inability to produce in spring training. "You'll be looking at him for a long, long while," predicted Casey, "Ten, fifteen, maybe twenty years. He's up to stay."

In his first tour around the league, Stan had attracted quite a bit of attention, especially when he came to the plate. His speed getting from home to first base on grounders, his defense, the level swing of the bat, the unorthodox peekaboo stance—all of this endeared Musial to baseball fans everywhere. In September, Stan had received his first national publicity when J. Roy Stockton, sports editor of the St. Louis *Post-Dispatch,* wrote an article for the *Saturday Evening Post* in which he named the Cardinal outfielder Rookie of the Year.

◆ ◆ ◆

The 1942 New York Yankees, a fearsome club led by manager Joe McCarthy, had won 103 games and breezed to the American League pennant with a comfortable nine-game margin over the second-place Boston Red Sox. Center fielder Joe DiMaggio, with twenty-one home runs, 114 RBIs, and a .305 batting average, was the heart and soul of the ball club, but hard behind him was left fielder Charlie "King Kong" Keller with twenty-six round-trippers and 108 runs batted in. The Yankee pitching staff was anchored by a quartet of righthanders: Ernie Bonham (21-6), Spurgeon "Spud" Chandler (16-5), veteran "Red" Ruffing (14-7), and the spectacular rookie Hank Borowy (15-4).

The Yanks had won eight World Series in eight tries since 1927 and had lost just four of their last thirty-six Series games. Confident of victory in the post-season championship, the Yankees couldn't hold a candle to the always arrogant New York newspapers. Manager Billy Southworth, placed in the unusual position of defending a team which had won 106 games, said, "They'll have to beat us out on the field, not in newspaper columns." The two deans of sportswriting were split on their votes.

Grantland Rice was firmly in the Yankee corner: "The Yankees don't think they can be beaten, even if the Series goes to extra innings in the seventh game." But Ring Lardner held a different view. "St. Louis pitching," he wrote, "in the long run, will overcome Yankee hitting."

The 1942 World Series opened at Sportsman's Park on September 30 before a crowd of 34,769. Red Ruffing and Max Lanier duelled through three scoreless innings until the Yanks took a 1–0 lead in the fourth on Buddy Hassett's two-out RBI double. The American Leaguers scored again in the fifth and seemed to put the game on ice in the eighth with two more runs. Ruffing was cruising along with a no-hitter until Terry Moore spoiled his bid for immortality with a two-out single in the eighth. Assisted by reliever Max Lanier's two errors, New York added another pair of runs in the ninth and Ruffing carried a one-hit shutout into the final frame. Musial opened the inning by fouling out, but Walker Cooper singled and one out later, pinch-hitter Ray Sanders worked Ruffing for a base on balls. Marty Marion's triple to right plated the first two Cardinal runs of the game and Ken O'Dea's single made the score 7–3, Yankees. Jimmy Brown stroked a safety to center and Joe McCarthy, taking no chances, brought in Spud Chandler to close out the game. Terry Moore's RBI single only heightened the drama and when Enos Slaughter beat out an infield hit, the winning run came to the plate in the person of rookie Stan Musial. Musial tried to get under one of Chandler's deliveries and power it out of the park, but all he could do was ground to first baseman Buddy Hassett. Hassett flipped to Chandler covering first, and the game was over. Stan had accounted for two of the three outs in the inning and hitless in five trips to the plate, had proven to be a bust in the first post-season appearance of his career. Although the ninth-inning Cardinal rally had fallen short, it dissipated any notions the club had that the Yankees were supermen.

The next afternoon was a meeting of twenty-game winners: Ernie Bonham, 21–5, vs. Johnny Beazley, 21–6. The Cardinals broke on top, 3–0, but the Yankees fought back to tie the score in the eighth. The Redbirds regained the lead with a two-out rally in the bottom of the inning when Enos Slaughter doubled into the right-field corner and scored on Musial's first hit of the series, an RBI single. Beazley faltered in the ninth, surrendering a leadoff single to Bill Dickey. Then Buddy Hassett lined a hit to right, but Enos Slaughter's strong throw to Whitey Kurowski nailed pinch-runner Tuck Stainback at third and broke the back of the inning. Red Ruffing flied to right and when Phil Rizzuto grounded to Marion to end the contest, the Series was tied at one game apiece.

At this point, the Musials had a travel decision to make. Sam Breadon provided a hundred dollars for expenses for each player's wife, but on Stan's meager salary, the couple decided it was too expensive to put Lil up in a hotel in New York for the middle three games of the Series. Lillian decided to take the Cardinals special train back east, get off at Pittsburgh, and return to St. Louis for the windup. Several other player wives made a similar decision. Those who failed to travel to New York would see no more of the 1942 World Series.

The Series resumed at Yankee Stadium on October 3 in front of a record crowd of 69,123. Spud Chandler (16-5) against Ernie White (7-5) seemed a mismatch, but White pitched the game of his career. The contest was scoreless when Whitey Kurowski drew a base on balls to lead off the third. Marty Marion bunted successfully, but the Yankees squawked that the ball had hit Marty's bat twice. Marion, required to bat over, swung away and beat out a slow roller toward third and White sacrificed both runners into scoring position. Second baseman Joe Gordon fielded Jimmy Brown's ground ball cleanly, but had no play at the plate, and the Cards led, 1–0. The Yankees threatened to tie the score all day. In the sixth, with two out and a man on first, Joe DiMaggio smashed a low liner to left-center. Musial broke for the ball, slipped, and went down, but Terry Moore made a spectacular catch on the dead run to end the inning. In the seventh, Musial backed up all the way to the left-field seats to grab Joe Gordon's bid for a home run, and a moment later, Enos Slaughter climbed the right-field wall to make an even greater catch on Charlie Keller's long drive. White finished with a six-hit, 2–0 shutout, the first time the Yankees had been whitewashed in the World Series since another Cardinal, Jesse Haines, had turned the trick in the third game of the 1926 championship.

Sunday, October 4, saw another record crowd when 69,902 fans turned out for Game Four, the hardest-hitting contest of the Series. Trailing 1–0, the Cardinals mauled Yankee starter Hank Borowy, 15–4 in the regular season, for six runs in the fourth. Musial started the big inning by beating out a bunt to the left side. Walker Cooper's single sent him to third and when Johnny Hopp walked, the bases were loaded. Whitey Kurowski's hit to left scored two and sent Hopp to third. Marion walked to load the bases again and pitcher Mort Cooper blooped a single into short right, scoring Hopp and Kurowski and knocking Borowy out of the box. Reliever Atley Donald retired Jimmy Brown on a fly ball to center, but Terry Moore came through with a clutch base hit, scoring Marion with the fifth run of the inning. Slaughter forced Moore at second and Musial doubled to right for his second hit of the frame, tying a record for most hits in an inning in a World Series and giving the Redbirds and Mort Cooper a seemingly insurmountable 6–1 lead.

But these were the Yankees, after all, and in the sixth, they demonstrated that their reputation was well-deserved. Phil Rizzuto singled to left, Red Rolfe walked, and Roy Cullenbine singled home a run. After DiMaggio popped out, Charlie Keller blasted a three-run homer into the lower right-field stands. The Cardinal lead was down to a run. Billy Southworth, having seen enough of Cooper, sent in reliever Harry Gumbert. Joe Gordon reached base on Whitey Kurowski's throwing error and one out later, Gerry Priddy's RBI double tied the score at six. But the Redbirds regained the lead with two runs in the next half-inning and padded their margin to 9–6 on Max Lanier's RBI single in the top of the ninth. Although Howie Pollet was the pitcher of record, the official scorer awarded Lanier the win for his three scoreless innings in relief.

As the lineups were being exchanged the next day at home plate, Yankee coach Art Fletcher demanded that the umpires keep clubhouse manager Butch Yatkeman out of the Cardinal dugout. The Yankees were testy and the pressure was showing in the form of petty meanness. Home plate umpire Bill Summers was sympathetic to the St. Louis club, but told Cardinal captain Terry Moore that under the rules, Yatkeman must leave the dugout. "That's all right, Bill," said Moore, "This is just one more reason why there's going to be no tomorrow in this World Series."

No one could remember the last time a team had swept New York three straight at Yankee Stadium, but the Cardinals did just that, ending the Series that afternoon. With the score tied at two, Walker Cooper led off the ninth with a single to right center. Although Whitey Kurowski had been hitting Red Ruffing hard all day, he was wearing the collar with an oh-for-three performance. But Ruffing put a pitch into his wheelhouse and the Cardinal third baseman sent a rifle shot into the left-field seats, just a few feet fair, to put St. Louis on top, 4–2. The Yankees did not go quietly in the bottom of the frame. Leadoff batter Joe Gordon opened the inning with a clean single to left, only his second hit in twenty-one Series at-bats. When second baseman Jimmy Brown bobbled Bill Dickey's grounder, the Yankees had the winning run at the plate. But, incredibly, Gordon strayed too far from second and was picked off. Gerry Priddy popped out and pinch-hitter George Selkirk, in his last major-league at-bat, grounded to second baseman Jimmy Brown, bringing the 1942 World Series to an end.

Whitey Kurowski was the center of the clubhouse celebration as the Cardinals lifted wizened old Judge Landis off the floor, tore National League president Ford Frick's hat to shreds, and sang "Pass the Biscuits, Mirandy."

Over in a somber Yankee clubhouse, Joe McCarthy was gracious in defeat. "They're a good ball club and they beat a good ball club," said Marse Joe. "They deserve all credit, but my boys weren't disgraced. That's what I told Southworth. The spotlight's on him now."

The 1942 World Series was generally considered to be the biggest upset since 1914, when the Miracle Braves had swept Connie Mack's heavily favored Philadelphia Athletics. Mack himself admitted, "I have to take my hat off to the Cardinals. They played the game the way it ought to be played. They took advantage of everything and didn't give anything. I think that's the greatest club I've ever seen."

The Cardinals had taken as many victories from New York in four days as eight National League clubs had won since 1927 as they became the first team to beat the Yankees in the fall classic since 1923. Each member of the Redbirds took home $6,193 for the Series win and Billy Southworth's season was made complete a month later when he was named Manager of the Year.

Musial had finished the Series with a .222 batting average on four hits, one a double, four bases on balls, two runs scored, and two RBIs. After the final game, Stan wired Lil at the Fairgrounds Hotel in St. Louis and told her he would be arriving the following afternoon on the Cardinal train. Rethinking his decision, Stan sent a second telegram, asking Lil to meet him in Donora instead. Musial's rookie season ended with him standing on the platform at Pennsylvania Station, watching his teammates pull out for St. Louis. He cried as he watched them go.

◇ 5 ◇

Holdout

---

*He shone in 1943 like a National League
Ty Cobb.*

SPORTSWRITER FRED LIEB

Less than a month after the 1942
World Series, Branch Rickey bade farewell to the Cardinals when he signed
a five-year pact with the Brooklyn Dodgers. Sam Breadon had notified
Rickey months earlier that his contract was not going to be renewed,
realizing the franchise couldn't begin to afford Rickey's big salary in the
lean war years ahead—Branch's share of the profits over the past two
seasons had been over $150,000. Then again, perhaps the Cardinal owner
had simply tired of playing second fiddle too often in his own organization.
No matter. Rickey was gone.

At Donora, Pennsylvania, Musial was employed at the zinc works when
he received his 1943 contract in the mail. (Unlike today's major leaguers,
ballplayers of yesteryear needed to supplement their modest baseball in-
comes by holding down regular jobs during the off-season.) Eager to get to
spring training and back on the ball field, Stan tore open the envelope, but
was disappointed to discover Breadon had offered only a thousand-dollar
raise. After talking it over with Lillian, Musial wrote back, asking for
$10,000. Stan suggested that with Terry Moore and Enos Slaughter in the
armed services, he would have to play "even harder." Musial's bid for more

money was immature and poorly thought out, and he had unwittingly played right into the hands of Breadon, who answered in a coldly worded letter. Stan would have to do no more in 1943 than he had in 1942, said Breadon, and he believed, perhaps wrongly, that Musial was "the kind of ball player that gave all you had in every ball game." Breadon closed his letter by saying he expected the "same in 1943, if you sign a contract with us."

The veiled threat must have been quite chilling to a young man who wanted nothing more than to play baseball. Musial countered by asking for $7,500, but Breadon was having none of it. "No one in our organization has been advanced faster than you have been," wrote the Cardinal owner. "We have had great outfielders on our ball club, including Hafey, Medwick, Moore and Slaughter, and none of them in their second year received a contract for as much as $5,500." In this war of words with an opponent far more canny than himself, Musial countered that a comparison with salaries of a decade earlier was unfair, but Sam wrote back: "We could write letters until the end of the season and get no place. Therefore, I suggest you come to St. Louis and if you do not sign a contract and want to stay out of baseball in 1943, we will pay your round-trip expenses."

There it was, out in the open. Breadon's threat was real now. Stan could either sign the contract he didn't want or continue to toil in the zinc works. Showing a lot of gumption for a youngster, Musial refused to take the trip back west. Breadon, perhaps panicking a bit himself, sent Cardinal farm director Eddie Dyer to Donora with a compromise offer of $6,250. Stan quickly agreed to the terms and his first holdout was ended.

With war raging in the Atlantic and Pacific, government travel restrictions forced baseball to change its plans for spring training in 1943. Commissioner Landis ruled that no club, with the exception of the Cardinals and Browns, could train south of the Ohio or Potomac Rivers or west of the Mississippi. The Redbirds, arriving for the first day of spring training at Cairo, Illinois, found Cotter Field under four feet of water, the result of levee seepage from the Mississippi River. Trainer Doc Weaver had written to the players, suggesting they bring hats, topcoats, and long underwear to camp. In the cold weather, they needed each item of clothing.

The Cardinals had lost pitcher Johnny Beazley, infielder Creepy Crespi, and outfielders Terry Moore and Enos Slaughter to the armed forces over the winter and would say goodbye to second baseman Jimmy Brown and pitchers Howie Pollet and Murry Dickson during the season. Manager Billy Southworth promoted infielder Lou Klein from Columbus to fill the void at second base, and Harry Walker became the regular center fielder. In June,

Breadon sent outfielders Coaker Triplett, Buster Adams, and Dain Clay to the Phillies for Earl Naylor and Danny Litwhiler. Litwhiler went to left, Musial was shifted to right, and Naylor was sent to Rochester. Pitcher Alpha Brazle earned an advance from the Sacramento farm club and hurlers George "Red" Munger and screwballer Harry Brecheen were promoted from Columbus.

Brazle was a colorful southpaw who managed to parlay the most limited of talents into a ten-year career on the mound. He was a poor fielder and threw a mediocre fastball, but he had good control and an effective sinker which, ironically, dipped better the more weary he got during a game. Red Munger was a giant right-hander with a good fastball and one of the best pickoff moves in the game, but he lacked the killer instinct. Despite flashes of brilliance, he enjoyed just two good seasons in a career which spanned a decade at the major-league level.

Harry Brecheen, on the other hand, was a different story altogether. Dubbed "the Cat" by sportswriter J. Roy Stockton for his fielding ability, Brecheen had won over a hundred games at the minor-league level and at age twenty-eight, was a little long in the tooth to be reaching the big time. But from 1944 through 1948, this bowlegged, stoop-shouldered left-hander was the most consistent hurler on the Cardinal pitching staff. Although not especially fast, Brecheen wasn't timid about knocking down an opposing batter when the situation warranted it, had amazing control, and could spot one of his dangerously deceptive screwballs anywhere in the strike zone. Ted Williams would later call him one of the smartest pitchers he ever faced.

Since 1922, no National League team that won the World Series had taken the pennant the following year, but the mood of the world champion Redbirds was exuberant as the club broke camp and headed north. To a man, the Cardinals were confident of winning the pennant.

Because rubber, a war-priority item, was scarce, A.G. Spalding & Brothers used re-processed rubber for its baseballs—the infamous dead balata ball. Lou Coleman, a spokesman for Spalding, confirmed what everyone already knew when he stated that the "shipment of baseballs sent out for the opening of the season, unfortunately, did not measure up to standard."

The Redbirds started the season unsurely, losing in eleven innings, 1–0, to the Reds. Musial, batting third in the lineup, collected his first triple of 1943 the next day, but the Redbirds failed to score again and went down to another 1–0 defeat at Crosley Field, this one in ten innings. Billy Southworth had already noticed the ball wasn't traveling the distance it should and instructed his charges to alter their playing technique. "We're back at the go-for-one-run style of baseball," said Southworth, "and the sooner we adapt ourselves to it, the better."

The Cards trailed in their third game of the season when Musial stole home in the sixth to break the St. Louis scoreless string at twenty-six innings. In the eighth, Stan singled, advanced to second on a single by Ray Sanders, made third on an error, and alertly came home with what proved to be the winning run on a passed ball. The following day, the Cardinals scored just once, but that tally was enough for Howie Pollet to capture a 1–0 win over the Reds. The Cards posted their second successive shutout the next afternoon when Mort Cooper five-hit the Cubs, but were white-washed by Chicago on April 29, 4–0. The Redbirds had played six games, five of which had been shutouts, had won every game in which they scored, and hadn't scored in any game they had lost. St. Louis continued the pattern the following day when they downed the Cubs, 4–3, in twelve innings.

Eleven games were played in 1943 before Joe Gordon of the Yankees hit the majors' first home run. Both league offices were concerned that the dreaded balata ball was going to kill interest in the sport, and teams which had 1942 baseballs on hand were given permission to use them. Those clubs which had no 1942 baseballs in stock quickly ordered some. On May 3, the Cards swept a doubleheader from Cincinnati, then left for their first extended road trip of the year. The following day, St. Louis racked up fifteen hits in an 11–3 win over the Cubs at Wrigley Field. The rabbit ball was back and nobody was happier about it than Musial, off to a slow start in his second full season at the major-league level. The new (old?) baseball had an electrifying effect on the Cardinals' newest star. Stan drove in a pair of runs and scored two others as Harry Brecheen downed the Dodgers, 7–1, on May 18, and four days later, Musial was five-for-ten with two RBIs and three runs scored against New York pitching, leading the Redbirds to a doubleheader victory at the Polo Grounds.

In late May and again in early June, Mort Cooper rallied the club when he became just the third pitcher in baseball history to throw back-to-back one-hitters. On Memorial Day, May 30, in the first game of a doubleheader at Sportsman's Park, Cooper one-hit the Dodgers. Brooklyn's only safety was an opposite-field, pop-fly double by Billy Herman in the fifth, inches fair and just a foot out of Musial's reach. Cooper's second one-hit perfor-mance came on June 5 against Philadelphia, and the Cardinals took over sole possession of first place the next day. Musial was hitless in his first two at-bats when he faced Philadelphia hurler Jack Kraus in the sixth inning with Lou Klein on second and one out. Stan singled Klein home and when the game was called after seven and a half innings because of darkness, the Redbirds and Howie Krist had a 1–0 shutout and Musial a twenty-two-game hitting streak. The following afternoon, Stan's string came to an end when the Cards and Phillies played to a 1–1 tie in a contest which was called after five innings because of rain. During his streak, Musial had come to the plate eighty-two times and made thirty-two hits for a .390 batting average, scored nineteen runs, and drove in eighteen.

On June 18, baseball commissioner Kenesaw Mountain Landis and Cardinal owner Sam Breadon presented the Redbird players with their 1942 World Series rings in pennant-raising ceremonies at Sportsman's Park. Three Cardinals in the armed forces, Enos Slaughter, Frank Crespi, and Johnny Beazley, were given leave to be present at the ceremony; a fourth, Terry Moore, was stationed in Panama and was unable to attend. His mother accepted the ring on his behalf.

By July 3, the two contenders for the 1943 pennant were tied for the National League lead. When the Cardinals opened a three-game series at Ebbets Field, the Cooper brothers, with Mort pitching and Walker catching, led the way as St. Louis downed Brooklyn, 5–3. Howie Pollet spun a masterful three-hit shutout in the first game of an Independence Day doubleheader. In the nightcap, the Redbirds roughed up Freddie Fitzsimmons and reliever Les Webber for four runs in the first inning en route to a 7–2 victory and a three-game lead in the standings.

Cardinal pitching was carrying the day. Mort Cooper blanked Boston, 7–0, on July 9, and Howie Pollet extended the St. Louis scoreless string to twenty-two innings when he hurled his third straight shutout the following afternoon, four-hitting the Braves, 6–0. (The celebration was a bittersweet one for Pollet, who received his orders to report to active duty in the U.S. Army Air Force on July 15.) Harry Gumbert whitewashed Boston in the opening game of a doubleheader on July 12, but the Cardinal scoreless streak was halted at thirty-one innings in the first inning of the nightcap when the Braves tallied two quick runs off Max Lanier. St. Louis rebounded to post a 9–6 victory and the Redbirds led the second-place Dodgers by five and a half games.

On July 13, at Shibe Park in Philadelphia, Musial made his first of twenty-four appearances in baseball's annual All-Star Game, lofting a sacrifice fly off Washington's Dutch Leonard in his initial at-bat. Stan slammed a double off Hal Newhouser later in the contest. The American League, declining to use a single member of the champion Yankees, won for the eighth time in the last eleven tries, pounding starting pitcher Mort Cooper for two walks, four hits, and four runs in two and one-third innings en route to a 5–3 victory. Despite the junior circuit's disdainful treatment of Cooper, Redbird manager Billy Southworth gave his hurler a vote of confidence. "Don't think I've weakened on Mort," said the Cardinal skipper. "If I am lucky enough to get into the World Series, he'll start for me."

Four straight losses to the Pirates following the All-Star break shaved the Cardinal margin to three and a half games, but a doubleheader sweep of the Bucs on July 19 helped the Birds close out their long road trip with sixteen wins in twenty-five games. St. Louis was about to open an incredible homestand at Sportsman's Park, one that would ultimately carry the club to the 1943 pennant.

First up were the New York Giants. Although three-hit in the opening game of a doubleheader on July 21, the Redbirds still won 3–1, then mounted a nineteen-hit attack in the nightcap and drubbed the Giants, 14–6. By day's end, Musial was leading all major-league hitters with a .342 batting average. Two more wins over New York increased the St. Louis margin over Brooklyn to five and a half games.

The Cardinals went on to win eleven consecutive games before the Phillies brought the winning streak to an end on July 26. And then the second-place Dodgers pulled into town, trailing St. Louis by nine games. Max Lanier, drawing Whit Wyatt in the opener of the four-game series, drove in the winning run with a ninth-inning single while scattering seven hits en route to a 2–1 win. In the sixth inning of the first game of a doubleheader the following day, the Cards were leading 6–1 when Brooklyn reliever Les Webber threw a fastball at Musial's head, then followed up with three inside pitches. For the only time in his career, Stan charged a pitcher. Musial's momentum was stayed when Dodger catcher Mickey Owen wrapped his right arm around his waist and eased the bat from his hand. While umpire Al Barlick attempted to reason with Stan, Cardinal coaches Mike Gonzalez and Buzzy Wares raced onto the field to protect their valuable outfielder. Walker Cooper was the next batter and he grounded out, intentionally stepping on Augie Galan's foot as he crossed first base. Owen, backing up the play, jumped on Cooper's back, but Cooper flipped him off, pinned him to the ground, and held him there. Both dugouts emptied onto the field and police were called out to separate the opposing catchers, both of whom were banished from the game. Musial was four-for-eight on the day as the Cards swept the twin bill and dropped the Dodgers into third place, a dozen games back. St. Louis made just six hits the next day, but used them to good advantage as the club scored seven runs in the first two innings and cruised to a 7–4 win behind Mort Cooper's fifteenth victory of the season.

The pennant race, while not mathematically ended, was effectively over. The Cardinals, who had begun their 18–4 homestand with a 48–28 record and a four-game lead over the second-place Dodgers, ended their stay at Sportsman's Park with a 66–32 mark, thirteen games ahead of runner-up Pittsburgh. It was just a matter of time before the club clinched the 1943 pennant.

Musial was leading all major-league hitters in batting average and his closest National League competition, Brooklyn's Billy Herman, was some thirty points distant. When asked about his improvement over 1942, Stan said, "That's easy. For one thing, I've more confidence than I had last year. Then again, I'm not swinging at the bad pitches they fooled me with in '42. Furthermore, I'm loose up there now with two strikes on me, whereas last year I used to tighten up after that second strike. They used to throw me a lot of balls in on my hands and I'd swing at them. I'd think the ball was going to be over the plate, but when I swung, the ball would be breaking in against my hands."

Remembering his days in the minor leagues, Musial added, "I've always been a good hitter, was a good one even when I was pitching. In fact, that's the reason I'm still playing professional baseball. If I hadn't been a good hitter, I'd no doubt be out of the pro game now, 'cause I hurt my arm in my third season and that washed me up as a pitcher."

With the Cardinal lead at fifteen games, the front office was taking orders for World Series tickets. The Yankees were thirteen-to-twenty favorites to win the fall classic.

On September 18, the Redbirds clinched the National League title on one of the earliest dates on record when they swept a doubleheader from Chicago. Nine days later, on September 27, Cardinal owner Sam Breadon announced that Billy Southworth had been signed to manage the club for 1944. "Southworth not only is a great manager, but a standout personality," said Breadon. "His efforts toward the success of the team have been tireless, off the field as well as on, for even in his hours away from the diamond he is thinking and working for the Cardinals."

A few days later, Stan and thirty-five other major-league ballplayers were selected to tour the Pacific war theatre in November, playing exhibition games for the men in uniform.

On October 1, the Cards were trailing the Giants, 1–0, when Musial dribbled a grounder to the right side of the infield. As he broke from the box, Stan caught his spikes in the dirt, twisted awkwardly on his left ankle, and sprawled in the dirt at home plate. Southworth, coaching at third base, rushed anxiously to the plate, but Musial was able to leave the field on his own steam. The ankle was examined in the clubhouse and found to be slightly wrenched. Frank Demaree was the starting right fielder the following day, but Stan pinch-hit in the seventh and kept intact his record of playing in every Cardinal game during the 1943 campaign. St. Louis wound up its regular season on October 3, one victory shy of their 106 wins of 1942. But the Cardinals' two-year total of 211 triumphs was the greatest in the National League since the 1906–07 Chicago Cubs had won 223.

In only his second full year in the majors, Stan Musial was well on his way to establishing himself as the National League's most dangerous left-handed hitter, leading the circuit in games played (157), hits (220), doubles (48), triples (20), total bases (347), on-base percentage (.425), and slugging average (.562), despite the meager total of thirteen home runs. With a .357 average, Stan captured his first of seven National League batting championships, becoming the tenth Cardinal since 1920 to win the title. For his efforts, Musial would win the Most Valuable Player award, beating teammate Mort Cooper, who finished second in the voting. Stan was the only player to be named on each ballot.

As in 1942, the Redbirds had won the pennant on the strength of their pitching staff. Mort Cooper (21-8, 2.30 ERA) and southpaw Max Lanier (15-7, 1.90) were the big winners in the rotation, but lefties Alpha Brazle (8-2) and Howie Pollet (8-4) chipped in with sixteen victories and ERAs of 1.53 and 1.75, respectively. Little Murry Dickson was 2–2 in relief and a perfect 6–0 in seven spot starts. Howie Krist was 9–4 in seventeen starts, won two games in relief, and saved three others, while rookie Red Munger came out of the bullpen to win four games and save two en route to a 9–5 record. Southpaw Harry Brecheen split ten decisions as a starter and posted a 4–1 record in relief with four saves. The owners of the three lowest earned run averages in the National League, Pollet, Lanier, and Cooper, all wore Cardinal uniforms.

◆ ◆ ◆

Joe McCarthy's new-look Yankees had swept to their third consecutive American League pennant with a thirteen-and-a-half-game lead over the Washington Senators. New York had lost shortstop Phil Rizzuto, first baseman Buddy Hassett, pitcher Red Ruffing, and outfielders Joe DiMaggio and George Selkirk to the armed forces and veteran third baseman Red Rolfe to a coaching job at Yale University. But the front office had made a key addition to the club in third baseman Billy Johnson, who would win Rookie of the Year honors for his .280 batting average and ninety-four RBIs. The Yankee pitching rotation was anchored by the American League's Most

Valuable Player, Spud Chandler, who won a league-leading twenty games while losing just four, topping all American League hurlers in winning percentage (.833), earned run average (1.64), complete games (20), and shutouts (5). The bullpen was anchored by veteran reliever Johnny Murphy, who had posted a 12–4 record in relief and saved eight games, while recording a 2.54 earned run average. The Yankees were ready and eager to erase the previous year's memory.

Because of continuing wartime travel restrictions, the first three games of the 1943 World Series were played at Yankee Stadium and the remainder at Sportsman's Park. Shaggy-haired and clad in a fur coat, Commissioner Kenesaw Mountain Landis was on hand to throw out the first pitch when the Series opened on October 5 before 68,676 fans, with Max Lanier opposing Spud Chandler. Going back on his promise at the All-Star break, Southworth elected to bypass twenty-one-game winner Mort Cooper because of his shockingly bad record against American League competition. In two World Series starts, Cooper had lasted thirteen innings and given up seventeen hits and ten runs (eight of which were earned) for an ERA of 5.54. In his two All-Star Game starts, Cooper had fared even worse—five and a third innings, eight hits, seven runs, an 11.82 ERA, and two losses, making him the only major-league pitcher in baseball history to lose two successive All-Star games. Indeed, the only bright spot in Mort's two starts was that he was part of, with Walker, the only brother combination to form a starting battery in the mid-summer classic.

The Redbirds drew first blood in the second, but the Yankees fought back to tie the score. In the sixth, with Frank Crosetti on third, Lanier unleashed a wild pitch. The ball rolled no more than fifteen feet from home plate, but catcher Walker Cooper couldn't locate it and Crosetti scored to put the Yanks up 3–2. Bill Dickey's single plated Johnson, and Chandler went on to finish with a seven-hit, 4–2 win. Following the game, McCarthy boasted, "We were playing the Cards' style of ball game today. We were running and they were standing still."

Southworth was reflective. "You know the winners can do the talking today, so don't put me on the spot. I'll pitch either Alpha Brazle or Mort Cooper tomorrow and we'll be right out there."

Walker Cooper refused to talk about the pitch that got away from him in the sixth. "You was out there just as much as I was," the Cardinal catcher grumbled to the press. "You won't get nothin' from me."

Late that night, as brothers Mort and Walker Cooper slept, their father died at his home in Independence, Missouri. Robert John Cooper, fifty-nine years old, had followed the first game of the Series on radio and listened in silent anger while Walker was criticized for not locating Lanier's errant pitch. The next morning, Southworth told the brothers to go on home. "I left them in a room alone to decide," said Southworth after the game. "It didn't take them a minute to make up their minds to stick it out."

"Dad would have wanted it that way," said Walker.

That afternoon, few of the sixty-eight thousand fans at the stadium knew of the Coopers' tragedy as they watched the only contest the Redbirds would win. Shortstop Marty Marion, with just one home run during the regular season, led off the third with a Chinese dinger that dropped into the left-field stands a scant 320 feet from home plate, and the Redbirds put the game on ice with three runs in the fourth. Leading 4–1, Cooper carried a four-hitter into the ninth. Billy Johnson's leadoff double to left-center was followed by a long triple by Charlie Keller. Nick Etten's one-out grounder sent Keller home and pulled the Yankees to within one run of a tie, but Joe Gordon fouled out, fittingly, to Walker Cooper, and the Series was tied. Cooper had temporarily shaken his American League jinx with a 4–3 win.

Both dressing rooms were quiet after the contest. Yankee hurler Ernie Bonham remarked that the Yanks had at least thrown a scare into St. Louis and McCarthy held forth with a long-winded discussion of how his club had lost the contest. Frank Crosetti proudly displayed a telegram which stated that he had just become a father of a ten-pound, four-ounce baby boy. "He must be as big as that bunt I hit over the first baseman's head today," quipped the Yankee shortstop.

Over in the St. Louis clubhouse, the phonograph was going full blast as the Cardinals entered. But after the first record, trainer Doc Weaver shut the machine off, sensing the mood of the ballplayers. Mort Cooper and his wife left for Independence immediately following the contest, but Walker remained with the club to backstop the next game.

On October 7, a Series-record 69,990 fans were present when Alpha Brazle took the hill against Hank Borowy. Brazle held a 2–1 lead when Johnny Lindell led off the eighth with a single and reached second when center fielder Harry Walker fumbled the ball. George "Snuffy" Stirnweiss pinch-hit for Borowy and bunted to first baseman Ray Sanders, who fired a rifle shot across the infield to Kurowski. Lindell and the Cardinal third baseman collided hard enough to chip one of Lindell's teeth. Umpire Beans Reardon signalled the baserunner out, then reversed his decision when Kurowski dropped the ball. An intentional walk to Crosetti loaded the bases for Billy Johnson, who spoiled Southworth's strategy with a long triple to left center. Suddenly, the Redbirds trailed by two runs. When Charlie Keller drew a base on balls, Southworth called to the bullpen for reliever Howie

Krist. As Brazle left the field, a sportsmanlike Yankee Stadium crowd gave him a standing ovation. Joe Gordon greeted Krist with a single to left, scoring Johnson, and Southworth immediately went to Harry Brecheen. Bill Dickey's ground ball hit Gordon on the leg. Gordon was automatically out, Dickey was credited with a single, and Keller was at third. Nick Etten singled to right for the fifth run of the frame, but Dickey was thrown out at third, ending the inning. The game ended in a 6–3 Yankee victory.

Following the loss, Southworth focused on Lindell's hard slide in the eighth. "I'm tired of seeing you shoved around," raged the Cardinal manager at his players. "We'll play that kind of ball from now on if that's what they want."

Yankee skipper McCarthy replied in kind, "It was no pink tea and Lindell had the right of way."

Sunday liquor laws were in effect on October 10 for Game Four, the first at Sportsman's Park. Lieutenant Johnny Beazley and privates Terry Moore, Howie Pollet, and Jimmy Brown were on hand to root for fifteen-game winner Max Lanier. McCarthy gambled and went with lefty Marius Russo, a 5–10 performer on the season. After seven innings Lanier had surrendered just four hits, but the Redbirds were trailing by a run and had Ray Sanders on third when Southworth reluctantly sent Frank Demaree to bat for the Cardinal starter. Demaree grounded to rookie third baseman Johnson, who bobbled the ball while Sanders streaked across the plate with the tying run. New York regained the lead the next half-inning on Frank Crosetti's sacrifice fly and went on to win the game, 2–1.

Southworth was uncharacteristically short with the press after the contest as he told reporters, "Ask your questions in a hurry and get the hell out of here."

Still fuming, Southworth closed the clubhouse the next morning. It was only when the starting lineup was announced that reporters knew the Cardinal manager had benched outfielders Harry Walker and Danny Litwhiler in favor of Johnny Hopp and Debs Garms. (Ironically, Hopp and Garms would go 0-for-4 in the game while Litwhiler and Walker would both single in pinch-hitting roles.) Southworth pencilled in Mort Cooper to start the contest against Spud Chandler. Cooper started strongly, fanning the first five Yankees he faced. His only serious lapse came in the sixth inning when, with two out and a man on base, he put a fastball in Bill Dickey's wheelhouse and the Yankee catcher lofted the pitch onto the roof of the right-field pavilion. The Cards put runners in scoring position in five different innings, but could never deliver the big blow. Musial, with a walk, two strikeouts, and a groundout, was held hitless for the first time in the

Series as Chandler scattered ten hits for a 2–0 shutout and the Yankees' tenth World Series championship. For Joe McCarthy, it was the last of an American League record (since broken) eight titles.

In a somber Cardinal clubhouse, manager Billy Southworth said, "We simply never played our game. We never got started, but we were beaten by a fine ball club and by McCarthy's great pitching. In baseball, you've got to take the sour with the sweet. Well, last year we enjoyed the sweet, so this year we've got to take the sour."

One reporter asked Cardinal owner Sam Breadon about Southworth's future with the team. Breadon replied, "Southworth still is the man who took the club when it was hopelessly mired in the second division in 1940 and finished third. He came in a good second in 1941, despite injuries which could have wrecked any other club, and he won two pennants with a total of 211 victories. Could anyone ask more of a manager?"

On behalf of the team, Walker Cooper gave Breadon a black marble desk set with the players' signatures etched on the bottom. The inscription read, "Presented to Sam Breadon as a token of good will and loyalty and with our congratulations on your success. With our hopes for many such years to follow. From your 1943 Cardinals."

Each Cardinal player took home $4,321.99 for his share of the Series, big money to Musial, a young man who had to consider himself lucky not to be carrying a gun on a foreign field. But Stan wanted to do something for the war effort. Several weeks after the season ended, Musial, teammate Danny Litwhiler, Pittsburgh manager Frank Frisch, Brooklyn's Dixie Walker, and Hank Borowy of the Yankees were fitted with standard Army-issue apparel and were off on a six-week tour of Alaska and the Aleutian Islands as part of a USO troupe. The little group showed World Series films and regaled American servicemen with baseball stories. Everywhere they went, they were received enthusiastically. (Pfc Howard Kosbau, sports editor of the servicemen's newspaper, *Sourdough Sentinel*, reported that one soldier had insisted "he'd rather talk to a major league ballplayer than Betty Grable.")

At Christmastime, Musial and his fellow band of ersatz entertainers found themselves stranded on a mountaintop above Dutch Harbor, the Aleutians. A ship was waiting at the bottom of the mountain to take them to Adak Island, but after a day and a half, the group decided no one was coming to their rescue, so they began walking down the mountain in the midst of a blizzard. Stan and his fellow ballplayers were forced to walk at a nearly forty-five-degree angle against the wind, but arrived just in time to board the ship. That was the easy part of the voyage. As Litwhiler later recounted the story, "We got into a terrific storm in the Bering Sea. We were prepared then for submarine attacks by the Japanese. About the second day of the storm, we were hoping they'd hit us, it was that bad. Everybody was sick."

Stan survived the tour without further incident, looking forward to 1944 and something far easier, like trying to hit one of Rip Sewell's fastballs.

◇ 6 ◇

The Trolley Series

*Musial reminds me of a housewife choosing
tomatoes at a market. She picks up one,
feels it and puts it down. She squeezes
another, pinches a third and then—ah!—
here's the one she wants. That's the way Stan
sorts out pitches.*

CARDINAL COACH BUZZY WARES

"I've got a far better club in the
Army than I can put on the ball field," said Cardinal owner Sam Breadon
of the toll the war was taking on his team. Dodger president Branch Rickey
was jealous. "I wish I had Sam Breadon's replacements," said the Mahatma,
and added, "All I can say is that we will have a large number of human
beings at the training camp."

Center fielder Harry Walker, second baseman Lou Klein, and pitchers
Alpha Brazle, Ernie White, and Howie Krist had entered the military service
over the winter, and hurler George Munger would be taken three months
into the 1944 season. Shortstop Marty Marion, catcher Walker Cooper, and
outfielder Danny Litwhiler had also been accepted, but none would be
called up during the season. 4-Fs on the club included outfielder Johnny
Hopp (back injury), rookie second baseman Emil Verban (punctured ear-

59

drum), catcher Ken O'Dea (hernia), staff ace Mort Cooper (trick knee), and rookie pitching sensation Ted Wilks (stomach ulcers).

Desperate for warm bodies, the Cardinal front office brought forty-year-old Pepper Martin back to the majors after he'd spent the previous three years managing in the farm system. The Wild Horse of the Osage reported to the Cardinal spring training camp at Cairo, Illinois, and said he was "holding down the fort for the ballplayers who are soldiers so that when they come home the game will be alive." Pepper would steal two bases during the year, hit .279, play twenty-nine games in the outfield, and in general, keep the club loose with his sense of humor. In one contest, when Musial lost a high fly in the bright sun, the ball glanced off his head on one bounce to Martin, who quickly retrieved it and fired to the relay man on the infield. After calling time to see if the bruised and embarrassed Musial was all right, Martin inquired politely, "Mind if I laugh?" When Stan replied, "Not at all," Pepper dropped his glove, laid down in the grass, and giggled until the umpire came out to see what was going on.

Musial had also been accepted for the draft, but was not called up during the season. The Cardinal outfielder neither sought nor accepted any special consideration. But draft boards in major metropolitan areas had some leeway in deciding who should be deferred, and apparently Stan was just lucky—not that Musial, who supported his parents and had a child born before Pearl Harbor, couldn't have applied for and probably received a deferment. Instead, the Redbird superstar asked for a three-year contract totaling $40,000; perhaps remembering his 1943 salary negotiations, he eagerly accepted Sam Breadon's counter-offer of $36,000. Stan was to be paid $10,000 for 1944, $12,500 in 1945, and $13,500 in 1946, the final year of the pact.

With World War II in its third year, all major-league teams had suffered player losses, some clubs more than others. All were now staffed with the aged, the infirm, and a wide variety of 4-Fs. Billy Southworth's Cardinals fared better than most clubs and after the Redbirds racked up the best record in spring training, they journeyed to Pittsburgh for the opening of the regular season. St. Louis was picked by all but ten of sixty-seven baseball writers to repeat as National League champions. In the season opener, Max Lanier faced Preacher Roe. The game was scoreless until the sixth, when Musial drove in the first Cardinal run of the year with an RBI single. Stan was the spark that ignited another rally in the eighth when he singled, stole second, and raced home on a hit by Whitey Kurowski. That was enough for Lanier, who blanked the Pirates on two hits, 2–0.

On April 22, Musial was ordered by his draft board in Pennsylvania to report for his physical induction examination. Stan asked that the exam be transferred to Jefferson Barracks in St. Louis and quipped, "Well, I've just written a letter to my wife and now I'll add a little postscript to it."

By the end of April, the Redbirds were 9–2 and Musial, leading the National League with a .447 average, was in the middle of what would prove to be a fourteen-game hitting streak. On the morning of May 16, Stan reported to Jefferson Barracks, Mo. After passing his physical, he was told that he had been accepted for service in the Navy. At twenty-three, Musial faced a possible early call, but it would be at least three weeks before he would be ordered to report.

On June 10, at Crosley Field, Mort Cooper was the lucky starter as the club mounted a twenty-one-hit attack and posted the most lopsided victory in Cardinal history, an 18–0 pasting of the third-place Reds, notable also for another bit of baseball history. St. Louis was leading 13–0 in the ninth when Cincinnati manager Joe McKechnie brought in rookie reliever Joe Nuxhall. At fifteen years, ten months, and eleven days old, he became the youngest player to enter a major-league baseball diamond in the twentieth century. Nuxhall retired George Fallon, then walked Mort Cooper. After Augie Bergamo popped out, Debs Garms coaxed a base on balls and Musial singled home the first run of the inning with his third hit of the day. Cincinnati's beleaguered youngster then hit a horrendous wild streak, passing Ray Sanders, Walker Cooper, and Danny Litwhiler and forcing in two more runs to give the Cards a 16–0 lead. When Emil Verban singled for two more tallies, McKechnie sent the rookie to the showers. Nuxhall, who had been pitching for his Hamilton, Ohio, high school team just two weeks earlier, wouldn't work in the majors again until 1952, but his first taste of major-league baseball could have been worse: the Cardinals tied a major-league record by stranding eighteen baserunners.

Years later, Nuxhall recalled his outing: "Musial got the first hit, a line drive to right field. I remember it well. He knocked the hell out of it, too. And later on when I thought about it, I was amazed. I'll never forget how he just dug in and stood up there. I'm throwing fastballs all over the place, everywhere, and he stood right up there like I was a needle threader. And when I finally got that first pitch in there, wham! If there was any good of it from my perspective, well hell, a Hall of Famer got the first hit off me."

The Redbirds captured an Independence Day doubleheader from the Giants and pulled out in front of the rest of the National League by ten and a half games, their largest advantage of the season and the greatest ever enjoyed by a Cardinal team on July 4. Three days later, Musial collected his one hundredth safety of the season in a 10–5 loss to the usually weak-hitting

Braves, but was blanked the next evening while the sensational rookie, Ted Wilks, scattered six hits and blanked Boston, 4–0, for his first major-league shutout. Just up from Columbus, the stringbean Wilks was nick-named "the Cork" because he was a stopper in relief. Nothing fancy about Wilks. Marty Marion once asked him how he pitched to a certain batter and Ted replied, "I don't know, I just throw it down the middle."

But the news wasn't all good. The Redbirds had already received the disconcerting tidings that Red Munger, 11–3 on the year, was to report to military service on July 11 and now discovered that starter Max Lanier was suffering from a sore elbow, an injury which would prevent him from reporting for All-Star duty. Suddenly, the ten-and-a-half-game lead didn't look quite so safe.

The 1944 All-Star game was played at Pittsburgh's Forbes Field on July 11. Musial, who played both center and right field, collected a single in four trips to the plate and drove in a run as the National League posted a 7–1 victory, its first since 1940.

By mid-August, the Cardinals had equalled a National League record, set in 1907 by the Cubs, by winning their seventy-third contest in their first one hundred games played. St. Louis had a whopping eighteen-and-a-half-game lead over the rest of the league. Billy Southworth was rewarded for his success when he was signed to a two-year contract, the first time Sam Breadon had given a St. Louis pilot an extended pact. Since Southworth had signed on in 1940, the Redbirds had won 452 games while losing 220, an amazing .673 percentage.

St. Louis swept a four-game set from the Dodgers on August 13–15, while Musial, slumping at the plate, found himself trailing Dixie Walker by two points in the race for the National League batting title. Stan's light hitting had not affected the team: the Cardinals had won eight of their last nine outings, eleven of thirteen, and twenty-five of thirty, while the second-place Pirates, winner of nine straight contests, had picked up just one game in the standings.

On August 16, the Redbirds captured a 5–0 win over the Giants, their nineteenth shutout and eightieth victory of the season, the earliest date on record a club had reached eighty wins. On August 28, St. Louis downed Cincinnati for its ninetieth win of the year, the earliest on record any club had posted ninety victories, shading by one day the previous record held by the 1906 Cubs. Ted Wilks, who hadn't lost since May 28, closed out the 19–3 homestand the following evening with his second consecutive three-hitter, blanking the Cubs, 3–0. The Cardinal lead had peaked at twenty games with the victory, but the Redbirds promptly fell into a prolonged slump which would see them lose fifteen of their next twenty outings.

By early September, Musial had dropped to .348 and trailed Dixie Walker by eight points. His chance to capture a second successive National League batting title was slipping away. Worse yet, in the final game of a series with Chicago, prior to which Stan had been honored as 1943's Most Valuable Player, Musial and Debs Garms collided at full-tilt as they raced into right-center field for a fly ball off the bat of Cubs catcher Dewey Williams. Garms was cut above his left eye and across the bridge of his nose, but Stan sustained a terrific gash under his chin and went into shock. Carried off the field, Musial was taken to St. John's Hospital, complaining of pain in his right leg and ankle. He was lost to the club for the next nine games.

The Redbirds dropped four straight to Pittsburgh and left town without their star player, who was in Donora, Pennsylvania, visiting his father. Lukasz Musial was seriously ill. St. Louis went 1–8 without Musial before Stan, limping slightly, his father out of danger, rejoined his teammates in Boston. On September 22, the Redbirds clinched the 1944 National League title with a doubleheader sweep of the Braves, but with fifteen losses in their last twenty games, the Cardinals celebrated quietly.

St. Louis posted win number one hundred on September 24 and when the Redbirds began their final series of the year, a four-game set at New York, Stan was on the bench the first two days to give his right leg some much-needed recuperation. The decision cost him his second two-hundred-hit season and perhaps a batting championship. On October 1, the Cards closed out the year with a doubleheader against the Giants. Musial was six-for-nine on the day, but failed to catch Dixie Walker, who at .357, had hit ten points higher.

The Cardinals' final margin of victory was fourteen and a half games, a few less than the club managed in 1943, but a dominating lead nonetheless. With a 105–49 record, identical to 1943, the Redbirds became the first team in the history of the National League to win a hundred games three years in succession. Billy Southworth became the first National League manager since John McGraw in 1921–24 to lead his club to three straight pennants. St. Louis had been out of first place just four days during the season and had topped the National League in runs scored (772), doubles (274), home runs (100), batting average (.275), slugging average (.402), pitcher strikeouts (637), shutouts (26), earned run average (2.67), fewest errors (112), most double plays (162), and fielding percentage (.982). Four Cardinals—first baseman Ray Sanders, third baseman Whitey Kurowski, outfielder Johnny Hopp, and shortstop Marty Marion—led the league in fielding percentage at their respective positions. Marion would become the first shortstop and perhaps the only eighth-place hitter to capture the National League's Most Valuable Player award. Slats took away a lot of hits at shortstop, as evidenced by his league-leading .972 fielding average, hit .267, and drove in sixty-three runs.

Because he had lost nearly two weeks of playing time after his collision with Debs Garms, Musial had finished his third full year with the Cardinals three safeties shy of his two-hundred-hit goal, a total which nonetheless tied him for the league lead with Chicago's Phil Cavarretta. Stan had led the majors in doubles (51) and slugging average (.549), and finished second in the National League in total bases (312), despite hitting just twelve home runs.

Mort Cooper was 22–7, the third straight year he had won twenty or more games. Rookie Harry Brecheen was 16–5 with a 2.85 earned run average, and Max Lanier won seventeen of his twenty-nine decisions. Red Munger posted a 9–2 record in twelve spot starts, won a pair of games in relief, and saved two more. Newcomer Fred Schmidt, 7–3 on the season, won three games out of the bullpen and saved five others. Rookie Ted Wilks had a phenomenal year, the likes of which he would never enjoy again, posting a 17–4 record with a league-leading .810 winning percentage.

Over in the American League, the Browns had gone to the final day of the season to capture their first pennant. St. Louisans were agog over the idea of an all-St. Louis World Series, only the third time in history an entire Series would be played in one park. Although the Redbirds were quoted by oddsmakers as two-to-one favorites, the Browns were the hometown favorites, having outdrawn the Cardinals at Sportsman's Park on the year. Mayor Aloys P. Kaufmann proclaimed the week of October 2 as "St. Louis Baseball Week" and on October 4, the 1944 World Series opened with the Cardinals as the home team. Mort Cooper started for the Redbirds, drawing as his opponent Denny Galehouse, 9–10 on the year. The contest was scoreless until the fourth when Gene Moore singled and Cooper surrendered a two-run homer to George McQuinn. Still stymied by his American League jinx, Cooper allowed just two hits in seven innings, but that was enough to send him to a 2–1 defeat.

The Redbirds tied the Series the next day in what proved to be the most exciting game of the championship. Aided by some sloppy defensive work by the Browns, the Cardinals broke on top in the third. Emil Verban singled to lead off the inning and Max Lanier reached base safely when Browns starting pitcher Nelson Potter bobbled his bunt, then threw wild to first. Verban reached third on the error and scored on Augie Bergamo's groundout. The Cardinals padded their lead to 2–0 in the fourth, and through six innings, Lanier had held the Browns to one hit, Gene Moore's fifth-inning bunt single. But with two out in the seventh, the Cardinal hurler surrendered a single to Moore and an RBI double to Red Hayworth. Frank Mancuso's pinch single tied the score at two-all and when the Redbird starter was tagged for a leadoff double by Mike Kreevich in the eighth, Billy Southworth went to the bullpen for reliever Blix Donnelly, who struck out the side. In the bottom of the eleventh, Ray Sanders started the winning rally with a single to right off Browns reliever Bob Muncrief. Whitey Kurowski bunted Sanders to second and Marion was walked intentionally, but pinch-hitter Ken O'Dea spoiled the strategy with an RBI single. The Cardinals had a 3–2 victory.

The Browns were the home team for Game Three in a duel of seventeen-game winners, Ted Wilks and Jack Kramer. Trailing 1–0, the Americans drove Wilks to the showers with a four-run third. Marty Marion's RBI single in the seventh closed the gap to 4–2, but the American Leaguers put a pair of insurance runs on the scoreboard in the bottom of the frame for a 6–2 win. Through the first three games, Musial was still having difficulty in post-season competition: three-for-twelve, Stan had no runs scored, no RBIs, and no extra-base hits.

Harry Brecheen drew his first start of the Series the next day. In the first, with Johnny Hopp on base, Musial uncoiled and blasted a Sig Jacucki delivery high over the right-field pavilion roof. What proved to be Stan's only home run in World Series competition was a 400-foot shot that gave the Cardinals a 2–0 lead. In the third, Danny Litwhiler singled with one out and Musial beat out an infield hit with two down. Walker Cooper's single drove in Litwhiler, and when second baseman Don Gutteridge booted Ray Sanders' grounder, Stan alertly raced home to put the Cards on top, 4–0. Musial doubled for his third hit later in the game and was now six-for-sixteen in the Series, leading all Cardinal hitters with a .375 batting average. Brecheen, who scattered nine hits and walked four, was on the ropes all day, but two double plays and four strikeouts bailed him out of trouble and he earned a 5–1 win. The Series was tied at two games apiece.

The attendance at Sportsman's Park on Sunday, October 8, was 36,568, the largest crowd of the Series. Mort Cooper again drew Denny Galehouse. Cooper wasn't as sharp as in his first start, but the results were more satisfactory for Cardinal fans. The contest was scoreless until the sixth when Ray Sanders tagged Galehouse for a solo home run. In the eighth, Litwhiler belted an even longer shot, the first homer of his career to right field. Those were the only two hits Galehouse surrendered after the third inning, but they were enough as the Redbirds cruised to a 2–0 win. Cooper ended the game in strong fashion, fanning three successive pinch-hitters, Milt Byrnes, Chet Laabs, and Mike Chartak. Galehouse whiffed ten in the game and Cooper twelve, establishing a new World Series single-game strikeout record. They were aided in part by the center-field background at Sportsman's Park, which made it difficult for a batter to see the ball whenever a crowd of fans with white shirts were jammed into the bleachers.

The 1944 World Series came to an end the next afternoon when Max Lanier and Nelson Potter hooked up for the second time. George McQuinn's RBI single gave the Browns a 1–0 lead in the second, but sloppy fielding again proved the Browns' undoing when the Americans helped the Cardinals push across three runs in the bottom of the fourth. With one out, Walker Cooper drew a base on balls and raced to third on Ray Sanders' single to center. Kurowski slapped a routine grounder to Vern Stephens, but the ball took a skittish bounce. Stephens, in his haste to start a double play, pulled Don Gutteridge off second with a bad throw and Cooper scored the tying run on the error. Emil Verban singled to left and Max Lanier's base hit sent Potter to the showers, trailing 3–1. Pinch-batter Floyd Baker fanned in the seventh for the eighty-eighth strikeout of the Series, a new record. In the ninth, George McQuinn fouled to left and reliever Ted Wilks ended the Series by striking out pinch-hitters Milt Byrnes and Mike Chartak. The Redbirds had their fifth world championship, becoming the first National League club to accomplish the feat.

Played entirely in Sportsman's Park, the Series had drawn just 206,708 fans, some seventy thousand fewer ticket-holders than in the two previous St. Louis appearances in the fall classic. Each Cardinal player took home $4,626 for the win, bringing their three-year draw to $15,141, more money than most of the Redbirds had made over the past season. Musial, who made the Cardinals' only error in the 1944 World Series, had connected for two doubles, a home run, two runs scored, and a pair of RBIs, but despite his .304 batting average, had once again generally proven to be a bust in post-season competition.

◆ ◆ ◆

Two months after the season ended, Stan and Lillian celebrated the birth of their second child, daughter Geraldine. Six weeks later, on January 23, 1945, Musial was drafted into the Navy and sent to the Bainbridge (Maryland) Naval Training Station for basic training. At boot camp, like any other rookie, Musial had his head skinned by the Navy barber, who said apologetically, "Why didn't you tell me who you were? I wouldn't have cut it so short."

At Bainbridge, where Musial played baseball to entertain the troops, athletic officer Lieutenant Jerry O'Brien inserted Stan at first base, a position he played clumsily at first. Aware that servicemen wanted to see home runs, not singles, Musial moved up in the batter's box and began swinging for the fences, an important step in his maturation as a hitter. Stan was assigned to Special Services and sent to Hawaii, where he was given ship repair duty at Pearl Harbor. The naval base had an eight-team league, and Musial was able to play ball every afternoon, a fortuitous turn of events that helped him keep in shape.

The Allies were victorious over the Nazis in May of 1945. Three months later, the war in the Pacific ended. Back home, Lukasz Musial contracted pneumonia before Stan had been rotated back to the states. Fearing the worst, Mary Musial appealed to the Red Cross for emergency leave for her son. By the time Stan arrived stateside in January 1946, his father was out of danger. The returning serviceman had another pleasant suprise in store for him when he arrived home. Five-year-old Dick had refused to let Lillian take down the Christmas tree and Musial enjoyed an emotional, if belated, Christmas.

When Stan's leave was up, he was assigned to the Philadelphia Navy Yard, where he helped dismantle a British destroyer. In March, the Cardinal slugger was discharged from the service. He returned to his home in Donora to prepare for the upcoming baseball season. The Chicago Cubs had taken the 1945 pennant by a margin of three games over St. Louis, a lead which probably would not have stood up had the Redbirds enjoyed the services of their best hitter. Cardinal fans were eager to see Musial return to the lineup.

◇ 7 ◇

Baseball Comes Marching Home

Stan, you've got two children. Do you want them to hear someone say, "There are the kids of a guy who broke his contract"?

EDDIE DYER

A month after the close of the 1945 season, manager Billy Southworth, with a year remaining on his Cardinal contract, approached Sam Breadon and asked for his release so he could accept an offer to manage the Boston Braves. Breadon flew to Houston, Texas, where he met with Eddie Dyer, who, after more than twenty years in the Cardinal fold, had resigned as director of the Redbirds' class AA farm clubs in 1944 to go into the oil business. Breadon persuaded Dyer to replace Southworth and returned to St. Louis to say, "I think I am the luckiest man in the world. With Eddie Dyer's knowledge of young players, gained through years of experience in our organization, there isn't another man in the country so fitted to run our post-war Cardinals."

Dyer, a former Cardinal hurler, would prove to be a popular manager with the players and more appreciative of what his charges went through on the road. Under Southworth, the Cardinals handled their own luggage and paid for their transportation to the ballpark. But Dyer had the ball club take care of such necessities. The new Cardinal skipper treated the players as adults and had few rules, one of which was no more poker games in the clubhouse or on the train. Pinochle was allowed, but only because it was a thinking man's card game. And if you were playing at Dyer's table, you'd be well advised to pay attention. "How can you play ball," the Cardinal pilot would demand, "if you can't even play pinochle?"

The Redbirds had a wealth of ballplayers returning from the war. Infielder Jimmy Brown, outfielder Enos Slaughter, and pitchers Murry Dickson and Howie Pollet had all been sent home from the armed services over the winter. George Munger, who would receive a late discharge on August 27, returned to the Redbirds in time to make ten appearances over the last two months of the season. Although no more eager to return to duty than any of his peers, Stan Musial was more able, having spent a large portion of his military service doing what he did best, playing baseball.

Some ballplayers came back damaged goods. Infielder Frank "Creepy" Crespi had broken his leg in a 1943 exhibition game at Fort Riley, Kansas, then rebroke the limb in a wheelchair race while convalescing at a military hospital. He never appeared in the big leagues again. Captain Johnny Beazley returned from the U.S. Army Air Force on March 17 suffering from a sore arm, the result of working too many exhibition games, and would win just nine more games over his major-league career. Johnny Grodzicki, one of the Cards' best pitching prospects before the war, had taken a couple of Nazi bullets through the thigh and found he could no longer pivot well enough to field his position. After limited service over the next two years, he was gone from the major-league scene. Outfielder Harry Walker hit only .237 in his first season back and Breadon traded him to the Phillies a year before he rediscovered his stroke and captured the National League batting title with a .363 average. After three years in the Navy, outfielder Terry Moore, now thirty-four years old, was discharged with leg trouble and he, too, was never the same. Perhaps the saddest story of all was Howie Krist. From 1937 to 1943, the tall right-hander had never suffered a losing season at the major-league level and with a lifetime 37–9 record, had a glittering .804 winning percentage. When Krist returned from the war, his fastball was gone. After posting an 0–2 record with a bloated 6.75 ERA in 1946, he exited the major leagues.

St. Louis fans who were curious about which of the excess wartime Cardinals would be let go didn't have long to wait for a flurry of front-office moves. Over the first six months of 1946, three players were sold to the Phillies, and no fewer than seven Cardinals were either traded or sold to

Boston, so many that wags in the press called the Braves the "Cape Cod Cardinals." Perhaps the most important move the Cardinal organization made was the sale of Jimmy Brown to the Pirates, a shift which ceded second base to second-year-man Albert "Red" Schoendienst, the club's versatile utility infielder.

Schoendienst had made the club in 1945, beginning a major-league playing career that would last until 1963. Today, almost fifty years later, coach Red Schoendienst still wears the uniform of the Cardinals. A quiet, gentle man, Schoendienst became Musial's closest friend on the club and his road roommate for the next eleven years, until the sure-handed second baseman was traded to the Giants. "He's the best second baseman I ever saw," said Stan, "with wonderful relaxed hands and a remarkable ability to roam far and wide for pop flies. A good hitter from either side of the plate, too." Indeed, Schoendienst was one of the best switch-hitters of his day and one of the catalysts of the Cardinal clubs of the 1940s.

In a pre-season poll of 119 sportswriters, the Redbirds were the overwhelming favorite to win the 1946 pennant, capturing 114 votes. "If we are no worse than five games behind on the Fourth of July," said Dyer confidently, "we should win."

The Cardinals trained at Waterfront Park in St. Petersburg, Florida, a field which had been used for military drill practice the last four years. Musial slipped in the sandy soil and strained ligaments in his left knee, an injury which would bother him periodically throughout the rest of his career.

Tuesday, April 16, was Opening Day, a raw, rainy afternoon at Sportsman's Park. Sentimentally, Eddie Dyer named Johnny Beazley to start the 1946 season, but Beazley's arm was gone and he was knocked out by the Pirates in the fourth. Musial singled his first time back from the service, but Whitey Kurowski committed a damaging error later in the contest that led to a pair of unearned runs and a 6–4 defeat.

On April 26, New York Giants manager Mel Ott threw a scare into major-league baseball owners everywhere when he announced that pitchers Ace Adams and Harry Feldman had jumped the club to play in millionaire Jorge Pasquel's newly founded Mexican League. Pasquel, a wealthy customs broker from Mexico, had already induced several other major leaguers to renege on their contracts and cross the border. On May 3, New York Yankees club secretary Arthur Patterson reported that George "Snuffy" Stirnweiss and Phil Rizzuto had turned down offers from Pasquel. In Brooklyn, outfielder Pete Reiser acknowledged he had received a three-year, $100,000 proposition to play south of the border. "If I thought this offer

71

was free of all United States taxes," said Reiser, voicing what many a major-league ballplayer was afraid to say out loud, "I would take it in a minute. It would take ten years or more at a good salary here to earn that much."

By the middle of May the Cardinals had sole possession of first place and Stan, batting .388, led all National League batters except Brooklyn's Dixie Walker, whom he trailed by a point. But after sweeping a pair of games from the Giants at the Polo Grounds, the club received its worst news of the year: second baseman Lou Klein, pitcher Max Lanier, and minor-league hurler Freddie Martin had jumped their contracts to play for Jorge Pasquel's Mexican League. Lanier, who had won seventeen games in 1944 and his first six starts in 1946, had asked for a $2,000 raise, but Sam Breadon had countered with an increase of only five hundred. Max was experiencing some pain in his elbow and was frightened for his future, so he leaped at the chance to sign a five-year pact with Pasquel that called for $20,000 a year and a $25,000 signing bonus. Lanier's departure was not without risks: Kenesaw Mountain Landis had died in November 1944, and the new baseball commissioner, A.B. "Happy" Chandler, ruled that any player who failed to return to the states immediately was automatically barred from American organized baseball for five years. (The ban would stick until 1949, when lawsuits by several of the outlaws forced Chandler to back down.)

In New York, the Yankees were seeking an injunction against Jorge Pasquel and his brother Bernardo to prevent the Mexican raiders from signing American baseball players. Jerome Hess, Pasquel's counsel in the United States, fought back, arguing that player contracts were "monopolistic, unconscionable, illegal," and kept players "in peonage for life," as lucid an argument against the reserve clause ever presented. Justice Julian Miller reserved decision on both motions and postponed until May 24 a similar suit brought by the New York Giants. Mark Hughes, attorney for the Yankees, stated flatly that none of his organization's players was complaining about the reserve clause.

Maybe not out loud. But just before the Redbirds arrived in New York, Robert Murphy, organizer of the newly formed National Baseball Guild, a precursor to the current-day Players Union, conferred with St. Louis players for more than an hour. "The validity of baseball contracts makes me laugh," Murphy told the Cardinals. "A baseball owner can do as he wants with a player on ten-day notice." Murphy then played his trump card, claiming he had enrolled more than ninety percent of the Pittsburgh players in his organization earlier in the week and that he had sent team president William

Benswanger a telegram asking for a meeting with Guild representatives "for bargaining purposes." Baseball was on the verge of one of its most serious labor crises.

Musial had also been approached in New York. Accompanied by former Brooklyn catcher Mickey Owen, who had jumped to the Mexican League before the season started, Jorge Pasquel came to Stan's hotel room and dropped five cashier's checks for $10,000 each onto the bed, telling the Cardinal outfielder he could consider the money a bonus. The Mexican League raider offered Musial a five-year contract for $125,000, a figure which looked pretty inviting to Stan, making just $13,500. But Terry Moore convinced Musial that in time, he would make more money playing for an American team.

To add insult to injury, on the same day that Lanier, Klein, and Martin jumped to the Mexican League, the Cards were stranded in New York by a train strike. Traveling secretary Leo Ward managed to charter a DC-3 bound for Cincinnati, but the flight encountered bad weather and was forced down at Dayton, Ohio, some fifty miles or so short of its goal. Ward rounded up taxicabs and a police escort and the Cardinal entourage raced to Crosley Field. When the hood of the cab in which Musial was riding kept popping up, the driver suggested one of the ballplayers take a perch in the open air to keep it closed. Instead, Stan offered to drive, and with the hack balanced on the hood of the car, Musial stuck his head out the side window and rolled into the parking lot, minutes before game time. Shaken by the bumpy flight and worried about more possible defections, the Redbirds dropped the game to Cincinnati, 5–1. The defeat gave Brooklyn first place, a position they would hold until August.

Breadon tried to put a happy face on his losses, noting that the club was now under the thirty-player limit due to go into effect on June 15. "The absence of those three," argued Breadon lamely, "will simply give other players a chance to perform. We have others on the team who have not worked much up to date. They'll get more opportunity now, especially the pitchers." At Cincinnati, manager Eddie Dyer announced that although Terry Moore, Enos Slaughter, and Stan Musial had received big offers from the Mexican League, all had rejected the money out of hand. Neither Musial nor any of the other loyal Cardinals were offered so much as a nickel for not jumping. Stan was with friends who were visiting from Pennsylvania and was unavailable for comment. (Later in the season, Dyer went to bat for several of the players, and in August, Breadon called Musial into his office and gave him a $5,000 raise, effective immediately.)

On the morning of May 26, Fred Martin and Max Lanier visited the

Cardinal clubhouse to gather up their things before leaving for Mexico. "I told them I thought they were making a mistake and would regret it," said Breadon, "but they said they were going through with it and I did not plead with them not to. What's the use? You can't force a man to work for you if he doesn't want to." On June 1, Musial dropped by Sam Breadon's office to quell persistent rumors that he was still entertaining the idea of jumping to the Mexican League. Stan gave the Cardinal owner his word that he would stick by his contract and remain with the club. A grateful Breadon released the news to the press. It appeared as if it might take very little for major-league baseball to be embroiled in a fight for its life, perhaps as little as the defection of one more player to the Mexican League. But Stan Musial was not going to provide that impetus.

Three days later, Stan mysteriously disappeared, giving rise once again to rumors that he was about to defect to the Mexican League. When a reporter spotted little Dick Musial at the Fairgrounds Hotel and asked what his father was doing, Stan's son created quite a stir when he replied simply, "Packing." As it turned out, Musial and Lillian were only moving from the hotel to a furnished bungalow in southwest St. Louis. Stan did acknowledge receiving another contract proposal from Pasquel that evening. Mickey Owen and Pasquel had telephoned the Cardinal outfielder and offered him more money than they had put on the table in New York. The contract had called for five figures, and Musial was sorely tempted. But once again he spurned the overture.

The next afternoon, a possible players' strike was averted at the eleventh hour when the Pittsburgh ball club voted to take the field against the Dodgers. Many of the Pirates cast their ballots to refuse to play the game of the seventh unless club officials allowed the players the right of collective bargaining. (Major-league baseball had not seen a strike since May 8, 1912, when the Detroit Tigers refused to play the Philadelphia Athletics because their Hall of Fame outfielder Ty Cobb had been suspended.)

Baseball owners feared the worst. When Robert Murphy issued a fiery statement the next day, trouble continued to brew. "I guarantee that there will be a strike tomorrow night unless the club comes across," threatened Murphy. "We're going to get tougher. If it goes another day, we're not only going to ask for recognition, we're going to start making actual demands. If a club can change a contract and not the players, what kind of contract is it?"

Indeed, the ballplayers were asking the very same questions. But on June 7, less than an hour before the Pirates were to take the field against the New York Giants, the players came back with a "no strike" vote. One anonymous Pirate stated, "The strike is over for keeps." The American Baseball Guild died aborning, and major-league baseball had dodged a bullet it would continue to dodge for another two decades.

The Cardinals left town in June for a fifteen-game road trip which would earn Musial his lifelong nickname. After winning five of their first seven outings on the road, the Redbirds pulled into Brooklyn, where they had high hopes of shaving the game-and-a-half margin which separated them from the league-leading Dodgers. The two teams split the first two contests, but the rubber game of the series went to the Dodgers, 4–2. Stan finished his stay at Ebbets Field with eight hits in twelve at-bats, including two runs scored and three RBIs. During the final game, whenever Musial came to the plate, St. Louis sportswriter Bob Broeg had heard the Dodger fans chanting, but couldn't quite make out the words. At dinner after the contest, he asked traveling secretary Leo Ward if he'd been able to decipher the Brooklyn accents.

"Every time Stan came up," Ward explained, "they chanted, Here comes the man!"

"That man, you mean," Broeg said.

"No, *the* man," Ward replied.

Broeg mentioned the anecdote in his *Post-Dispatch* column, and Musial had his nickname—an ironic honor, considering it came to him from the fans of his fiercest rivals.

At the All-Star break, the Cards were five games behind the league-leading Dodgers. In the mid-summer classic, Boston Red Sox slugger Ted Williams had four hits in his home ball park, two of them home runs, scored four runs, and drove in five as the American League crushed the Nationals, 12–0, in the most one-sided defeat in All-Star history. Musial was a bust, hitless in two trips to the plate.

Shortly after the All-Star break, the Dodgers arrived at Sportsman's Park for a four-game set, still leading St. Louis by four and a half games. It seemed as though every meeting between Brooklyn and St. Louis throughout the 1940s was steeped in drama, and this one was no exception. And even though Musial gave a hundred percent regardless of his opponent, he could always reach back for a little extra when the Dodgers came to town. This series was more of the same.

Before a packed house in a doubleheader on July 14, Stan walked in the first, reached third after a hit and an error, then stole home under the tag of Dodger catcher Bruce Edwards as the Redbirds took an early lead. The score was knotted at three-all when Musial singled in the eighth to start a two-run rally that gave the Cards a 5–3 win. In the nightcap, Brooklyn southpaw Vic Lombardi blanked St. Louis until the eighth, when Stan tripled and scored the tying run on Whitey Kurowski's sacrifice fly. In the twelfth, it was Musial again, as The Man homered on Lombardi's first pitch of the inning to give the Redbirds a 2–1 victory and a sweep of the twin bill. The next afternoon, before a standing-room-only crowd, the Cardinals pounded five Brooklyn pitchers for a decisive 10–4 victory in which Stan collected two singles, a triple, and a two-run homer, number eight on the year. On July 16, the Cards completed the sweep when pinch-hitter Erv Dusak slugged a three-run, ninth-inning homer to cap a 5–4 win, earning him a nickname of his own, "Four Sack" Dusak. St. Louis was now just a half game back. Musial had put on a one-man hitting clinic in the four contests with nine hits in eighteen at-bats, including a steal of home, two triples, a pair of home runs, three RBIs, and five runs scored. His average now stood at .365, third-best in the National League.

A few days later, a win over the Phillies gave the Cards sole possession of first place for the first time since the morning of May 21. From this point of the season until the end of the year, no more than three and a half games would separate Brooklyn and St. Louis.

On August 10, the St. Louis *Globe-Democrat* published a photograph of what was purported to be a letter written by Stan to Mexican League president Jorge Pasquel back on July 5 and postmarked Wingdale, New York. The letter stated:

Dear Sir,

I would like to reconsider the offer you made to me to play baseball for your team. After thinking it over I realize that my days in baseball are numbered. Please forward the promised bonus.

I will be in Mexico City by August first.

Yours truly
Stanly Musiel

Stan had been in St. Louis on July 5, and the letter's handwriting came nowhere near to matching his own. If further proof was needed that the letter was a hoax, the misspelling of his own name might have offered a clue. Having long ago made his decision about the Mexican League, Musial declined any comment on the letter when questioned by reporters.

In early September, the Redbirds closed out a 13–5 homestand with a two-and-a-half game edge over Brooklyn, their widest margin of the season. By winning twenty-three of their last thirty-one games while the Dodgers were posting a 16–13 record, St. Louis had picked up six full lengths on the Bums. Over the next three weeks, both teams played well. On September 18, at Boston, a group of Red Sox players led by Ted Williams and manager Joe Cronin scouted the Cardinals for the upcoming World Series. St. Louis, at 91–53, held a paper-thin lead over the 88–54 Brooklyn Dodgers. What the Red Sox saw must have cheered them up as Johnny Sain posted his nineteenth victory of the season, a 2–1 squeaker over the Redbirds.

As the pennant race entered the final week of the season, the National League title was still up in the air. On September 23, Harry Brecheen preserved the slim Cardinal lead with a 1–0 shutout of the Cubs. The next day, St. Louis increased its lead to a full game over the idle Dodgers with a dramatic 2–1 win over the Reds. Musial drove in the tying run with two out in the ninth and Erv Dusak won the contest with a solo home run in the tenth. The following morning, Reverend Benney J.F. Benson, pastor of the Brooklyn Dutch Reformed Church, knelt on the steps of Brooklyn Borough Hall and prayed for the Dodgers to win the National League title. God looked like he might have been a Cardinal fan, because Benson's prayers went unanswered when Brooklyn went down to an 11–9 defeat. The Redbirds, whitewashed by Cincinnati's Bucky Walters, fared no better. St. Louis had held sole possession of first place since August 28, but that streak came to an end on September 27 with a 7–2 loss to the Cubs as the idle Dodgers moved into a tie for the National League top spot. Branch Rickey, counting his chickens, took the opportunity to quip, "I have had the feeling that we were going to win the championship for the past few weeks. We have two games to go and we won't lose any more. So the least we can get is a tie. Frankly, I did not expect to win this year, that is, until the last few weeks."

On September 28, Brooklyn kept the pressure on with a win over Boston ace Johnny Sain. The victory had already been posted on the scoreboard when St. Louis took the field for a night game against the Cubs. Musial drove in the first Cardinal run and Harry Brecheen scattered four hits for a clutch 4–1 win, bringing the entire season down to the final day, Sunday, September 29. The Dodgers lost, 4–0, to the Braves while at Sportsman's Park, the Cubs cruised to an easy 8–3 win over St. Louis. For the first time in the seventy-one-year history of the major leagues, two contenders had finished the season in a dead heat.

The National League constitution provided for a best-of-three playoff. League President Ford Frick arranged a three-way telephone conversation among himself, Sam Breadon, and Dodger manager Leo Durocher to choose the site for the first game. Frick flipped a coin and Breadon called heads. The coin came up tails and Durocher elected for the series to open in St. Louis, leaving the final two games for Brooklyn's home park, Ebbets

Field. On the year, the Bums had won just eight of twenty-two meetings with the Redbirds, and Durocher was scrambling for as much of an advantage as he could get. What he hadn't counted on was the twenty-six-hour train trip to St. Louis, a fatiguing journey that left the Dodgers exhausted before the first game even began.

The 1946 National League playoffs opened on October 1 before 26,012 screaming fans at Sportsman's Park. Manager Eddie Dyer tapped Howie Pollet for the first game while Durocher went with Ralph Branca, who had three-hit the Redbirds in the biggest game of his life just two weeks earlier. Joe Garagiola's RBI single in the first gave the Redbirds an early lead, but Brooklyn tied the score when Howie Schultz blasted a Pollet change-of-pace into the left-field seats for a home run in the third. In the bottom of the frame, a walk to Musial plus singles by Enos Slaughter, Garagiola, and Harry Walker put the Cards on top, 3–1. The Dodgers closed the gap with a single tally in the seventh, but Musial tripled and scored in the bottom of the inning to give St. Louis a 4–2 lead. The Dodgers put a pair of runners on in the eighth, but failed to score, and Pollet set the side down in order in the ninth for his twenty-first victory of the season.

Meanwhile, the Boston Red Sox were attempting to stay sharp by playing a pair of exhibition games with American League all-stars at Fenway Park. The makeshift series had an unforeseen consequence when Bosox left fielder Ted Williams was struck by a pitch and suffered a bruised right elbow. Williams, angered by the delay, said, "I'll be glad to finish this baseball season. It certainly hasn't helped my disposition to have things drawn out so long."

After a day off for travel, the National League playoffs resumed at Ebbets Field. The Dodgers touched Murry Dickson for a first-inning run, but St. Louis scored twice in the second, then drove Brooklyn starter Joe Hatten to the showers in the fifth with a two-out rally. Musial doubled, Whitey Kurowski was walked intentionally, and Enos Slaughter scrambled Durocher's strategy with a ringing triple to right center. Erv Dusak's single stretched the St. Louis margin to 5–1. Marty Marion's squeeze bunt gave the Redbirds another run in the seventh, and the Cards widened their lead to 8–1 with two more tallies in the eighth. Dickson, who hadn't allowed a hit since the second inning, worked to the Dodgers in the ninth.

Holding a seven-run lead with three outs to go, the diminutive Cardinal hurler should have disposed of Brooklyn easily. Dickson had a strong arm, good control, and a large assortment of pitches including a fastball, change fastball, curve, change curve, slider, sinker, knuckleball, and screwball. He threw each pitch overhand, three-quarters, sidearm, or submarine, making it impossible for the befuddled batter to guess what was coming next. In one start against the Dodgers, Dickson threw Carl Furillo seven straight curveballs on a 3–2 count, then shouted, "What do you think you're going to get next?" A bewildered Furillo replied, "Another curve?" "Right," answered Dickson, "but neither of us knows from what angle." Furillo went down swinging a moment later on a slow, overhand curveball. Regardless of the game situation, he was always experimenting with his repertoire, earning him the nickname "the Tom Edison of the mound." Harry Walker said years later, "When he'd pitch, he'd get two strikes on a guy and then ball one, ball two, ball three. Drove us nuts. By the sixth inning we were wore out, back on our heels, not as alert as we should be. So we were more prone to errors."

Sure enough, Dickson tried to work too fine. Leadoff hitter Augie Galan doubled and after Dixie Walker was retired, Ed Stevens tripled home Brooklyn's second run of the game. An RBI single by Carl Furillo, a wild pitch, and a walk to Pee Wee Reese brought a frustrated Eddie Dyer to the mound. Harry Brecheen trotted in from the bullpen and promptly surrendered a run-scoring single to rookie backstop Bruce Edwards and a base on balls to pinch-hitter Cookie Lavagetto. With the tying run at the plate, Brecheen struck out Eddie Stanky. Howie Schultz pinch-hit and gave Cardinal fans a good scare when he blasted the first pitch down the left-field line, just outside the chalk mark. Brecheen ran the count to three-and-two before sending in the most fearsome screwball of his career. Schultz almost fell down swinging, and the 1946 National League season was over.

For the fourth time in the last five years, the Cardinals had dominated the National League. St. Louis led all National League clubs in runs scored (712), fewest runs allowed (545), doubles (265), batting average (.265), slugging average (.381), fewest errors (124), fielding percentage (.980), shutouts (eighteen), and earned run average (3.01). Enos Slaughter had hit an even .300, blasted eighteen home runs, scored a hundred runs, and collected a league-leading 130 RBIs. Whitey Kurowski had slumped slightly, but still finished with fourteen homers, eighty-nine RBIs, and a .301 batting average. Musial had proven to be an adequate first baseman, fielding his territory with occasional flair, but saving his heroics for his work with the bat. Musial had topped all National League batters in hits (228), doubles (50), triples (20), total bases (366, eighty-three more than runner-up Enos Slaughter), runs scored (124), at-bats (624), and slugging average (.587), while capturing his second batting title with a .365 average.

The Boston Red Sox, who hadn't appeared in the fall classic since 1918, had clinched their pennant in mid-September, coasting to a twelve-game lead over the second-place Detroit Tigers. Boston's lineup boasted three .300 hitters, Johnny Pesky, Dom DiMaggio, and the Red Sox franchise, Ted Williams. The Splendid Splinter had hit .342 with thirty-eight home runs and 123 RBIs. As deep as Boston's hitting was, the club's pitching staff could be even more fearsome, especially in a short series. Dave "Boo" Ferriss (25–6), Cecil "Tex" Hughson (20–11), Mickey Harris (17–6), and Joe Dobson (13–7) had posted nearly three-quarters of the Red Sox's 104 victories. Thus, it wasn't suprising when gamblers made Boston the odds-on favorites in the upcoming Series. Many sportswriters predicted the Redbirds would let down after their tense playoff with the Dodgers, but Cardinal players preferred to view the two games with Brooklyn as a tune-up for the Series.

The 1946 World Series opened October 6 at Sportsman's Park with a heartbreaking ten-inning defeat for Howie Pollet, the eighth time in nine World Series the Cardinals had lost the opening game. After both sides went down in order in the first, superstar Ted Williams led off for the Sox in the Boston second. Manager Eddie Dyer implemented the Williams Shift, squeezing all four of his infielders between first base and just a few feet to the left-field side of second base, while in the outfield, everyone moved toward right. Ignoring the defensive realignment, Williams refused to lay down a bunt and take the sure base hit, grounding instead to Red Schoendienst for the first out of the inning. But Pollet hit Rudy York with a pitch, Bobby Doerr walked, and Pinky Higgins singled to center to give Boston a 1–0 lead.

Bosox right-hander Tex Hughson nursed his slim advantage until the sixth, when Schoendienst singled and scored the tying run on Musial's two-out double. In the eighth, Whitey Kurowski singled and came home when center fielder Dom DiMaggio, one of the game's greatest outfielders, lost Joe Garagiola's high fly in the sun. The ball dropped in for a two-out RBI double. Pollet carried his one-run margin into the ninth and struck out leadoff hitter Bobby Doerr, but Pinky Higgins slapped a low grounder through short for a single. Pinch-hitter Glen Russell singled pinch-runner Don Gutteridge to third, but Roy Partee struck out and Pollet slipped two quick strikes past Tom McBride to come within one pitch of ending the contest. But he never got that third strike. McBride grounded a bad-hop single to the right of third baseman Kurowski into left field to tie the score at two-all. Then, with two out in the tenth, Boston first baseman Rudy York slammed a towering home run into the last row of the left-field bleachers, some four hundred feet from home plate, to give the Sox a 3–2 victory.

"Pollet pitched a wonderful game, but they got the breaks," said Eddie Dyer.

The temperature was in the mid-eighties the next afternoon when a standing-room-only crowd swarmed into the park, hoping to watch Harry "The Cat" Brecheen even the Series. Sox manager Joe Cronin called on his leading southpaw, seventeen-game winner Mickey Harris. The contest was scoreless until the Cardinal third when Del Rice doubled and came home a moment later on Brecheen's two-strike single to right. In the fifth, Rice started another rally with a single to left. When Brecheen bunted to Pinky Higgins, the Boston third baseman threw the ball away and the Redbirds had runners in scoring position. One out later, Terry Moore slapped a base hit off second baseman Bobby Doerr's glove, driving in the Cardinals' second run. Musial forced Moore at second, but Bobby Doerr's relay throw to first was a split second too late and Brecheen crossed the plate to give the Cards a 3–0 lead. That was all she wrote for the Red Sox.

In his Boston *Globe* column, "Ted Williams Says," the Bosox slugger complained, "Brecheen's pitches look nice to hit at, but when you try to hit him the ball just isn't where you think it's going to be." Teddy Ballgame was so completely fooled by Brecheen on one pitch that the bat slipped from his hands and cartwheeled into the Cardinal dugout. Red Schoendienst characterized him as looking "pitiful" at the plate. Indeed, an oh-for-four performance did look bad on the scorecard. Musial didn't fare any better, hitless in four attempts himself.

The Series shifted to Fenway Park on October 9. The Sox struck back with a shutout of their own, scoring all the runs they needed when Rudy York smashed a three-run homer off Cardinal starter Murry Dickson in the first. In the third, Williams faced the shift again, but this time the Splendid Splinter bunted into left field for a hit, prompting the Boston *Globe* to headline its account of the contest, "TED BUNTS!" Sportswriter Red Smith wrote:

> The Kid's bunt was bigger than York's home run. Thirty-four thousand, five hundred witnesses gave off the same quaint animal cries that must have been heard at the bonfires of witches in Salem when Williams, whose mission in life is to hit baseballs across Suffolk county, pushed a small, safe roller past third base.

The Cardinal infield played Williams normally after this hit, but the shift had thrown the Boston legend into a psychological funk from which he never recovered: for the Series, he would be held to five singles in twenty-five at-bats for a .200 batting average.

Boo Ferriss scattered six hits and completely dominated the Cardinals, who failed even to threaten until the ninth when Musial, who had suffered the ignominy of being picked off second base in the first inning, tripled with two out, becoming the first St. Louis baserunner to reach third. But Enos Slaughter struck out to end the contest, handing Ferriss his fourteenth straight victory at Fenway Park.

Over thirty-five thousand Red Sox fans swallowed hard the next afternoon as the Cardinals pounded six Boston pitchers for a Series record twenty hits and a crushing 12–3 win to tie the Series at two games apiece. Dyer reluctantly gave Howie Pollet his second start of the Series the following day, but the Cardinal lefty failed to survive even the first inning. Leadoff hitter Don Gutteridge singled off Musial's glove at first, Johnny Pesky laced a hit to right, and after Dom DiMaggio forced Gutteridge at third, Pollet surrendered an RBI single to Ted Williams, the only RBI the left fielder would record in the Series. The Redbirds tied the score the next inning, but Don Gutteridge's RBI single put Boston back ahead in the bottom of the frame and Leon Culberson's solo home run in the sixth gave the Sox a two-run margin. Boston put the game on ice with three runs off reliever Al Brazle in the seventh, and Joe Dobson cruised to a 6–3 victory.

Slaughter, struck on the right elbow by a pitch during the contest, had been forced to ask his manager to take him out of a ballgame for the first time in his career and was thought to be lost for the rest of the Series. On the train back to St. Louis, Doc Weaver worked on the Cardinal outfielder with hot and cold packs all night, and team physician Dr. Hyland reluctantly ordered Enos to the bench. But the never-say-die Slaughter wouldn't hear of it, despite the threat of amputation if the blood clot at his elbow should move.

The Series returned to Sportsman's Park for Game Six on October 13. Everyone expected Boston manager Joe Cronin to start twenty-five-game winner Boo Ferriss, but Cronin held out his ace for the seventh game and went with Mickey Harris instead. Harry Brecheen started for the Cardinals and despite giving up four hits over the first two frames, held the Sox scoreless. The Redbirds bunched five safeties in the third for a 3–0 lead and Brecheen, after his rocky start, held the Red Sox to just three hits for the remainder of the contest. The 1946 season had come down to one game.

On Tuesday, October 15, 1946, the front page of every newspaper in the country was filled with articles about the eleven Nazi war criminals who would meet death on the gallows that day. In St. Louis, the story competed for space with the upcoming seventh game of the World Series.

Boo Ferriss was working on five days' rest against Murry Dickson, his opponent from Game Three. Through five innings, the Cardinals led, 3–1. After surrendering a leadoff hit to Bobby Doerr in the second, Dickson had retired eighteen of the next nineteen men he faced before he suddenly found himself in an eighth-inning jam when pinch-hitter Glen Russell singled and raced to third on George "Catfish" Metkovich's pinch double. Eddie Dyer called to the bullpen for a weary Harry Brecheen, who fanned Wally Moses on a screwball. Johnny Pesky lined out, but Dom DiMaggio silenced the thirty-six thousand Cardinal fans with a ringing double off the right-center field wall, knotting the score at three-all. DiMaggio pulled into second with a charley horse and had to limp out of the game. The next batter was Ted Williams. In a move guaranteed to whet the lips of second-guessers everywhere, manager Eddie Dyer elected to pitch to the slugger with first base open. With an opportunity to put the Red Sox on top, Williams could raise only a feeble pop fly on the infield.

When the Red Sox took the field in the bottom of the eighth, Leon Culberson had replaced DiMaggio in center and Boston had a new battery of Roy Partee and premier reliever Bob Klinger, a 3–2 performer on the season with a league-leading nine saves. Slaughter, still swinging with difficulty, greeted Klinger with a line single to center, but Kurowski popped out, attempting to bunt. Del Rice lifted a fly ball to Williams in left for the second out. Then Harry Walker, six-for-sixteen in the Series, lined a pitch into left-center and Slaughter, off with the pitch, raced toward home without so much as a glance at third base coach Mike Gonzalez. Remembering the play years later, Slaughter said, "In an earlier game in the Series, Mike Gonzalez, our third-base coach, had stopped me at third on a bad relay throw and we lost that ball game. I went to Eddie Dyer and told him I thought I could have scored easily if I hadn't been held up. Well, he said, from now on if you think you've got a legitimate chance with two out, you go ahead and try it and I'll back you up. To me that was just another play. It was just heads up baseball. When I got to second, the ball hadn't hit the ground yet. I said to myself, I can score. I just kept running. I could've walked across the plate."

The relay from center fielder Leon Culberson came to the infield, but shortstop Johnny Pesky's throw to the plate pulled Roy Partee up the third-base line and Slaughter slid across the plate with the lead run. Most Red Sox fans believed Slaughter would never have scored or even tried to had Dom DiMaggio still been in the outfield. Not the hitter his more famous brother was, Dom was considered Joe's superior on defense.

Boston had three more at-bats. Brecheen opened the ninth by surrendering singles to Rudy York and Bobby Doerr. Paul Campbell pinch-ran for York and the Cardinal infield huddled on the mound, discussing how to defense the bunt. When Higgins pushed the ball to third, Kurowski quickly scooped the ball and forced Doerr at second while Campbell pulled into third with the tying run. Musial made a fine running catch of Roy Partee's high pop foul for the second out of the inning, then threw a strike to the plate to keep Campbell at third. Pinch-hitter Tom McBride sent a grounder to Red Schoendienst and the hearts of Cardinal fans everywhere stopped beating when the Redhead couldn't get the ball out of his glove. But Schoendienst recovered in time to flip to Marion, who stepped on second and forced Higgins as the potential tying run was crossing the plate. The Cardinals were world champions. Although he blew the save, Harry Brecheen had surrendered just one run in twenty innings and became the first left-hander to win three games in a World Series since Stan Coveleski had turned the trick for the 1920 Cleveland Indians.

Manager Eddie Dyer summed the season up simply: "We never lost a game we had to win."

The World Series melon was small in 1946. Each Cardinal player's share was only $3,742.34, and the Red Sox drew post-season paychecks of just $2,141, partly because both Sportsman's Park and Fenway Park had such small seating capacities. (Ted Williams, disgusted by the small amount, supposedly gave his share to Johnny Orlando, the Fenway Park clubhouse boy.) The head-to-head competition between the two best hitters in baseball, Ted Williams and Stan Musial, had proved to be somewhat less than dramatic. Musial had driven in four runs on six hits, including four doubles and a triple, but had batted just .222 for the Series. Williams fared even worse, batting .200 with no extra-base hits and one RBI in twenty-five at-bats.

The 1946 season had one last pleasure in store for Musial. Of the twenty-four sportswriters voting the Most Valuable Player award, twenty-two cast their ballots for Stan, who garnered 319 of a possible 336 points, ranking him 177 points ahead of Brooklyn's Dixie Walker. Because he had played the outfield when he captured the 1943 honor, Musial thus became the first man in National League history to have won the award at two different positions.

◇ **8** ◇

Letdown

---

*The 1947 Cardinals were a fine bunch of
guys as well. I was proud just to be there.
Just to know them. Just to walk on the same
field with Stan Musial. We all wore the same
uniform. That was a thrill in itself.*

DEL WILBER

Following victory over the Red Sox
in the World Series, St. Louis fans could hardly have been more hopeful
for 1947. Who would have thought nearly two decades would pass before
the Redbirds would make another post-season appearance?

Spring training began with Musial a salary holdout for the second time
in his career. Stan had hit .365, won the 1946 National League Most
Valuable Player award, and felt entitled to a big raise, but Sam Breadon felt
very strongly about what he viewed as spiraling salaries. Breadon's first
contract offer called for $21,000, an increase of just $2,500 over Musial's
1946 pact. Stan wanted his salary nearly doubled, to $35,000. Musial's
request was not out of line: in the American League, Detroit slugger Hank
Greenberg was drawing $65,000 and Ted Williams had already gone on
record as saying he would be asking for $80,000, the same salary Babe
Ruth had drawn in 1930 and 1931 and the most money ever paid a
major-league ballplayer for a season.

In February, Musial and Breadon crossed paths when the Cardinal first baseman received the Sid Mercer award as the best major-league player of 1946. Breadon had increased his offer to $27,000 and was eager to announce the signing at the banquet. But Musial stood firm. Stan officially became a holdout when spring training began, and he took Lil and the children to St. Petersburg, Florida, where they stayed at the Bainbridge Hotel. One evening, as Musial and his family were dining, Breadon entered the restaurant. Stan invited the Cardinal owner to join them for dinner. When the meal ended, he asked for both checks. Breadon would not let Musial pay for his meal, but neither did he offer to pay for Stan's. A few days later, as in 1943, Eddie Dyer approached Musial in the role of arbitrator to discuss compromise. Stan came down from $35,000, Breadon raised his latest offer, and the pair settled on a final figure of $31,000. Musial and Breadon had an enormous amount of respect for each other and neither man exhibited any hard feelings over the difficult negotiations. But at a press banquet the night before the St. Louis home opener, Breadon gently chided Stan when he said, "I believe it is a great credit to our organization that a ball club good enough to win four of the last five National League pennants, good enough to win three of the last five World Series, was signed this spring with only one mild holdout."

If Musial took offense at the remark, there was no mention of it in the newspapers.

The Cardinals were the overwhelming favorite to win the 1947 title in the annual pre-season poll of sportswriters. But Howie Pollet, who would struggle all year long and slump from 21–10 to 9–11, lost the season opener in Cincinnati. "Every pitch hurt," said Pollet at the end of the year. "I couldn't follow through. I began to pitch with a half-motion, using my elbow instead of my back. I stopped midway. My control was terrible and I began to feel a lump in my elbow. It frightened me. I was afraid I was through."

The next day, Musial's first hit of the season, an eighth-inning homer off Reds' hurler Eddie Erautt, tied the score in a game the Cardinals ultimately won. The Cardinals raised the 1946 National League pennant in pre-game ceremonies on April 18, beat the Cubs, 4–1, then dropped their next three games before embarking on an equally disastrous road trip. Batting just .135, Musial was questioned by reporters about his slow start. "I'm in fine physical shape," insisted Stan. "I have no worries of any kind and I'm signed to a good contract. I see the ball good, too, but my body and my swing are not working together. I'm hitting late at the pitches instead of meeting the ball out front. I'll break loose out there one of these days."

But Musial's problem was more serious than he knew. And although the Cardinal outfielder hit a little better in New York, three-for-twelve including another home run, the Redbirds lost all three contests and extended their losing streak to eight games. The last defeat dropped the 1946 world champions into the National League cellar. The Redbirds trained to Boston, where they lost their ninth straight in the opener of a doubleheader at Braves Field, but Harry Brecheen stopped the long slide in the nightcap when he hurled the first Cardinal shutout of the year, blanking Boston on five hits in a rain-shortened, 9–0 victory. Added to the Cardinals' miserable showing on the diamond were unhealthy rumors: some of the St. Louis players were planning to refuse to play on the same field with Dodger rookie first baseman Jackie Robinson.

Jackie Robinson wasn't the best ballplayer in the Negro Leagues after the war. That honor probably would have gone to Monte Irvin, who later played for the New York Giants. But Robinson had the character and integrity that Brooklyn's Branch Rickey was looking for in the first black man to play major-league baseball since the nineteenth century. After Rickey purchased Jackie's contract from the minor leagues, a group of five Dodger players approached manager Leo Durocher in spring training, threatening a revolt. Durocher quickly quelled the uprising. "I don't care if the guy is yellow or black or if he has stripes," said Leo. "I'm the manager of this team and I say he plays. What's more, I say he can make us all rich."

Despite Durocher's dictate, many of Robinson's teammates were cold and indifferent initially. Many of the Dodgers refused to sit near Robinson; some even declined to speak to him. When the Phillies played at Ebbets Field in mid-April, Philadelphia owner Bob Carpenter pleaded in vain for Rickey to bench Robinson. If not, said Carpenter regretfully, I'll have to pull my team off the field. "I'll be only too happy to accept a forfeit," replied Rickey. The threat remained just that. When the series opened, the Philadelphia ballplayers, egged on by manager Ben Chapman, subjected Robinson to some of the worst heckling experienced by any man, anywhere. "Hey, nigger, why don't you go back to the cotton field where you belong?" and "We don't want you here, nigger," were two of the milder slurs Robinson heard. Ironically, the abuse helped to unite the Dodger club behind their new first baseman.

In his biography years later, Musial took pains to note that while there was unrest over Robinson, the dissension was felt throughout the league and was not exclusive to the St. Louis club. In any event, there was no strike when the Cardinals arrived at Ebbets Field for the first time in 1947.

The Dodgers, atop the National League with a two-and-a-half game edge over the Pirates, won the opener of the three-game set, but the Redbirds came back to take the next two. In the series finale, Musial failed to report to the ballpark, remaining in his room at the Hotel New Yorker to nurse "a sick stomach," according to the St. Louis *Globe-Democrat.* Stan's slump attracted national attention when *Time* magazine highlighted his inability to hit: "I've had the whole team advising me, and I all but take the bat to bed with me," said Musial, who blamed his lack of productivity at the plate on playing too much golf in the winter and spring. But when the magazine reached the newsstands, Stan knew better: the hotel physician had diagnosed his problem as appendicitis.

Then all hell broke loose.

A week earlier, New York *Herald-Tribune* reporter Rudd Renny had spoken with Cardinal team physician Dr. Robert Hyland, who had confirmed the possibility of a players' strike. Renny called his editor, Stanley Woodward, who phoned National League President Ford Frick. Woodward told Frick he was hesitant to run the story without confirmation. Was a Cardinal strike possible? Frick wouldn't deny the story. On May 9, the Associated Press reported that Sam Breadon had informed Frick his team might strike rather than take the field with Robinson. Frick was quoted as saying, "I didn't have to talk to the [Cardinal] players myself. Mr. Breadon did the talking to them. From what Breadon told me afterward the trouble was smoothed over. I didn't know what he said to them, who the ringleader was, or any other details."

Breadon, allegedly, had asked Frick for guidance. The National League president had said to tell the ballplayers, "If you do this, you will be suspended from the league. You will find that the friends you think you have in the press box will not support you, that you will be outcasts. . . This is America and baseball is America's game." He added, "Tell them that if they go on strike, for racial reasons, or refuse to play in a scheduled game, they will be barred from baseball even though it means the disruption of a club or a whole league."

At odds with Frick's alleged remarks was Breadon, who stated flatly in the same AP story that reports of a strike were "ridiculous." The Cardinal owner said the club minded its own business and added, "They're always starting something about us."

Musial, in his autobiography years later, said this: "A story broke in the *Herald-Tribune* that the Cardinals had threatened a protest strike against Brooklyn's use of Robinson. Only Breadon's intercession and league president Ford Frick's counter-threat of indefinite suspension had averted the strike, the newspaper charged. I, for one, was just too sick to be indignant. There never had been a strike voted by Cardinal players because no vote ever had been taken. I ought to know—I was there."

There was no shortage of Cardinal denials. Manager Eddie Dyer, quoted the day after the Brooklyn series ended, said, "The report my club threatened a strike against Robinson is absurd. At no time to my knowledge did my players consider such a foolish action. They never discussed it. No one ever discussed it with them. As for Mr. Frick, he can investigate all he wants to. He will find that at no time did my players discuss anything resembling a strike of any sort."

Cardinal outfielder Enos Slaughter, in his autobiography, *Country Hardball: The Autobiography of Enos "Country" Slaughter,* hotly refuted his role—even though he, along with teammate and fellow Southerner Harry Walker, was named as one of the ringleaders. Shortstop Marty Marion years later said, "I've read stories that a strike was imminent, but I don't remember that at all." Infielder Red Schoendienst recalled, "I know that there were a lot of things being written that we objected to playing against the Dodgers being Jackie Robinson was there, but it wasn't true at all. I can't remember anybody talking about Jackie Robinson or the Dodgers for bringing up Robinson." Schoendienst's statement seems naive at best, a lie at worst. The Dodgers and Cardinals, after all, were mortal enemies. That the St. Louis ballplayers would not have discussed a new addition to the Brooklyn club seems unlikely. That they would not have spoken about the first black man to play major-league baseball in sixty years is impossible to believe.

Was a strike averted? Perhaps the truth will never be known, but two things seem reasonable to assume. First, Renny's story was probably just that: more story than fact. There is little hard evidence to support any of his charges. And secondly, if the Cardinal players had discussed a strike, they would not have done so in a team meeting, but in small groups, clandestinely. If the gentle and easygoing Musial denied any knowledge of an uprising, it is because he would probably have been the last person team dissidents would have approached in a strike vote.

On May 9, accompanied by reserve catcher Del Wilber, Stan left the club for St. Louis, where he was examined by Dr. Robert Hyland. Confirming the diagnosis of appendicitis, Hyland gave Musial the unhappy news that he had tonsilitis as well. Certain that surgery would sideline the Cardinal superstar at least a month, Hyland suggested freezing the appendix. Added to Stan's physical discomfort was the idle gossip that he had returned to St. Louis from New York, not due to his bout with appendicitis, but because he and teammate Enos Slaughter had gotten into a fistfight. Musial and Slaughter were not without their differences: Stan was a Northerner, Slaughter a Southerner, and the two cultures in which they were raised were vastly diverse. The North was far more tolerant of blacks than the Southern states. But regardless of their dissimilarities, both men vehemently denied the rumor.

On May 14, the Cardinals, with a 7–14 record, were in last place and seven games behind the league-leading Chicago Cubs when Musial, pale and several pounds underweight, returned to the lineup. Stan was oh-for-four in a 6–4 loss to the Giants, hitless in five trips to the plate in an 8–2 win over Boston, and blanked in his next six at-bats in a pair of losses to the Braves. Musial was shut out in five trips to the plate in the opener of a twin bill with the Phillies on May 18 and went until the seventh inning of the nightcap, twenty-five straight at-bats without a hit, before he broke what would prove to be the longest drought of his career with a drag bunt down the third-base line past southpaw Ken Raffensberger. Both Raffensberger and Al Brazle, the Cardinal starter, went the distance in the game, but the Cards ultimately lost, 1–0. Stan added another single in the twelfth, but was clearly not on his game.

(This was the season in which sportswriters began saying, "As Musial goes, so go the Cardinals." In April, Stan hit .146 and the Cardinals found themselves in last place with a 2–9 record. In May, he hit .227 and the Redbirds broke even in twenty-six games. In June, he would shatter his slump with a .330 average, while St. Louis won eighteen and lost ten. In July, Stan would hit .320 and the Cards were 18–10 again and in August, when Musial singled off Pittsburgh's Jim Bagby to reach the .300 mark for the first time in the season, the Redbirds reeled off an eight-game winning streak.)

On June 27, the Cardinals raised the world championship pennant and received their World Series rings from National League President Ford Frick. Baseball commissioner Happy Chandler, citing a "previous engagement," snubbed St. Louisans by not attending. The Redbirds swept a twin bill from Cincinnati in their last outing before the All-Star Game and reached the mid-summer break two games above .500. Despite Stan's poor performance in the early going, National League fans voted him a spot as a reserve on the National League All-Star team. The 1947 contest was played at Chicago's Wrigley Field and resulted in a 2–1 win for the American League, the junior circuit's tenth win in fourteen meetings. Musial grounded out as a pinch-batter.

A month later, on August 20, the Robinson-Cardinal feud resurfaced in a four-game series at Ebbets Field. The Dodgers had won two of the first three games, opening up a five-and-a-half-game lead over St. Louis. The final contest of the series, filled with excitement and controversy, was played on August 20 with Murry Dickson opposing Ralph Branca. Branca was near-perfect, hurling a no-hitter for the first six innings. In the seventh, Enos Slaughter grounded to Dodger second baseman Eddie Stanky and was thrown out on a bang-bang play at first. As he crossed the bag, he spiked first baseman Jackie Robinson.

Red Barber, in his book, *1947: When All Hell Broke Loose in Baseball,* could be accused of some hyperbole when he said, "The career of Jackie Robinson came within an inch of being ended." *New York Times* sportswriter Roscoe McGowen was perhaps closer to the truth when he wrote the next morning, "Jackie hopped around a minute or two and [Brooklyn] Doc Wendler came out, but Robbie stayed in the game, apparently not seriously hurt."

Branca, who believed the action was intentional, said, "Don't worry, Jackie, I'll get that son of a bitch for you," but Robinson insisted on handling matters himself. Jackie singled in the eighth inning. Standing at first, he told Musial he was going to knock second baseman Red Schoendienst "into center field." Schoendienst was Stan's roommate and close friend, but Musial quietly replied, "I don't blame you. You have every right to do that." A fierce competitor himself, Musial didn't care for Slaughter's actions either. The Cardinal superstar understood and accepted the concept of an eye for an eye, but his comment took the competitive fire out of Robinson. When Pete Reiser grounded into a double play, Jackie slid hard into second, but made no more than the normal attempt to take Schoendienst out of the play.

Whitey Kurowski's eighth-inning single spoiled the no-hitter. The Cardinal third baseman cemented his lock on hero-of-the-day honors when he homered in the twelfth to give the Redbirds a 3–2 victory and an unexpected split of a series that had begun with two losses. The Cards left town right where they had started, four and a half games back. It was the closest to first place the club would get for the rest of the season. St. Louisans waited in vain for Brooklyn to collapse, but the inevitable came on September 22 when the Dodgers, enjoying a day off, clinched the 1947 pennant while St. Louis split a doubleheader with the Cubs. One-for-nine in the twin bill, Musial fell to .299. With seven games remaining, he was in need of a minor miracle to finish the season above .300.

The pressure of the pennant race now removed, Musial could concentrate on his batting and he did just that. Stan collected ten hits in his next fifteen trips to the plate, raising his average to .312 and marking the first time all year he had led his own club in batting average. Despite suffering from appendicitis throughout the season, Musial had appeared in 149 games, collected 183 hits, thirty doubles, thirteen triples, nineteen homers, and ninety-five runs batted in. But former teammate Harry Walker had bashed National League hurlers for a .363 average and became the first player in baseball history traded in midseason to win the batting title. It was the only time in Walker's career he hit above .318.

Just before Thanksgiving, Sam Breadon stunned the Mound City by selling the club to St. Louis businessman Fred Saigh Jr. and former Postmaster General Robert E. Hannegan. Saigh and Hannegan paid $3.5 million for the Cardinals and their twenty minor-league affiliates. The team had drawn 1,247,931 paying customers in 1947, a record for the club and the most financially successful season in the franchise's history, and the white-haired Breadon, seventy years old, reckoned the organization's worth was at its peak. At the press conference announcing the sale, his voice breaking, Breadon read a statement to the press that said, in part, "It is hard for me to leave the association of the men who have built up the Cardinal organization and to whom I am under great obligation. I want to thank the fans of St. Louis whose loyalty has helped make the Cardinals the greatest organization in baseball."

Hannegan promptly announced that the new owners would keep the organization and the team intact. "I am confident," said Hannegan, "that all members of the Cardinal family will work with me and give the same ardent cooperation they have given Sam Breadon. The future is bright for the Cardinals. With all our teamwork, I am confident that when the 1948 season closes, the judgment of the people of St. Louis and of the nation will be: St. Louis Cardinals, winners and champions."

◇ 9 ◇

The Cape Cod Cardinals

*Of all the teams I've seen so far,
Musial is the best.*

PHILADELPHIA MANAGER EDDIE SAWYER

Musial had his appendix and tonsils removed shortly after the close of the 1947 season and spent the winter in lazy recovery. In February, a few weeks before the official opening of spring training, Stan and Lillian took the children to St. Petersburg, Florida, for a vacation. If Musial was hoping the new owners, Fred Saigh and Robert Hannegan, would give him a pay raise, he could think again. Hannegan, handling the delicate negotiations, reminded Stan that he'd had an off-year in 1947 and told him the club was offering the same terms as he'd played for the year before, $31,000. Astonished, Musial pointed out that he'd given more than his all in 1947 and had even played the entire year with appendicitis! But Hannegan was firm. He did say, however, that if Stan had a good year, his contract could be adjusted in mid-season.

At twenty-seven, Musial was being returned to right field in order for manager Eddie Dyer to insert hard-hitting prospect Nippy Jones into the lineup at first base. Healthy again and more determined than ever before,

Stan was about to enjoy the finest season of his career and one of the most remarkable in baseball history.

But not right away. Stan was hitless as St. Louis opened the season by splitting a pair of games with Cincinnati at Sportsman's Park. Musial enjoyed his first multiple-hit performance in the third contest of the year and on April 25, he collected the one-thousandth hit of his career, a fourth-inning triple. After the game, sportswriter Bob Broeg encouraged the Cardinal superstar to shoot for three thousand. "That's a long way off," said Stan. "Too many things could happen. But keep reminding me."

In just a little more than five years in the majors, Musial had averaged close to two hundred hits a season. To reach the coveted three thousand mark, he would have to do the same for the next ten years while avoiding any serious injuries.

On April 29, Redbird reliever Ted Wilks lost to Cincinnati, 5–4, in fourteen innings, his first defeat since September 3, 1945, a string of seventy-seven straight appearances and twelve consecutive victories. Musial, three-for-five in the contest, drove in all his team's runs, blasting a two-run homer in the fourth and singling across two more runs in the fifth. The next day, Stan put on a one-man hitting exhibition at Cincinnati. Musial's RBI single in the first put the Cards on top, 1–0, but the Reds tied the score in the bottom of the frame and went ahead 5–2 in the third. Stan crashed a two-run homer in the fifth to pull the Birds within a run and when he batted in the seventh, the score was tied at five-all. His double started a seven-run rally in which he scored the first tally and drove in the last two with another single. Musial doubled again in the ninth and with five hits on the day, accounted for two runs scored and four RBIs in the 13–7 victory. For the year, he was batting an even .400.

On May 7, Musial came in for some criticism from St. Louis *Globe-Democrat* sportswriter Robert L. Burnes. In his column "The Bench Warmer," Burnes reproached Stan and five other ballplayers for appearing in cigarette advertisements. "Watch a ball game on any corner lot," wrote Burnes, "and you'll see the youngsters imitating Musial's batting stance or running like Enos Slaughter or pitching with the whip-like motion of [Ewell] Blackwell. They wear their caps the same way. Kids are natural imitators. So they're inclined to the belief that if it's all right for a major league ballplayer to smoke, it's all right for them. You can't tell the youngsters that it's a dangerous habit to form in their early years. They look at you in disdain, then point to the picture and say, 'What about this?'"

Musial was always sensitive to constructive criticism, especially that offered by his close friend Burnes. Stan did few endorsements throughout his playing career, but he soon stopped appearing in cigarette advertisements.

In mid-May, at Ebbets Field, Musial led the Cards to a 14–7 win over Brooklyn with two RBIs, five runs scored (one short of a National League record), three singles, a double, and a triple. This was the second of four five-hit days for the Cardinal superstar on the year. The next afternoon, Stan collected a single, two doubles, and a home run as St. Louis again roared past the Dodgers, 13–4, for their sixth straight win and thirteenth in the last sixteen games. Musial's nine hits in two successive games were a modern-day National League record, leaving him convinced that if he could have hit at Ebbets Field all year, he would have batted .400.

Musial extended his hitting streak to thirteen games and was now batting .399, trailing only Pittsburgh's Frankie Gustine, at .412. But the Cardinals were slumping, having lost five games in a row. By mid-June, the Redbirds had fallen to second place. And although the Cardinals remained in contention for the rest of the season, they never again regained the top spot.

On June 21, the Redbirds arrived in Boston for their biggest series of the year, a three-game set with the league-leading Braves. St. Louis was trailing Boston by three and a half games. No National League hurler had pitched a complete game against the Braves in the past twenty-four games, but that evening Al Brazle went the distance in a 1–0 win over Warren Spahn. The next night, Musial recorded his third five-hit game of the season. Stan singled in the first, bunted safely in the third, singled in the fifth, and singled again in the seventh. When he picked up his bat in the ninth, the score was tied at 2–2 and the bases were loaded. "Hey boy," shouted Eddie Dyer playfully. "I'm afraid I'm going to have to send up a hitter for you."

Stan chuckled, but when he got to the plate he was all business. Musial pasted reliever Clyde Shoun's first delivery through the middle for his fifth safety of the contest, a two-run single that won the game for Harry Brecheen. Brecheen, like Brazle the night before, also worked a complete game. Howie Pollet went the distance on the twenty-fourth as the Cards crushed Boston, 11–2, and closed to within a half-game of first place. Two days later, Musial was all over the Dodgers. Stan collected four hits, including two singles, a double which drove in the Cardinals' first run, and his sixteenth home run of the season. Now hitting a league-leading .408, Musial trailed only Boston Red Sox slugger Ted Williams, at .415. The next evening, Dyer was holding a pre-game meeting when someone knocked on the visitors' clubhouse door at Ebbets Field. It was Dodger pitcher Preacher Roe, who announced he had developed a new, albeit unusual, method of getting Musial out.

"Walk him on four pitches and pick him off first," chortled Roe, out the door.

Musial clubbed his seventeenth home run of the season that night as the Cards downed Brooklyn, 6–4. Stan was in the midst of a twelve-game hitting streak which would boost his average to .406, the best mark in baseball. Just before the All-Star break, Cardinal owner Robert Hannegan called Musial into his office and made good on his pre-season promise, giving Stan a $5,000 raise that boosted his salary to $36,000. On July 13, at Sportsman's Park, Musial blasted his first All-Star Game homer, a two-run line drive atop the right-field pavilion in the first inning off Washington's Walt Masterson. Stan singled later in the game, but his round-tripper gave the National League its only two runs of the contest as the senior circuit went down to a 5–2 defeat.

In late July, the Redbirds took two of three from the league-leading Braves at Boston. In the series finale, Musial was having one of his worst nights ever at the dish. In the first and fourth, he grounded into double plays, and in the fifth, he struck out. But Stan had once told Marty Marion, "To be a good hitter and to have a good average, you have to bear down every time you walk up to the plate. Every single time, you try to get a base hit." Perhaps Musial was remembering his own advice, because he doubled and scored in the eighth and singled home a run in the ninth, helping pace St. Louis to a 9–6 win, a victory which sparked the Redbirds to reenter the National League pennant race.

On August 17, Musial clubbed his thirtieth home run of the year, pulling into a tie with Ralph Kiner for the league lead. Stan was now batting .384, tied with Ted Williams for baseball's highest average and fifty-two points ahead of the National League's second-best hitter, Chicago's Andy Pafko. Stan usually won games with his bat, but he was literally all over the park on August 20, playing right field for the first six innings, moving to center in the seventh, and back to right for the final two frames. In the first, with a man on base, Stan quelled a Pittsburgh uprising when he raced into right-center and made a shoestring catch of Ralph Kiner's certain base hit. In the second, Eddie Stevens lined a ball off the screen in right-center, but Musial held him to a long single when he artfully played the ball on the rebound. One out later, Danny Murtaugh hit a sinking liner down the right-field line for what appeared to be a sure double. But Stan made a somersaulting catch, and after righting himself and planting his foot, threw the ball on a line to first base to double Stevens off the bag. As if his defensive output wasn't enough, it was Musial's bunt single which sparked a four-run sixth inning and eventually gave the Cards a 7–4 victory.

In late August, the *Globe-Democrat's* Robert Burnes took *Sport* magazine to task for an article entitled, "Who Is the World's Greatest Ballplayer?" *Sport* had offered just two choices, Ted Williams or Joe DiMaggio, and then effectively rebutted its own selections by pointing out that DiMaggio wasn't the hitter he once was and that Williams left something to be desired as a team player. Burnes noted that neither Williams, leading the American League in batting and runs scored, nor DiMaggio, leading the American League in home runs, was ahead of Musial in either category. As if to prove the columnist's point, Stan provided the winning runs in both ends of a doubleheader sweep the next afternoon over the Giants. In the opener, Musial's bases-loaded double plated the first three Cardinal runs, pacing the Redbirds to a 7–2 win, and it was Stan's two-run homer in the ninth that gave the Redbirds a 7–5 victory in the nightcap. Coupled with Chicago's sweep of Boston in a twin bill at Wrigley Field, Musial's only two hits of the day were, perhaps, his biggest of the year as the Cards moved back into second place, two and a half games off the pace. But by September 11, the Redbirds had fallen to fourth place, six games back. It was now just a matter of time before Boston clinched the title.

On September 22, Musial's left wrist was jammed and his right hand bruised, the result of an outfield tumble a few days earlier. Both wrists were taped when he took batting practice before the Cardinal game with the Braves, winners of their last eight straight. A Boston victory would mathematically eliminate the Cardinals and clinch the pennant for the Braves. The wind was blowing out at Braves Field, a fact which sportswriter Bob Broeg pointed out. "Yeah, but I can't hit like this," responded Stan, showing his wrists. Just before game time, Musial tore off the tape. In the first, Musial went with the pitch and looped a single into left field. In the third, on a 3–2 count, he hit to left again, driving a double over Jeff Heath's head. In the fourth, against reliever Charlie "Red" Barrett, Stan slammed a 2–0 changeup into the right-field stands for a home run, number thirty-eight on the year. In the sixth, he dribbled a single past Al Dark into left field. With Al Lyons on the mound in the eighth, Musial came to the plate with a chance to tie Ty Cobb's 1922 record of four five-hit games in a season. When Lyons went to a 2–0 count, the Cardinal bench began to ride him to get the ball over the plate. Determined to get that fifth hit, Stan decided to swing at anything near the plate. The next delivery was a bit outside, but Musial grounded a single into right field for the record-tying safety. Sparked by Stan's one-man hitting clinic, the Redbirds breezed to an 8–2 win. Not until the game ended did an observant sportswriter note that Musial had swung at only five pitches during the contest, each swing bringing forth a base hit.

The Redbirds staved off elimination for the next three days, but on September 26, the "Spahn, Sain, and pray for rain" Braves held on for a 3–2 victory over the Giants, clinching their first National League flag in thirty-four years. On October 1, Musial collected two singles and a double as the Redbirds came from behind to down Chicago. Stan's double was his 102nd extra base hit of the season, equalling a club record for long hits set by Rogers Hornsby in 1922. In the next-to-last game of the season, a 9–0 shutout of the Cubs, Musial punched a double into right field to eclipse Hornsby's record.

The Cardinal team batting average had dropped from .270 to .263 while the staff ERA had climbed from 3.53 to 3.91, a combination guaranteed to lose pennants. Less Stan's contributions, the Redbirds would surely have finished further behind the Braves than six and a half games. Musial had enjoyed a season that mere mortals could barely imagine, leading all National League hitters in nearly every offensive category, much the same as another Cardinal, Joe Medwick, had done in his Triple Crown year of 1937. Stan topped the major leagues in batting average (.376), hits (230), doubles (46), triples (18), total bases (429), on-base percentage (.450), and slugging average (.702, the first .700 slugging percentage in the National League since Hack Wilson's .723 in 1930), and led the National League in RBIs (131) and runs scored (135). He finished second in the home run race to New York's Johnny Mize and Pittsburgh's Ralph Kiner, both of whom were tied with forty. Musial missed winning the Triple Crown by a single home run, but became the first hitter since Hank Greenberg in 1937 and the last ever to record over a hundred extra-base hits in a year. With 429 total bases, the most by any National League player since 1930 and sixth on the all-time list for most total bases in a single season, the Cardinal superstar became the only player on the top ten total-bases list to that time who did not accomplish the feat between 1921 and 1937.

The Dodgers were Musial's favorite patsies: at Ebbets Field in 1948, Musial was 25-for-48 for a .521 batting average, with ten singles, ten doubles, a triple, four home runs, and a slugging average of 1.021. Indeed, had Stan been able to hit on the road all year, he might have torn the National League record books up, as a comparison of his home/road statistics shows:

	G	AB	R	H	2B	3B	HR	RBI	SB	AVG
Home	77	293	56	98	17	9	16	55	1	.334
Road	78	318	79	132	29	9	23	76	6	.415

Perhaps more telling than any other statistic was the Redbirds' record in games in which Musial was held hitless. St. Louis finished the season with an 85–69 mark for a winning percentage of .552, but in the thirty-four contests in which Stan failed to produce, the club was 12–21–1, a winning percentage of .364. Conversely, in the games in which Musial collected a hit, the Cards were 73–48 for a winning percentage of .603. In recognition of his year at the plate, Stan was voted his third Most Valuable Player award in the last five years, the first National League player to record three such honors. (Musial and Carl Hubbell had previously been the only two-time winners in the National League.)

Less than a week after the season ended, on October 8, a burglar broke into the Musials' new home in southwest St. Louis and stole a three-hundred-dollar check, several pieces of Lillian's jewelry, the watch presented to Stan for winning the 1943 National League Most Valuable Player award, and a ring he received from the Cardinals after the club won the 1946 pennant.

Stan and his wife had only recently decided to make St. Louis their home, and when the Donora smog weakened Musial's father, he and Lillian invited Lukasz and Mary to come live with them. But the move did little for Lukasz's health. Stan's father died that winter.

◇10◇

Near Miss

---

*I always talked to Musial. He would come to
bat and of course the fans didn't know this,
but I'd say, "Stan, pop up." Course he'd say
something back like, "I can't afford it,
Preach." And then I'd say, "Well, you already
had two hits." And he'd say, "I gotta hit a
respectful .340, Preach."*

PREACHER ROE

The death of his father brought Musial face to face with his own mortality for the first time. Stan had been thinking for some time about a career outside baseball. He wanted something that would support him and his family when his playing days were over, and his thoughts turned to Garagnani's Club 66, a modestly successful, two-story brick restaurant located on Chippewa Street, a few minutes from his new home and owned by Julius "Biggie" Garagnani. Playing golf with Musial one day, Biggie asked Stan if he wanted to become partners. Garagnani was a shrewd businessman and realized Musial's good name would pull new patrons into the restaurant, so he made the Cardinal superstar an offer he couldn't refuse: Stan could pay for the partnership with his share of the profits. The deal was sealed in January 1949. Added to the sign over the entrance awning that said "Biggie's Charcoal STEAKS" was a new billboard which read, simply, "Stan Musial."

Musial signed a new contract for 1949, one which would pay him $50,000, plus $5,000 more if the Redbirds drew over 900,000 paid admissions into the park. But Stan had outsmarted himself at the negotiation table: Robert Hannegan had originally offered $45,000 plus an additional $5,000 for every hundred thousand people over 900,000 paid admissions. The Cardinals would go on to set an all-time St. Louis attendance record, 1,430,676 fans. Under the terms of the offer he had spurned, Musial would have earned seventy thousand dollars.

Before the season began, Hannegan sold his interest in the ballclub to Fred Saigh, who now controlled approximately ninety percent of the Cardinal stock. One of Saigh's first moves was the sale of pitcher Murry Dickson to the Pirates for $125,000, a decision which would gravely affect Cardinal pennant hopes when Dickson went on to defeat his former teammates five times during the season, the margin of difference in the race for the title. Terry Moore was through as an active player, having taken to the coaching lines, and Whitey Kurowski, his arm irreparably injured, was replaced at third by rookies Eddie Kazak and Tommy Glaviano.

Musial was hitless in three at-bats on Opening Day, April 19, as the Redbirds dropped a 3-1 decision to Cincinnati, and the Cards were shut out by Johnny Vander Meer the following evening. Stan celebrated his return to Sportsman's Park with a double and his first home run of the season as the Redbirds rolled over Chicago, 9-2, then cracked another homer the following evening in an 11-7 loss to the Cubs. A day later, Stan blasted home run number three to give the Cards a lead they never relinquished as they coasted past Chicago, 9-3. The red-hot Musial was a perfect three-for-three on May 1 when St. Louis downed the Cubs once again, 8-3.

On May 10, the baseball world was shocked when former Cardinal owner Sam Breadon died of cancer. To a man, the Cardinal players expressed regret at Breadon's passing. "I'm terribly sorry to learn about Mr. Breadon's death," said Musial. "He always treated me swell and I know that he acted that way with all with whom he ever came in contact."

By May 18, the Redbirds had slumped to 10-15 and seventh place, while Musial, with just seven hits in his last forty-eight trips to the plate, had lost more than a hundred points off his batting average, falling from .353 to .213. The following afternoon, Stan was presented with the John A. "Bud" Hillerich award, consisting of a plaque and five hundred dollars, signifying his league-leading .376 batting average the year before. On May

22, Musial was ranked second only to Ted Williams as baseball's best player by Joseph Reichler, the Associated Press sportswriter who would later become the game's greatest statistician. Perhaps taking heart from Reichler's appraisal, Stan clubbed a two-run homer the next evening to give the Redbirds a 3–1 win over Boston at Sportsman's Park and on May 26, blasted his sixth home run of the season, pacing the Cards to a 13–6 win over Pittsburgh.

A day later, the newspapers were full of the first rumors of Musial's career that he might be traded. According to the stories, Stan and pitcher George Munger were going to the Pirates for hurler Bob Chesnes, catcher Clyde McCullough, and a whopping $300,000. Ignoring the trade gossip, Musial had his biggest day of the year on May 30 when he collected four hits in eight trips to the plate as the Cards swept a doubleheader from Cincinnati and moved into a second-place tie with the Reds, two games behind Boston, Brooklyn, and New York, knotted in a three-way tie for the National League lead.

The race remained close through June. Late in the month, St. Louis edged past Brooklyn into first place with an 8–4 win over Boston. But the Cardinals' perch atop the National League lasted just twenty-four hours. On June 25, the Dodgers mauled Pittsburgh, 17–10, while the Redbirds and Harry Brecheen were taking a 10–6 beating at the hands of the Braves, despite three singles and a brace of RBIs from Musial. Prior to the Cardinal contest of the twenty-sixth, Commissioner A.B. "Happy" Chandler presented Stan the Kenesaw Mountain Landis Memorial Award for being voted the National League's Most Valuable Player in 1948. Musial was given a bouquet of flowers at home plate, which he sheepishly carried to his wife, seated in a front row box seat with the children. Stan drew a base on balls and scored in the first, providing the only run Cardinal starter Red Munger needed in a 2–0 win.

The Redbirds reached the All-Star break with a 47–32 record, a half game behind the Dodgers. Musial was the darling of the National League in an 11–7 loss to the junior circuit in the 1949 All-Star Game. After the Americans tallied four runs in the top of the first, Stan cut into the lead with a two-run homer in the bottom of the frame, singled in the third, beat out an infield hit in the fourth, was thrown out in the sixth, and walked in his final plate appearance in the eighth. Musial led all batters with three hits and tied Pittsburgh's Ralph Kiner for the most runs batted in, two, of any National League hitter. It was the twelfth loss in the last sixteen games for the National League.

By July 22, when the slumping Cardinals arrived at Ebbets Field for a four-game series with the Dodgers, Brooklyn had widened its lead to two and a half games. Led by a red-hot Musial, who hit for the cycle in the third game, the Cards took the first three. With the fourth game tied at four-all after nine innings, the game was called to allow both teams to catch a train. The Redbirds were in first place by half a game. Stan had collected six RBIs, seven runs scored, three singles, two doubles, two triples, and two home runs in fifteen trips to the plate for the series. Over his last two years at Ebbets, Musial was batting .531.

Less than a week later, hundreds of Cardinal fans stood in line, some for as long as eighteen hours, for the seven thousand unreserved seats for the game against the Dodgers on July 29. There were over thirty thousand loyalists crammed into Sportsman's Park by the time the game began, delayed by a steady downpour until 10:13. Preacher Roe was off his form and the Cards took an early 3–0 lead only to watch as Brooklyn tied the contest with two runs in the eighth and a single tally in the ninth. The Redbirds loaded the bases in the bottom of the frame and put a pair of men on in the tenth with one out, but failed to pull the trigger, and the game ended at 1:09 a.m. because of baseball's rule that no inning could start after 12:50 a.m. (The tie was scheduled to be replayed at Sportsman's Park on September 21.) The next evening, the Redbirds came from behind twice to pull out an exciting 7–6 victory and widen their gap over Brooklyn to two and a half games. The series concluded on July 31 when right-hander Don Newcombe went the distance and posted a 4–2 win. It was the first time the Redbirds had lost in their last eleven games counting the two ties with Brooklyn.

By August 7, the Dodgers and Cardinals were once again tied, a situation that prevailed for the next four days. Over the next two weeks, the league lead changed hands several times. On Labor Day, September 5, in a pair of games which would have a resounding effect on the pennant race, the Cards split a doubleheader with Pittsburgh. In the second inning of the nightcap, Enos Slaughter slid hard into Pittsburgh second baseman Danny Murtaugh, slashing him with his spikes. Slaughter's conduct aroused the Pirates, who played as if the pennant depended upon this one game. The contest went into overtime and Murtaugh got his revenge when he doubled and scored the winning run in the tenth. If the Dodgers were feeling any pressure, they failed to show it as they swept a pair of doubleheaders from Boston, reducing the Cardinal lead to a single game.

The September 5 issue of *Time* magazine included a short article on Musial which summed up the feelings of sportswriters everywhere, who felt the frustration of reporting on a ballplayer who so utterly shunned controversy in every phase of his life. The article said, in part:

> If he has an iota of fire and imagination, he succeeds in keeping it veiled behind his deadpan Slavic features. The umpires know that Musial has a deadly eye and that he can separate the balls from the strikes more accurately than most. They are also disconcerted when Musial makes his strongest protest: a calm, openmouthed stare that seems to say, "How can you be so wrong?" Such placidity makes him the despair of sportswriters who follow the Cards all season and dig in vain for Musial "color," but there is color in every move he makes on the field.

September 7 was Stan Musial Night at Sportsman's Park. Prior to the contest with the Cubs, Stan was presented with a DeSoto station wagon, a plaque from his teammates, telegrams from friends and fans around the nation, and $6,000 in United States Government savings bonds. Musial singled that evening, raising his average on the year to .324, third-best in the league behind Enos Slaughter's .337 and Jackie Robinson's .348. Even without a contribution from their best hitter, the Cards pulled out a 3–2 squeaker from Chicago, but it did them little good as the Dodgers downed the Braves at Ebbets Field. On September 15, the Pirates downed Brooklyn while the Redbirds edged the Braves and seventeen-game winner Warren Spahn for their ninetieth win and seventeenth victory in the last twenty-one games. Cardinal pennant hopes soared as the Redbirds held a two-and-a-half game lead with fourteen contests remaining on the year.

The Cardinals set a new home attendance record of 1,256,388 as they administered a 15–3 drubbing to the third-place Phillies on September 18. Musial scored two runs, slammed his thirty-third homer of the year, and raised his average to .332, nine points behind teammate Enos Slaughter and twelve behind league-leader Jackie Robinson. Two days later, Stan had to leave the game against Philadelphia with a pulled groin muscle after running out a triple in the fifth. He was expected, however, to suit up for the doubleheader with Brooklyn the next day as the Dodgers made their final trip of the year to Sportsman's Park for a crucial three-game series.

The Cardinals and Dodgers split their doubleheader on September 21, but the final game of the series marked one of the worst setbacks of the year for the Redbirds. The Bums blasted Cardinal starter Red Munger for three quick runs in the first; by the time the game ended, Eddie Dyer had trotted in five more pitchers while Brooklyn racked up nineteen hits and thirteen walks en route to a 19–6 overhaul of the Cardinal pitching staff.

On the year, the Cardinals had won twelve of twenty-two meetings with the Dodgers, but they'd lost four of their last six encounters and their lead was down to a half game.

On September 25, while the Dodgers were losing to Philadelphia, the Redbirds downed the Cubs in their final game of the year at Sportsman's Park. There were nearly thirty-one thousand fans in the park, bringing attendance for the year to 1,430,676, a mark which would remain a club record until the Cardinals moved into their new ballpark in 1966. The Redbirds were now leading the Dodgers by a game and a half with just five games to go. Tickets for the 1949 World Series were due to be delivered to the Cardinal front office from the printer the next afternoon, an off-day for both St. Louis and Brooklyn.

At Pittsburgh on September 27, the Pirates were still fuming over Slaughter's hard slide into Danny Murtaugh in the Labor Day doubleheader. Rookie Tom Saffell's grand-slam home run was the big hit in a 6–4 win over St. Louis. With four contests remaining in the season, the Cardinal lead was at one game. On September 29, former Cardinal Murry Dickson became the only opposition hurler to defeat the Redbirds five times in 1949 when he scattered six hits as the Pirates beat St. Louis and Gerry Staley, 7–2. At Ebbets Field, the Dodgers beat Boston's two best pitchers, Warren Spahn and Johnny Sain, and for the first time in six weeks, moved into sole possession of the league lead. Brooklyn had two games remaining with the third-place Phillies and the Cardinals had three against the last-place Cubs.

The Redbirds opened their series at Wrigley Field on September 30, a day when nothing went right. Max Lanier, riding a five-game winning streak, was knocked out of the box, George Munger failed in relief, and the always reliable Musial lost a fly ball in the sun that dropped in for a damaging two-run double. St. Louis went down to a devastating 6–5 defeat and now trailed Brooklyn by one game with two to go. Optimistic Cardinal fans, looking forward to two more games with the feckless Cubs, were daring to hope for a replay of the 1946 season, which ended with St. Louis and Brooklyn tied for the National League title.

On October 1, while Brooklyn was losing to Philadelphia, Chicago scored three quick runs for Bob Chipman and the Cubs held on for a 3–1 win over the Cardinals. Chipman, a herky-jerky pitcher who threw nothing but junk to the plate, worked a typical game in this crucial contest, surrendering nine hits and four walks. But the Redbirds squandered opportunity after opportunity and left twelve men on base. The defeat marked the first time during the season that St. Louis had lost four straight. The losing streak could not have come at a worse moment. On the final day of the season, Musial slammed two home runs and a single while Howie Pollet won an easy 13–5 victory over the Cubs. Following the victory, Cardinal players adjourned to the clubhouse to listen to the conclusion of Brooklyn's game with Philadelphia. The Dodgers had already blown a 5–0 lead and were tied at seven-all with Pee Wee Reese on second and Duke Snider coming to bat in the top of the tenth. Ken Heintzelman served up a pitch a little too fat and Snider lined a single up the middle, putting Brooklyn into the lead. The Dodgers went on to post a 9–7 win over the Phillies and capture the National League title, leaving the frustrated Redbirds in second place for the third straight season. The Cardinal players were a solemn bunch as they rode the train back to St. Louis.

Musial had an off year, for Musial that is—the result of swinging for too many home runs. Before spring training began, recalling Ralph Kiner's remark that "singles hitters drive Fords, but home-run hitters drive Cadillacs," Stan had announced that he was going for the home-run title. Both greedy and wrong, Stan went for the bleacher seats and tried to pull the ball too often. He overstrode at the plate, lost his timing, and played right into the pitchers' hands. It took two months before he realized home runs had to come naturally. Musial finished the season at .338, trailing Jackie Robinson by four points in the batting title, but had led all National League batters in total bases (382), on-base percentage (.438), runs scored (128), hits (207), and doubles (41), and tied for the league lead in triples (13).

At Sportsman's Park, a grim Cardinal front office began plans to return $1.5 million in World Series applications. Although no one knew it, the salad days were over. The Cardinals wouldn't finish this close to a pennant again until 1957.

◇ **11** ◇

The Slide Begins

---

*If I could roll the ball up there, I think that's
the way I might have pitched him.*

WARREN SPAHN

The decade began for Stan and Lillian with the birth of their second daughter, Janet. Musial used the new addition to the family as an excuse to cut back on his numerous speaking engagements, and he spent most of the winter at home in St. Louis.

The Dodgers were emerging as a dynasty. The nation's sportswriters picked them to win the first pennant of the 1950s, while the Cardinals ranked second in the pre-season poll. After a lackluster spring training, the Redbirds opened the year with a 4–2 win over Pittsburgh at Sportsman's Park on April 18, the first opening game in major-league history to be played under the lights. Red Schoendienst and Musial homered off Bob Chesnes in the contest, but it was Joe Garagiola's tie-breaking single, delivered during a light snow, which put the Cards ahead to stay in the sixth. Stan added another home run a day later, but the Redbirds made seven errors in the final two games of the opening series of 1950 and lost both contests, an inauspicious beginning, to say the least, for the new decade.

On April 28, Musial suffered the first serious injury of his career. Stan was already two-for-three in the contest at Pittsburgh and the Cards held a 5–2 lead when their $50,000 right fielder drove a ball to deep right-center at Forbes Field. Digging hard for second base, Musial slipped in the soft dirt and somersaulted hard on the ground. Stan rose and started for the dugout, thinking he wasn't hurt seriously, but as soon as he put his full weight on his left foot, he nearly collapsed. Leading the major leagues with a .448 batting average, Musial was lost to the club indefinitely. "I tried to get up once," Stan recalled years later, "but I couldn't and fell back. I said to myself, This is it, I'm through. Thank God for the restaurant."

Team trainer Doc Weaver applied icepacks after the game and Stan kept hot-water bottles on the knee during the night, but the joint had stiffened by morning. Musial had hoped to suit up for the afternoon game with Pittsburgh, but after taking diathermy treatments all morning, decided otherwise. It was the first time the Cardinal superstar had watched a game from the grandstand since the end of the 1947 season. Stan was convinced he would miss no more than a day or two, but Doc Weaver and team surgeon Dr. Robert F. Hyland shared the opinion that he should stay out of the lineup a week or so.

When Musial returned to right field for seven innings a few days later, he collected two singles in four times at bat, scored one run, and drove in another, as the Redbirds eked out a 6–5 win over the first-place Dodgers. Concentrating on just making contact with the ball, Musial had begun a fifteen-game hitting streak. Two weeks later, he was hitting .467 and his closest competition was Philadelphia's Dick Sisler, eighty-five points distant. Perhaps a little knee injury wasn't so bad, after all.

Stan's fifteen-game hitting streak came to an end in a doubleheader split with the Phillies. During the skein, Musial had come to the plate sixty-four times, made thirty hits, including ten doubles and two triples, scored thirteen runs, driven in nine, and batted .469, just a tuneup for a thirty-game streak which would begin eight weeks later. Thirty-two games into the 1950 season, Stan was leading the major leagues with a .447 average and causing some early speculation about his chances to hit .400 for the year.

On June 1, the Redbirds moved into a first-place tie with a tense 5–2 win over Brooklyn, a victory capped by Marty Marion's grand-slam home run. Musial, oh-for-three in the contest, saw his average drop to .397. Cardinal pennant hopes took a turn for the worse that afternoon when catcher Joe Garagiola suffered a shoulder separation in a collision with Dodger second baseman Jackie Robinson. (Batting .347 at the time, Garagiola looked to be a certain choice as the All-Star Game catcher, but the injury would keep him out of the lineup until September and shorten what was a promising career.) The Cardinals' brief stay atop the National League ended the next evening when Dodger hurler Don Newcombe five-hit the Redbirds, 8–1, ending the St. Louis winning streak at six games.

Throughout June the Cardinals battled first Brooklyn, then surprising Philadelphia, for possession of first place. Stan's single contributed nothing to a 2–1 victory over Pittsburgh on July 2, but the Cardinal superstar was honored nonetheless when he was selected as the senior circuit's starting first baseman in the upcoming All-Star Game, leading all National League players save Jackie Robinson in vote-getting. His average down to .350, Musial trailed the red-hot Dodger second baseman in the race for the batting title by thirty points. Stan extended his hitting streak to fourteen games by the All-Star break while the Redbirds closed out the first half of the season with a 43–30 record, trailing the Phillies by a game.

On July 11, in the All-Star Game at Comiskey Park in Chicago, the National League downed the junior circuit, 4–3, on Cardinal second baseman Red Schoendienst's home run in the fourteenth inning off Detroit's Ted Gray. Musial, after his three-for-four performance the year before, was a complete bust in the 1950 contest, hitless in five trips to the plate.

When the second half of the season resumed on July 14, Stan's hitting streak was jeopardized when he twisted his knee in the loose dirt surrounding first base in a 4–2 win over Philadelphia. Limping slightly, Musial was in uniform the next day, collecting two hits as the Cards lurched to an 8–6 victory over the Phils and moved back into a tie for first place. In the race for the National League batting title, Stan had now narrowed the gap with the slumping Jackie Robinson to just eight points, trailing .348 to .356. On July 16, despite a 10–2 clubbing at the hands of the Dodgers, St. Louis backed into sole possession of first place when the Phils dropped a doubleheader to Chicago. The next day, Brooklyn knocked the Cards out of the top spot by sweeping a twin bill. Musial extended his hitting streak to twenty games with a double in both contests. Just one game separated the top four teams in the National League and if baseball fans thought the race couldn't get any closer, they were wrong. When the Cards posted a 5–3 decision over the Dodgers on July 18, St. Louis, Philadelphia, and Boston were tied for first place with identical 46–34 records. Brooklyn, at 43–34, was a game and a half out.

On July 27, Musial's thirty-game hitting streak came to an end. The Cardinal superstar grounded out in the first, bounced into a forceout in the third, popped out in the sixth, and flied out in the eighth. Oh-for-four and with little possibility of coming up again in the ninth, it looked as if Stan's streak was finally over. But the Cards tallied three times in the final frame and loaded the bases, bringing Musial to the plate and nineteen-year-old rookie reliever Billy Loes into the game. Shortstop Pee Wee Reese and second baseman Jackie Robinson huddled with Loes on the mound and burst out laughing a moment later. When the players returned to their positions, Stan sent a grounder right to Jackie Robinson for an easy double play. The Redbirds went on to score three more runs in the frame, en route to a 13–3 pasting of the Dodgers. At batting practice the next day, a curious Musial asked Pee Wee Reese what had been so funny. Reese said he had asked Loes if he was aware that the Cardinal superstar had a thirty-game hitting streak on the line. The cocky rookie had said yes, and he was going to throw one right down the middle, too!

During his streak, Stan had come to the plate 121 times, scored twenty runs, drove in thirty-one, and collected forty-seven hits for a batting average of .388.

With two-thirds of the 1950 season gone, the Cardinals had slumped to fourth place, four and a half games back, when they arrived at Philadelphia for a five-game series. It was all downhill from there. The pennant race was effectively over for Cardinal fans a week or two later. By September, St. Louis was fourteen games back and struggling to avoid its worst finish since 1938. Rumors were afloat that Eddie Dyer was one of four major-league managers who would lose his job at the end of the season. Just six weeks earlier, the Cards had been in the National League top position, but since that time, the Redbirds had played at a 15–25 clip and compiled a dismal 3–11 mark in one-run games. In eight of their twenty-five losses, the Cards had gone down to defeat in the final frame. Musial, despite enduring a fourteen-at-bat hitless streak at the end of August, had virtually clinched another batting title, leading Jackie Robinson by some thirty points. No one criticized Stan when he took half a dozen games off late in the month because of a chest cold and twisted knee. Robinson was out of the Dodger lineup for perhaps the rest of the season with a hand injury and had no chance of catching the Cardinal slugger.

St. Louis ended the season in fifth place, with a disappointing 78–75 record, twelve and a half games behind the champion Phillies. It marked the first second-division finish for the Cardinals since 1938, and the only time since Musial had joined the club that the Redbirds had failed to place first or second. The day before the season ended, team owner Fred Saigh had given manager Eddie Dyer a no-confidence vote by saying he would withhold his decision on Dyer's future until after the World Series, but the team's poor showing had cost Dyer his job. The Cardinal skipper beat Saigh to the punch and handed in his resignation two weeks later, taking full blame for the disastrous season. On November 29, the Cardinals announced that shortstop Marty Marion was retiring as an active player and had signed a one-year contract to manage the club.

Musial had played first base and all three outfield positions for Dyer during 1950 and finished the year with a .346 batting mark, his career average to that time. Stan led the National League in batting and slugging average (.596), finished second to teammate Red Schoendienst in doubles (41 to 43), second in hits (192), and fifth in runs scored (109), the seventh straight season he had topped the one hundred mark. The effect of playing four different defensive positions for a mediocre team had caused Musial's offensive statistics to slump for the second straight year, but the coming season would see a virtual across-the-board improvement for the Cardinal slugger.

◆ ◆ ◆

In February 1951, in the midst of the Korean War, Musial departed the states for Germany to entertain the Army of Occupation at the request of the War Department. With him were Jim Konstanty of the Philadelphia Phillies, Chicago Cubs manager Frankie Frisch, Boston Braves manager Charley Grimm, and National League umpire Larry Goetz. Stan learned how to play a zither and was photographed umpteen times wearing a Bavarian hat and the familiar Musial grin.

Back in the States, Musial signed what he thought was a $75,000 contract for 1951. But two months later he got the bad news that the Wage Stabilization Board had instituted a salary ceiling on each major- and minor-league baseball club and that his expected $25,000 raise had been denied. The board ruled that wages paid baseball players in 1951 must conform generally with club payroll practices of 1950 which, in effect, said that any ballplayer on the club could be given a salary equal to Musial's, but that Stan could not be paid more. An individual plea for an exception could be made, but Musial would not see his raise until the following season.

The Redbirds headed north from the Grapefruit League with a 16–16 record, picked by most baseball writers to finish no better than fourth for the season. The Cardinals featured rookies Steve Bilko at first, Tom Richmond at third, and Sol Hemus at short. A week into the season, the only veteran on the infield, Red Schoendienst, was struck in the face by a foul tip off his own bat and was lost to the club for two weeks. Dick Cole was inserted at second base, giving the Redbirds an all-rookie infield. Manager Marty Marion opened the season with another first-year player, Tom Poholsky, on the mound. Poholsky, 18–6 at Rochester in 1950, was the first rookie in

Cardinal history to work an Opening Day game. St. Louis dropped its 1951 season debut to Murry Dickson and the Pirates, 5–4, in the midst of a snowstorm at Forbes Field. Musial, looking to become the first National Leaguer to repeat as batting champion since Rogers Hornsby, contributed a single in four trips to the plate.

Back at Sportsman's Park for their home opener on April 19, the Cardinal players were sporting new uniforms: dark blue, long-sleeved turtle-necks under their jerseys; dark blue caps with a red insignia; and a new, fatter Redbird on the front of the shirt, standing on a gold bat instead of the previous year's blue one. Musial was hitless in two official at-bats as St. Louis downed the Cubs, and it took until April 28, the ninth game of the year, before Stan collected his first extra-base hit, a double in a 6–3 win over the Cubs. Musial blasted his first home run of the year a day later, but was having trouble getting untracked at the plate. He wasn't alone. As a team, the Redbirds were batting just .218, and many of Stan's teammates were suffering from the flu.

On May 8, when the Cardinals arrived at the Polo Grounds for a three-game series with the Giants, the club was racked with illness. Seven members of the squad, including trainer Doc Weaver, were confined to their hotel rooms with the flu and nine other players or club personnel were ill. Starting pitcher Harry Brecheen was one of those left back at the Hotel New Yorker and mound duties fell to rookie Joe Presko, who was roughed up for eight hits in four innings as the Redbirds lost, 6–2. It was the last day during 1951 the club would occupy first place. Four St. Louis pitchers were rocked the next evening for twenty-one hits as the Giants rolled over the ailing Redbirds, 17–3. Stan shifted to center field for the night, but was himself bedridden the next evening as St. Louis dropped the series finale for the club's fourth loss in a row.

Near the end of May, Musial embarked upon one of the most extended home run binges of his career. Stan clubbed a three-run homer against the Reds on May 24 and a two-run shot a day later. The following evening, Musial crushed a pair of round-trippers in a 6–1 win over Cincinnati and the next night, he collected his ninth homer of the year and fourth in his last six at-bats, giving the Redbirds a 6–5 win over the Pirates. Number ten broke a 3–3 tie and sent the Cards on to a 4–3 win over Pittsburgh the following day. In twenty-three trips to the plate, Stan had pounded out thirteen hits, including six homers, three doubles, and a triple. But the Cards couldn't put a solid winning streak together, and by the All-Star break they were nowhere near first place.

On July 1, Musial had received word that he was baseball's biggest vote-getter in the annual balloting for the All-Star game, collecting 1,428,383 votes. In their final series before the break, the Redbirds split four games with the Pirates at Forbes Field. Stan collected seven hits in seventeen trips to the plate and was now hitting .369, best in the major leagues and thirteen points higher than second-place Jackie Robinson.

On July 9, on the eve of the 1951 All-Star Game in Detroit, Yankee hurler Eddie Lopat confided to Brooklyn's Preacher Roe that he had figured out a way to pitch to Stan Musial. But with the score tied at one-all in the top of the fourth the next day, Musial shattered the theory when he slammed Lopat's first pitch for a home run into the upper right-field stands at Briggs Stadium. "Hell," shouted Roe from the dugout, "I know how to pitch him that way." Stan added a single later in the game, won by the National Leaguers, 8–3.

By mid-July, Musial was no longer feeling the heat from Jackie Robinson, but was being chased by Philadelphia center fielder Richie Ashburn. Ashburn had raised his average sixteen points to .362 in the last three weeks, but still trailed Stan by five points. On July 15, the Redbirds opened a three-game series with the Phillies at Connie Mack Stadium with a twi-night doubleheader. Enjoying the head-to-head competition, Stan singled and crushed two homers in the opening contest. The second blast was one of the longest ever hit in Philadelphia, clearing the right-field wall and sailing far over 20th Street, finally coming to rest on the rooftop of a second-story flat. Musial added two singles in the nightcap and was five-for-nine on the day. Ashburn, two-for-eight in the twin bill, fell to .359, fourteen points behind the Cardinal superstar. Musial was one-for-five the following day, but Ashburn was hitless and remained fourteen points off the pace.

Beginning in late July, St. Louis embarked on a disastrous streak during which the club lost fifteen times in nineteen outings, falling twenty games behind the league-leading Dodgers. Musial achieved a personal milestone on August 9 when he legged out an inside-the-park home run against the Cubs, the two hundredth round-tripper of his career. A week later, Musial slammed his twenty-eighth home run of the year, equalling his entire output for 1950. On August 28, Musial was honored at Connie Mack Stadium by the United Polish-American clubs of Philadelphia. National League president Ford Frick was on hand for the festivities, during which Stan was presented with a plaque and wrist watch. One-for-three in the contest, Musial scored what proved to be the winning run.

On September 23, the Redbirds closed out their home season with a doubleheader sweep of the Cubs. While the Giants and Dodgers were winding up their epic struggle for the 1951 pennant, St. Louis split its last four games and quietly finished the year in third place with an 81–73 record, fifteen and a half games out.

Musial had another fine year at the plate, hitting .355 to capture his fifth batting title. Stan blasted thirty-two homers and drove in 108 runs, the only Cardinal to finish the year with more than sixty-five RBIs. Musial led the National League in runs scored (124), triples (12), and total bases (355). For his career, he stood 171 hits short of two thousand, twenty-seven doubles short of four hundred, and seventy-seven RBIs short of a thousand. Stan's lifetime batting average was .3473, a mark which gave him a slight lead over Ted Williams, at .3466. *The Sporting News,* for the second time in Musial's career, named him Major League Player of the Year.

Marty Marion, who asked for a two-year contract, was fired instead and wound up managing the Browns in 1952. On December 11, the Cardinals traded pitcher Max Lanier and outfielder Chuck Diering to the Giants for second baseman Eddie Stanky, an ask-no-quarter-and-give-none player who would become the Redbirds' playing manager for 1952.

A young Stan Musial in a typical batting shot from the 1940s. *(NBL)*

Musial *(standing, second from right)* and his teammates from the 1938 Donora High School basketball team. *(Sporting News)*

A member of the 1942 World Series champion Cardinals, Stan still had to supplement his income by working in his father-in-law's grocery store in the off-season. *(Sporting News)*

The keen batting eye and unwavering concentration that won seven National League batting titles. (NBL)

Musial shares a cup of coffee with a fellow sailor while serving in the Navy, 1945. (NBL)

The 1946 Cardinal fly-catchers and one of the greatest National League outfields ever: Enos Slaughter, Terry Moore, and Stan Musial. Between them, they played 52 years and collected more than 7,000 hits. *(Sporting News)*

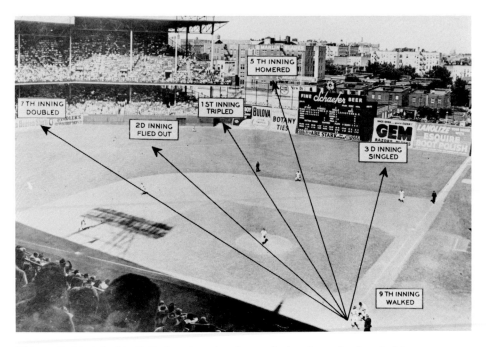

Ebbets Field, July 24, 1949. Stan hits for the cycle for the only time in his career as the Cardinals trounced the Dodgers, 14–1. *(Sporting News)*

(From left) Del Rice, Alpha Brazle, Bill Howerton, Musial, and Johnny Lindell relax in the clubhouse with a friendly game of hearts. *(Sporting News)*

Stan jokes with Enos Slaughter, Dizzy Dean, and Terry Moore. *(NBL)*

He may have started his baseball career as a pitcher, but Musial's only major-league appearance on the mound came as an embarrassing publicity stunt at the end of the 1952 season. *(Sporting News)*

Stan uncoils at the plate with the stance and swing described by Branch Rickey as "ideal in form." *(Sporting News)*

A posed batting shot from 1954, the year Stan did something none of the other Hall of Fame sluggers had ever accomplished—hit five home runs in a doubleheader. *(NBL)*

Musial and his two biggest fans, mother Mary and
wife Lillian. Nearing 37, Stan said he expected to
play "a couple more years." *(Sporting News)*

Musial prepares to cut the cake that commemorates him
breaking the National League record for most consecutive
games played. With Stan are Al Dark *(left)*, Larry Jackson, and
manager Fred Hutchinson *(standing)*. *(Sporting News)*

The M&M boys, Musial and New York Yankees slugger Mickey Mantle, pose before a spring training game, 1957. *(NBL)*

Musial, Gene Oliver, and Ken Boyer pose for a very fishy publicity shot during spring training, St. Petersburg, Florida, 1960. *(NBL)*

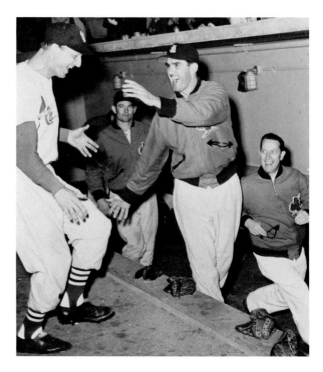

Musial is welcomed to the dugout by pitcher Ernie Broglio after he breaks Honus Wagner's National League record for career hits on May 19, 1962. *(Sporting News)*

Cardinal broadcaster Harry Caray emcees one of the many ceremonies honoring Musial in 1963. *(NBL)*

Stan and Lillian in front of the white Cadillac that bears his
personalized license plate. The date is September 29, 1963.
(Sporting News)

Musial, on the day of his retirement, poses with Baseball Hall of Fame director Sid
Keener *(center)* and National League President Warren Giles. *(NBL)*

Stan, with Lillian and his daughters, on the day he retired. *(NBL)*

Musial and Boy Scout Howard Johnson in pre-game ceremonies, September 29, 1963. *(Sporting News)*

Cardinal owner August A. Busch Jr. clasps Stan's hand warmly after presenting him with a painting during Musial's retirement ceremonies. *(Sporting News)*

Musial and President Lyndon B. Johnson, 1964. Stan has just accepted the post of national director of the President's Council on Physical Fitness. *(NBL)*

Stan and Attorney General
Robert Kennedy, 1964. *(NBL)*

Stanley Frank Musial and his plaque in the Hall of Fame, 1969. *(Sporting News)*

Musial and his family. *(Sporting News)*

Retirement rests easily on Musial at Busch Stadium, early 1980s. *(Sporting News)*

Stan the Man. *(NBL)*

◇12◇

Now Pitching, Stan Musial

With the departure of Joe DiMaggio [to retirement] and Ted Williams [to the military service] Stan Musial is the only diamond brilliant left for most fans to follow.

GRANTLAND RICE

F red Saigh had offered Musial a contract for $75,000 with a $5,000 attendance clause in 1951, but Stan had not been able to get his raise because of the Korean War freeze on pay hikes. In January 1952, while Musial was seated next to Secretary of Labor Maurice Tobin at a dinner in Washington, he mentioned his pay increase problem. Tobin told Stan to bring his lawyer to Washington. Stan did, and Tobin took the Cardinal superstar before the Wage Stabilization Board, which voted a "hands-off" policy on baseball salaries. In a press conference a few days later, Saigh handed Musial a blank contract and said, "I know this puts you on the spot, Stan, but I think you've given some thought to what you want. Anything short of your owning the ball club tomorrow morning is all right with me."

Musial, wearing his patriotism on his sleeve, signed for the same amount he had received in 1951: $75,000 with a $5,000 bonus if the Cardinals reached one million in paid attendance.

On January 28, 1952, the Cardinal franchise was thrown into turmoil when Saigh pleaded nolo contendere to income tax evasion. Saigh, who had bought out Robert Hannegan following the 1948 season, was sentenced to fifteen months in jail and a $15,000 fine, necessitating a search for a new owner when he was ordered by major-league baseball to divest his control of the club. Anheuser-Busch, the giant St. Louis brewery, was interested.

Less than a month before the 1952 season opened, Ty Cobb penned a controversial article for *Life* magazine entitled "They Don't Play Baseball Any More." The always fiery Cobb opened his diatribe against modern-day ballplayers by saying:

> There are only two players in the major leagues today who can be mentioned in the same breath with the oldtime greats . . . Phil Rizzuto and Stan Musial . . . No man has ever been a perfect ballplayer. Stan Musial, however, is the closest to being perfect in the game today. I've seen greater hitters and greater runners and greater fielders, but he puts them all together like no one else, except the way George Sisler did. He's certainly one of the greatest players of all time. In my book, he's a better player than Joe DiMaggio was in his prime. Stan Musial will score from first on a single. You don't see much of that kind of running around today. He plays as hard when his club is away out in front of a game as he does when they're just a run or two behind. He'll go after a ball, even in an exhibition game, diving for a shoestring catch, as if the World Series depended on it. He's my kind of ball-player . . . He plays anywhere you put him, left field, center field . . . He has the power of Napoleon Lajoie. He has the stamina of Eddie Collins. He is as steady as old Honus Wagner.

Cobb's statements were undeniably self-serving—he was, after all, one of the "oldtime greats"—but that did not detract from his assessment of Musial. Four months later, Cobb passed through St. Louis and was interviewed by St. Louis *Globe-Democrat* sportswriter Bob Burnes, who asked the Hall of Famer to elaborate on his comments. "When I wrote the article," said Cobb, "fans asked, Why not DiMaggio? Why not Williams? For one thing, Musial is a better hitter. The record proves it. He hits to all fields, he runs the bases, he plays well defensively, he helps the ball club. What more do you want?"

Stan, for his part, was as modest as ever. "I don't want to argue with Ty Cobb," said Musial. "Cobb is baseball's greatest. I don't want to contradict him, but I can't say that I was ever as good as Joe DiMaggio. I don't think there was ever a day when I could reach Joe DiMaggio, when Joe was in his top form. That DiMaggio was the best, the greatest ballplayer I ever saw on any diamond anywhere . . . That's all very nice for Ty Cobb to say all those things about me but I think he's off base this time."

Grantland Rice may have been guilty of some hyperbole when he said that Stan was the only "diamond brilliant left for most fans to follow," but his words held the ring of truth when applied to the 1952 Cardinals, a team which boasted little more than the hitting of Musial, the hustle of Enos Slaughter, and the splendid defensive work of second baseman Red Schoendienst. The Brooklyn Dodgers started the year by winning eight of their first nine games, but the Cardinals were going the other way. By the time the season was barely a month old, St. Louis had fallen into the second division. When the Redbirds reached the .500 mark in mid-June, the club trailed Brooklyn by seven games.

On June 18, Stan collected career hit number 1,900, a two-run homer which broke a 1–1 tie and propelled the Redbirds to a 7–1 win over the Phillies. Musial drove in another run later in the contest, the fifteenth straight game in which he had hit safely, and was within forty RBIs of a thousand, a goal which seemed attainable in 1952. Over the last seven games, Stan had collected twelve hits in twenty-nine at-bats and had raised his average to .336, tops in the National League. The Cardinal slugger hit safely in every game for the next nine days, but on June 28, the weatherman accomplished what National League pitchers had failed to do for nearly a month. Stan drew a base on balls in the first and lined out in the fourth before rain halted the contest in the sixth and along with it, Musial's twenty-four-game hitting streak. During the skein, Stan had collected thirty-six hits, including three doubles, three triples, and four home runs, in ninety at-bats for an even .400 average.

Musial was the starting center fielder for the National League and the top vote-getter for the 1952 All-Star Game, played at Shibe Park in Philadelphia on July 8. Stan was hit by a Bob Lemon pitch and was on base when Chicago's Hank Sauer slammed a two-run homer which provided the margin of victory in a rain-shortened 3–2 National League victory. Officially, Musial was hitless in two at-bats. Five days later, National League president Warren Giles presented Musial with the J.A. "Bud" Hillerich Memorial Award, a certificate and silver bat valued at five hundred dollars, symbolic of the 1951 batting title. Giles, one of Stan's biggest fans, lauded Musial's character and ability and said he was the greatest player in baseball and one of the greatest of all time.

The Cardinals mounted an eight-game winning streak in mid-August and took over second place as they prepared to meet the Dodgers for a four-game series beginning on the twenty-fourth. Seven and a half games back, if the club stood any chance of making a run at the 1952 pennant, this was it. Musial was three-for-four with two singles, a double, and two runs scored in the opening contest, but the Dodgers mounted an early 8–0 lead and coasted to a 10–4 win. Stan drove in the only Cardinal tally in the first game of a doubleheader the next day as John Rutherford two-hit the Redbirds, 3–1, then scored one run and drove in another in the night-cap, but the Dodgers tallied five in the ninth for a 9–5 victory. The next evening, Musial's two-run homer in the fifth helped stake Stu Miller to a 3–0 lead, but the rookie self-destructed and Brooklyn completed the series sweep with a 4–3 triumph. St. Louis fell to third place, eleven and a half games off the pace, and the 1952 pennant race was effectively finished. Musial, holding steady at .330, was still leading all National League hitters in the race for the batting title.

On September 9, Stan became the only active major-league player with two thousand hits when he rapped a single off Philadelphia's Curt Simmons. In the middle of a hitting streak which would eventually run to fourteen games, Musial was nonetheless struggling to maintain his lead in the race for the batting championship: Chicago outfielder Frankie Baumholtz, batting .322, had closed the gap with Stan to nine points.

The Cardinals were eight games behind the Dodgers when they arrived in Brooklyn for a two-game series on September 12. St. Louis went down to an 8–5 defeat in the opening contest, but Stan had one of his best days of the year. Musial had already walked, singled twice, and doubled when he blasted a Joe Black delivery high over the right-field screen for his sixteenth home run of the season and RBI number one thousand of his career.

On September 19, the Cards met Chicago for the first of three games which would see the National League's two leading hitters go head to head. Entering the opening contest, Musial was hitting .336 and Frankie Baumholtz .330, but Stan mustered just one hit to Baumholtz's two and Musial's lead was down to three points. The following afternoon, while the Cardinals were mathematically eliminated from the pennant race with a 4–1 loss to the Cubs, Baumholtz collected one hit, but Musial flied out twice, fouled to the catcher, and looked at a called third strike. Batting .333, Stan now held just a one-point edge over the Chicago right fielder. In the rubber game of the series, Baumholtz was hitless in two at-bats, his average dropping to .330. Musial slammed a two-run homer and raised his mark for the year to .334. With one hundred runs scored, Stan surpassed his own modern National League record by scoring a hundred or more runs for nine straight years.

A week later, on September 29, the Cardinals closed out the season at home with a bit of silliness when manager Eddie Stanky talked Musial into making his major-league pitching debut against the Cubs. Stan faced just one batter: right fielder Frankie Baumholtz, the man he'd beaten for the batting title. Baumholtz turned around to bat right-handed and reached base when third sacker Solly Hemus bobbled his grounder. Embarrassed by the spectacle, Musial never again pitched in the majors.

Under Stanky, the Cardinals had wound up in third place with eighty-eight victories, a mark which would be the club's highest total of the decade. Musial captured his sixth batting title and third in a row, the first time since 1920–25 that any National League batter had won three consecutive titles. Stan had led all National League batters in batting average (.336), hits (194), doubles (42), total bases (311), slugging percentage (.538), and tied for the league lead in runs scored (105). But for the first time since 1947, Stan had finished with fewer than a hundred RBIs. Musial lamented a season which, for most major-league hitters, would have been a career year. "I wish I could have done better," said Stan. "My timing was off."

Still, Musial was one of the few ballplayers, as the September 15 issue of *Life* magazine had said, "that the fans still come out to see regardless of wind, water or club standing."

◆ ◆ ◆

On February 20, 1953, Fred Saigh sold the Cardinal franchise to St. Louis-based Anheuser-Busch. The brewery assumed $1.125 million in indebtedness and purchased 1,665 shares of Saigh's stock for $1,491.65 per share, a total asking price of $2,483,597.25. Anheuser-Busch stockholders overwhelmingly approved the deal and on March 11, the brewery officially took over operation of the Cardinal organization. On April 9, less than a week before the 1953 season was due to open, brewery owner August Busch bought Sportsman's Park from St. Louis Browns owner Bill Veeck for $800,000 and announced that the park's new monicker would be Budweiser Stadium. (Harangued by local citizens and pressured by the commissioner's office, Busch swiftly changed his mind about naming the stadium after a beer and called it Busch Stadium instead.) The Cardinals were about to enjoy an open field in St. Louis: Veeck, seeing the handwriting on the wall, would transfer his club to Baltimore for the 1954 season, the first franchise shift in baseball since 1902.

The St. Louis home opener was a near disaster. Most of the fireworks display fizzled in the forty-degree temperatures. The rooftop elevator broke down. Governor Phil M. Donnelly had a sore arm and barely managed to throw out the first ball, and singer Phil Regan, scheduled to sing the national anthem, developed a sore throat. The only high spot of the evening was the game itself, as Cardinal starter Harvey Haddix blanked the Cubs on four hits, 3–0. Musial scored the first run in the "new" stadium when he singled in the sixth and trotted home a moment later on Enos Slaughter's home run. St. Louis' first April snow in fourteen years canceled the second game of the homestand the next evening, and flurries were coming down the following night when Musial's fifth-inning, solo home run broke a 3–3 tie and gave the Cards a 4–3 win over the Braves. Beginning a twelve-game hitting streak, Stan was off to a hot start in his drive for a fourth consecutive National League batting title before he was embroiled in one of the silliest controversies in the history of major-league baseball.

In early May, St. Louis Browns manager Marty Marion had implied that Mickey Mantle was a greater ballplayer than Musial. At a Pittsburgh Junior Chamber of Commerce Luncheon on May 4, Cardinal manager Eddie Stanky responded. "Maybe in seven, eight, or nine years he will surpass Stan Musial," said Stanky, "and he may even be greater than Stan is today, but as of now, we, with good common sense, will take Stan Musial as the greatest ballplayer of the present time. I am aware of Mickey Mantle's great potential, but I believe he should be given a chance to establish himself before comparing him to Musial."

Prior to the 1953 season, Musial had played in 1,524 National League games, accumulated 2,023 hits for a lifetime .346 batting average, and collected 415 doubles, 133 triples, and 227 home runs. Mantle, beginning just his third season in major-league ball, had played in 238 games and collected 262 hits in 890 trips to the plate for a .294 mark. Among his 262 hits were forty-eight doubles, twelve triples, and thirty-six home runs. More telling, perhaps, were Mantle's 185 strikeouts in his first two seasons, more whiffs than Musial had rung up in his first seven years in the major leagues, and since he had been swinging for the long ball, more than he had collected in the past five years combined. The very day Stanky made his comments, Mantle had left the tying runs on base in the ninth inning when he struck out in a 10–8 loss to the last-place Detroit Tigers.

A week later, Marion, who had seen Mantle play less than thirty games, offered a mild rebuttal. "I never once said Mantle was a better ballplayer than Musial was five years ago," argued the Browns manager. "I said he's better than Musial is today. Ask Stanky, ask anyone in baseball today, who'd they rather have on their ball club, Musial or Mantle? Nobody would try to deny Musial's the best they ever saw, but you can't compare them today. Mantle's twenty-one and just coming up and Musial's going out, though he's got several good years left."

Two days later, St. Louis *Globe-Democrat* sportswriter Bob Burnes, a close friend of both Musial and Marion, put a cap on the controversy in his column, "The Bench Warmer." Musial, wrote Burns,

> doesn't need any protection. He doesn't need defense, statements or arguments from the likes of me. Stan has always been the only spokesman Musial ever needed—and he has done his talking with his bat, his team spirit and his general makeup which has class written all over it . . . There is only one other yardstick by which the greatness of an athlete may be measured. That is on his value to the ball club. On that one, there is no point in debating the issue. Musial's finest trait, more so even than his hitting, has been his usefulness to his ball club. A man such as Marty Marion should know that better than anyone else. He was with Stan long enough to know all about that.

Musial, mired in the middle of a one-for-twenty-four slump during which his average had fallen off to .233, was unable to defend himself. On May 12, Stan took a one-hour hitting drill at Busch Stadium, working with coach and former National League batting champion Dixie Walker, who pointed out that the Cardinal slugger was overstriding at the plate. "I was glad to discover what I was doing that was wrong," said Musial after the workout, "but there's nothing wrong with my hitting that a few hits won't cure."

Stanky, asked his opinion, replied, "You'd never know that fellow was in a slump. He's a real thoroughbred, never a change in his disposition as you'd find in other players."

The hitting drill paid immediate dividends: Musial was three-for-five the next night, scored twice and singled the following evening, then batted in what proved to be the winning run in a 9–3 win over the Dodgers on May 15. Prior to the contest, National League president Warren Giles presented Stan with the silver bat which was emblematic of the 1952 league batting title.

Still struggling with the bat, Musial came to the plate to face Cincinnati starter Clyde King on May 22. The Cards and Reds were tied at two-all when Cincinnati manager Rogers Hornsby directed his hurler to knock Musial down. "Rogers," objected King, "over the years I've gotten Musial out, I guess as good as anybody, and there's no point in knocking him down." But Hornsby wasn't asking King to knock Stan down. He was ordering him to. "Sure enough, I knocked him down," said King. "The ball went right up here [under the chin] and the bat went one way and his body went another way. And he hit the next pitch on the roof in right field. Home run! He killed it."

The round-tripper was Musial's first in over a month. Stan drove in another run later in the contest as the Cards downed Cincinnati, 4–2. A day later, in the opening contest of a three-game series at Wrigley Field, Musial had his biggest day of the year, blasting two home runs and a single, good for six runs batted in, as the Cards crushed Chicago, 14–3. Outwardly, at least, Stan's poor performance at the dish wasn't bothering him. "I just haven't been hitting the way I should," he said simply. "My timing is off. It has been off practically from the start of the season. Don't ask me why, I just don't know. All I know is that the pitchers are making a sucker out of me. And I'm not hitting in hard luck either. I'm just not getting good wood on the ball. I'm certain I'll snap out of it soon, but right now I just can't seem to do anything right. I know I've been pressing because I've been taking too many good pitches and swinging at too many bad ones, but that's the way it goes when you're in a slump."

Musial had not yet given up hope of winning his seventh batting title and fourth in a row. "I'm not discouraged," he said. "Whenever I begin to feel real low, I recall the bad start I had in 1947 and wound up hitting over .300. What I need is a good splurge for about three or four days. That will get me going. And I'm going to get 'em real soon, just watch. I'll get even with those pitchers who are having a picnic with me now."

Always charitable, Musial grinned and added, "Well, I've got one consolation. My roomie, Red Schoendienst [currently leading the National League in batting] is having a great year. I'm rooting for him to win the title if I can't do it. At least it will be in the family."

Musial regained his batting stroke in late June. Riding a ten-game hitting streak, Stan collected nineteen hits in twenty-seven at-bats, a mind-boggling .704 batting average, and crested the .300 mark for the first time since the early days of the season. Musial had little to say about coming out of the slump. "All I know is that my timing is improved," he declared. When reminded of an earlier comment that he would settle for a .300 mark by the All-Star Game, Stan added, "I won't be satisfied with .300 now. I want all I can get." The Redbirds, led by Musial's bat, had closed to within a single game of the Braves and Dodgers, tied for the league lead.

On July 3, Stan received the news that Chicago's Ralph Kiner had out-polled him in fan voting and would be the National League's starting left fielder for the 1953 All-Star Game. The following afternoon, Independence Day, Musial was four-for-nine in a doubleheader split with the Cubs and entered the ranks of the National League's top ten hitters for the first time in over two months. By the All-Star break, Stan had just realized his goal of batting .300. With thirty-eight hits in his last ninety at-bats, including eleven doubles, three triples, and five home runs, Stan had tattooed National League pitchers for a .422 average and arrived at the break with a .304 batting mark. The 1953 All-Star Game was held on July 14 at Crosley Field in Cincinnati. Musial singled twice in four trips to the plate, but the contest belonged to his thirty-seven-year-old teammate, Enos Slaughter, who drew a base on balls, singled twice, stole a base, and scored two runs. The National League won handily, 5–1.

The Cardinals resumed the second half of the season with a four-game, do-or-die series against the Dodgers at Ebbets Field. The opening contest was decided in the first fifteen minutes when Gil Hodges blasted a first-inning grand-slam home run to pace Brooklyn to an easy 9–2 win. The following day brought even worse news to St. Louis fans when the Dodgers routed Wilmer "Vinegar Bend" Mizell with seven runs in the first and coasted to a 14–0 victory in the first game of a doubleheader. The Redbirds lost the nightcap, 7–4, on Jackie Robinson's three-run homer in the bottom of the eighth. St. Louis held a 6–2 lead in the series finale, but the Bums once again went to the big stick, scoring nine times in the fourth to post a 14–6 triumph. The four-game sweep dropped the Redbirds into fifth place, eight games back.

July 24 saw Musial involved in one of the more unusual incidents of his career. When player-manager Eddie Stanky handed the lineup card to the umpires before the game with Philadelphia, he had written in shortstop Solly Hemus as the leadoff hitter, himself second, and Stan third. But when the contest began, Stanky batted first and was called out on a third strike. Hemus followed with a single and when Musial took a pitch from Bob Miller, Phillies' manager Steve O'Neill trotted out to home plate umpire Bill Jackowski and pointed out Stanky's error. Hemus was sent to the dugout and Musial was called out for not batting in turn. In the sixth inning, with the Cards trailing by a run, Stan stole home for the first time in his twelve-year career, but Granny Hamner's ninth-inning home run gave the Phils a 2–1 win.

On August 3, club president Gussie Busch signed Eddie Stanky to a three-year contract, the longest since Branch Rickey had penned a five-year deal back in 1923. The Redbirds celebrated Stanky's new pact that evening with an 8–3 win over the Phillies. A day later, the St. Louis Navy recruiting station made Musial an "Honorary Navy Recruiter," in appreciation for Stan's appearances at various Navy affairs and functions since he received his discharge following World War II.

But the Redbirds had fallen seventeen and a half games behind the Dodgers, who were running away from the rest of the league. "It's no use fooling ourselves," said Stanky. "As of right now, the Dodgers are in a class by themselves. The rest of us have got to do something about building ourselves up to their level." Stanky said the Cardinal front office would be active in the trade market over the winter, but when asked if trade plans included Musial, he replied, "Stan's my number one guy. We're going to build our 1954 team around him, him and Red Schoendienst and a couple of other old reliables on the club."

By early September, Musial had scored his one hundredth run of the year, the tenth consecutive season for the Cardinal superstar, adding to his own National League record. A solo home run on September 15 gave Stan one hundred RBIs for the year, the sixth time in his career the Cardinal superstar had crested the one-hundred-RBI plateau. With less than a week to go in the season, Musial was trailing Carl Furillo (sidelined with a broken hand), teammate Red Schoendienst, and Duke Snider in the race for the National League batting title when he launched a last-ditch effort to capture his fourth straight crown. In a doubleheader split against the Braves on September 22, Stan collected five hits in nine trips to the plate, raising his average to .333, and he rapped out another two hits the following evening in a 2–1 loss to the Braves. To take the batting title, Musial would have to hit safely at least ten times in his next twelve trips to the plate.

On September 25, rookie Harvey Haddix posted his twentieth victory of the year, downing the Cubs, 11–2. Schoendienst, four-for-six on the day, raised his average to .342 while Musial, who singled and smashed his twenty-ninth home run of the year, now stood at .336. The following afternoon, Schoendienst slipped to .3416 with one hit in four at-bats while Musial, two-for-four including his thirtieth home run, was virtually eliminated from the title. For Stan to surpass Furillo's .34446, he would need seven hits in seven at-bats in the final game of the season. The only goal Musial had remaining on the 1953 season was to collect two hundred hits and to do that, he needed two safeties. The Cubs shaded St. Louis in the season finale, 3–2, but the big story involved Schoendienst and Musial. Stan's roommate needed at least three hits in four at-bats, but was two-for-five and ended the campaign trailing Furillo by two points. Musial singled and doubled for hit number two hundred, the sixth time he had reached that mark.

The Redbirds had closed out another unsuccessful campaign, in fourth place, a staggering twenty-two games behind the pennant-winning Dodgers. About the only highlights of the team were the good work of third baseman Ray Jablonski and outfielders Harry "Peanuts" Lowrey and Wally Moon. Jablonski had made a spectacular debut. "Jabbo" hit .268, slammed twenty-one homers, drove in 112 runs, and played in a rookie major-league record 157 games. Veteran outfielder and pinch-hitter extraordinaire Peanuts Lowrey came off the bench fifty-nine times and tied a National League record for pinch-hits with twenty-two, equalling the 1932 mark set by New York's Sam Leslie, who had thirteen more at-bats.

Back on June 14, Musial had been hitting .249, but from that point on, he had scorched National League pitchers for a .375 average. Since late August, Stan had hit safely in twenty-nine of thirty-one games for a blistering .437 mark. No one doubted Chicago manager Phil Cavarretta when he said, "Another week of the season, and Stan would have won the title." Ironically, Musial had a better year across the board than 1952, batting one point better than in his previous title-winning year, and even though he failed to lead his own club in batting average for the first time in his career, Stan still topped all National League hitters in doubles (53) and walks (105), finished second in hits (200) and runs scored (127), third in total bases (361) and batting average, and fourth in slugging average (.609). For the sixth year in a row, and the ninth time in his career, Musial had collected more than three hundred total bases. That equalled Joe Medwick's consecutive-season record from 1934–39 and surpassed Rogers Hornsby's National League record eight seasons.

◇13◇

Are Those Power
Boys Watching?

*Once he timed your fastball, your infielders
were in jeopardy.*

WARREN SPAHN

Anheuser-Busch was peeling off the
banknotes, trying to come up with a winner, but the Cardinals were an old
ballclub and the players weren't getting any younger. The front office took
steps to correct the situation. Four days before the 1954 season was due to
begin, the Cardinals traded veteran outfielder Enos Slaughter, the star of
the 1953 All-Star Game, to the Yankees for pitcher Mel Wright and outfielders Bill Virdon and Emil Tellinger. The deal made the 1954 season the first
in which Musial, Slaughter's teammate since 1941, was the senior member
of the team. Enos, a few weeks shy of his thirty-eighth birthday, got the
news following an exhibition game with the Baltimore Orioles. Stan was
the last one out of the clubhouse after the game and when he found
Slaughter in the parking lot, the two old war horses looked at each other
and burst into tears. "This is the biggest shock of my life," Slaughter said
bitterly. "I never expected this to happen. I've given my life to this organization, and they let you go when they think you're getting too old. I guess
that's baseball."

Stan had signed for $80,000, his third successive pact at the same figure and the first with the brewery, and the Redbirds had plodded through another mediocre spring training. They opened the regular season in the same vein on April 13 when rookie Wally Moon blasted a home run in his first major-league at-bat. Musial also homered, but the outcome of the contest exposed the greatest weakness of the 1954 team, pitching, as the Redbirds went down to a 13–4 defeat at the hands of the Cubs. The season promised to be a long one when on April 17 at Wrigley Field, the Redbirds played one of their worst games in decades, losing to the Cubs by a football score: Chicago 23, St. Louis 13.

Two weeks later, Musial was limping slightly because of a charley horse. But he took the field against the New York Giants on May 2, a day on which the Cardinal superstar did something none of the great sluggers— Lou Gehrig, Ted Williams, Jimmie Foxx, Hank Greenberg, Rogers Hornsby, not even the legendary Babe Ruth—had ever accomplished.

Stan hadn't taken batting practice at Busch Stadium because of an early-morning rain, so he took a long look at southpaw Johnny Antonelli in the first, finally drawing a base on balls. In the third, Musial popped his first home run of the day, a solo shot off one of Antonelli's slow change-ups. The Giants were ahead, 4–3, when Stan batted in the fifth, but his two-run, 354-foot shot off an Antonelli fastball down and in put the Cardinals back on top, 5–4. In the sixth, Musial singled off reliever Jim Hearn's slider for his third straight hit and in the eighth, with the score tied at six and two teammates on base, Stan slammed one of Hearn's sliders for a three-run shot onto the right-field roof to put the Cards up, 9–6. St. Louis won the game, 10–6, and Musial, for the first time in his major-league career, had hit three home runs in a single contest. Between games of the doubleheader, Stan was relaxing in the clubhouse, a glass of milk in one hand and a ham and cheese sandwich in the other, when he received a call from Lillian, who hadn't been able to make it to the park that day. Laughing, Lil reminded him of the day in 1941 when her husband, playing for Class C Springfield, had belted three round-trippers against Stockton. Lil had been at the park that day, but diaper duties had taken her out of her seat every time Stan had homered.

In the twi-night contest, Don Liddle walked Musial in a three-run first, drawing boos from the partisan hometown crowd. In the third, Stan drove a Liddle fastball to deep right-center, 410 feet from the plate, but Willie Mays hauled it down. The Giants were leading, 8–3, in the fifth and had their best reliever, Hoyt Wilhelm, on the mound when Musial came to the plate with Red Schoendienst on base. Stan waited patiently while a couple of knuckleballs floated by, then slammed a slow curve out of the park and onto Grand Avenue, tying the major-league record for most home runs in a doubleheader. New York was still leading by two when Musial blasted his fifth homer of the day, a solo shot to right-center off a Wilhelm knuckler in the seventh. As Stan trotted around the bases for the fifth time that day, he could clearly be seen laughing. The lights were on at Busch Stadium when Stan faced reliever Larry Jansen in the ninth with a shot at a sixth homer. But Musial was overeager and could only lift a high pop fly to first as the Redbirds went down to a 9–7 defeat.

Six other players—Jimmie Foxx, Earl Averill, Jim Tabor, Bill Nicholson, Ralph Kiner, and Gus Zernial—had clubbed four home runs in a twin bill, but Stan's five round-trippers were a new record. Musial's twenty-one total bases are still a record for a doubleheader, although the five home runs in a doubleheader were tied by San Diego's Nate Colbert on August 1, 1972. Reporters crowded around Musial in the clubhouse after the contest, hanging on his every word. Having just raised his batting average to an even .400, third-best in the National League, Stan quipped, "How far am I behind Ruth?" He was open-mouthed in disbelief when told what he had accomplished. "You mean," he asked, somewhat naively, "that none of those real sluggers, Ruth, Gehrig, Kiner, and the others, none of them ever hit five in one day?"

When Stan walked into his living room that evening, his thirteen-year-old son Dick gently chided him. "Gee, Dad," he said. "they must have been throwing you fat pitches today." The bat with which the Cardinal superstar slammed those five home runs is now on display at the Baseball Hall of Fame in Cooperstown, New York.

The Cardinals had lost all eleven of their meetings with the Dodgers at Ebbets Field in 1953 and the Bums continued the jinx when they coasted to a 10–3 triumph on May 12, making it an even dozen successive victories over St. Louis in their home park. Manager Eddie Stanky offered a new suit of clothes to the first Cardinal hurler who could post a victory against Brooklyn on the road, and Vic Raschi collected the next day with a 10–1 win. Musial drove in the run that put the Cards ahead to stay and blasted a two-run homer later in the contest, giving him a .390 batting average and thirty-one RBIs for the year. In the rubber game of the series, Tom Poholsky three-hit the Dodgers, but went down to a 1–0 defeat, the first time on the year the Redbirds had been shut out. When asked to appear on a post-game show, Musial, who had one of the two Cardinal safeties, said modestly, "Not me, didn't do anything. Tell 'em to get Poholsky, someone who did something."

A few days later, Stan slugged his twelfth home run of the year as the Redbirds posted an 8–0 victory over the Phillies. "Are those power boys watching?" joked Musial after the win, which propelled St. Louis into a three-way tie for first place with Philadelphia and Brooklyn.

By early June, fifty games into the season, Stan was leading the National League with a .387 average and twenty home runs, two games ahead of Babe Ruth's sixty-home-run pace. But Musial insisted, "I'm still only a singles hitter. The homers are coming to me. I'm not going after them, but just getting out in front of the pitch at times with good wood on a lively ball."

A 7–4 loss to the Dodgers on June 10 featured one of the more unusual incidents of Musial's career, and in anecdotal fashion pointed up the Cardinal superstar's easy-going reputation. With a man on first in the seventh, Musial grounded to shortstop Pee Wee Reese, who fumbled the ball, but recovered in time to get off a hurried throw to first base. Stan was called out on a bang-bang play by umpire Frank Dascoli and when he wheeled around to dispute the decision, Dascoli, stunned that the gentlemanly Musial would argue a call, whirled away and promptly thumbed Cardinal first-base coach Bill Posedel out of the game. Posedel, who had begun to put up the mildest of pleas for his baserunner, left the field in a daze.

Stan suffered through a one-for-nineteen drought in mid-June as his batting average dropped to .341, sixth-best in the National League and thirty-three points behind Brooklyn's Duke Snider. While Stan was laboring, so were the Cardinals, who fell to sixth place, ten games behind the Dodgers. Musial had led all major-league players in All-Star voting and in the 1954 mid-summer classic at Cleveland's Municipal Stadium, Stan singled twice and scored a run in five trips to the plate as the American League captured a wild 11–9 victory with three runs in the bottom of the eighth.

The Redbirds hit their lowest point of the year on July 18 in the first game of a twin bill against the Phillies at Busch Stadium when manager Eddie Stanky used seven pitchers, but could not prevent an 11–10 defeat. A blinding rain had caused a long delay in the ten-inning contest and as a result, the nightcap didn't start until just a few minutes before 7:00. After several arguments and a few inside pitches from Redbird hurler Ellis "Cot" Deal to Philadelphia first baseman Earl Torgeson, Cardinal ballplayers were stunned to hear St. Louis fans cheering plate umpire Babe Pinelli for forfeiting the game to the Phils. Fearing a possible riot, police officers escorted the Philadelphia players and the umpires off the field. Stanky, who issued a public apology for his part in the debacle, was given a five-day suspension and a hundred-dollar fine by National League president Warren Giles, while

Torgeson and Yvars received two-day vacations. The forfeit was the last to date in National League history.

On July 26, before an exhibition game with the American League Indians, Stan Musial, Rip Repulski, and Cleveland sluggers Larry Doby and Al Rosen put on a home-run hitting exhibition. Each batter got ten pitches over the heart of the plate; the winner was the one who could put the most balls into the stands. Repulski and Rosen batted a pair of "homers," Doby one, but Stan drove seven balls out of the playing field at League Park. He was so happy at his display of power that he promised bullpen catcher Greg Masson, the man who pitched the exhibition, a new suit of clothes.

A week later, Musial enjoyed one of the biggest days of his career in the rubber game of a series at Ebbets Field. With two men on base in the third, Musial blasted a Preacher Roe fastball over the scoreboard in right field. In the next frame, with two teammates on base again, Stan parked an Erv Palica curveball just to the left of the same scoreboard for his one hundredth RBI, the first man in the major leagues to crest that mark in 1954, giving the Cards an 8–2 edge. Three innings later, Musial drove in Wally Moon with a sacrifice fly, his seventh run batted in of the day and the biggest single-game RBI output of his career. Stan always hit well at Ebbets Field, but he modestly downplayed his hitting after the contest. "I'm always expected to do it here anyway," he laughed.

Back in May, artist John Falter had done a striking illustration of Musial signing autographs, a portrait which had been featured on the cover of *The Saturday Evening Post* magazine. (The artwork was later donated to baseball's Hall of Fame in Cooperstown, New York.) In mid-August, the *Post* published "The Mystery of Stan Musial," an article written by his close friend, Bob Broeg, in which the sportswriter attacked the notion that Stan was a "colorless automaton." Broeg described Stan as a

> bright-eyed, lighthearted thirty-three-year-old businessman who laughs heartily at all jokes, including his own, performs parlor magic tricks with a professional patter and thrives on everyday living. He has a zest for conventional diversions such as sprinkling his sun-parched patch of lawn in a ranch-style section of Southwest St. Louis. He gave this up, though, after incurring a painful, strength-sapping sunburn . . . In the locker room he beats out jukebox tunes with a slide whistle, and drums coat hangers on an aluminum-backed chair.

That Stan laughed at his own jokes and watered his lawn wasn't exactly headline news; Broeg had unwittingly added to the idea that the Cardinal legend was, indeed, colorless.

Late in September, with seven meaningless games remaining in the season, Stan trailed Duke Snider by ten points, and it looked as if he was going to fall short of his seventh batting title. But Musial was always toughest when he was chasing a goal. Over the next five games, he banged out seven hits in seventeen trips to the plate, raising his average to .334. Snider, slumping to .340, had fallen behind Willie Mays, at .347. With no hope of capturing the batting title, Stan still had a slim chance of reaching two hundred hits for the year, but collected just two safeties in his final seven at-bats and finished five hits shy of the mark. The Cardinals ended the season in sixth place, twenty-five games behind, with a 72–82 record, the team's first sub-.500 showing since 1938. St. Louis had led the league in offense, but the pitching staff gave back all but nine of the 799 runs the club scored. The team ERA of 4.50 was nearly a run and a half worse than the champion New York Giants.

Through June 9, roughly the first third of the season, Musial had compiled some staggering statistics, matching and even bettering his banner year of 1948. But Stan had slumped horribly for the rest of the year, as the following chart shows:

	AB	H	2B	3B	HR	R	RBI	AVG.
First fifty games	199	77	14	4	20	53	66	.387
Projected season	609	236	43	12	61	162	202	.387
Actual season	591	195	41	9	35	120	126	.330

Musial's batting average had fallen to .330, seven points lower than in 1953, but still good enough for fourth place in the race for the batting crown. Stan led all National League batters in doubles (41), tied for the league lead in runs scored (120), finished third in hits (195) and walks (103), and fourth in triples (9), RBIs (126), slugging average (.607), and total bases (359). Musial garnered another post-season honor when *Real* magazine, in a poll of all sixteen major-league managers, named him the greatest player in baseball in 1954.

◆ ◆ ◆

After a mediocre 15–14 spring training, the Cardinals opened the 1955 season with Musial back on first base to make room for Bill Virdon, who would go on to become Rookie of the Year, the second successive season a St. Louis outfielder had captured the honor. Another rookie, Ken Boyer, was on third, a position he would anchor for the Cardinals the next eleven years.

Opening Day, April 12, saw the Cards slammed by Chicago, 14–4, but Bill Virdon's eleventh-inning home run the next day left eleven thousand Cardinal fans gasping for breath as the Redbirds evened their record with an 8–7 victory. Musial was off to his second slow start in the last three years and by late April, with just ten hits in forty-four at-bats, was batting a lowly .227. "My timing has been off," explained Stan, "but I'll be there."

And then the inevitable happened. On April 28, in his St. Louis *Globe-Democrat* "Bench Warmer" column, sportswriter Bob Burnes told of a letter he'd received from a fan suggesting Musial be traded. "Sure, he's a great man, seldom equalled, seldom excelled," said the anonymous fan, "but how much better can he get? I doubt any. Therefore, while he's still in his prime, trade him to any baseball club in either league and they would give you their entire pitching staff! The Man has been the team for many years. But that's just the problem. It should be a TEAM and not one man."

Burnes, ever Stan's close friend and defender, took the letter-writer to task:

> Musial's usefulness is far from ended. As usual he is having a difficult spring. But more important, when the time comes, and we hope it is some distance away, that Musial no longer can help, we believe he will be the first to recognize it and will gracefully step down into retirement.

Stan must have been reading the newspapers, because he clubbed two home runs in his next three starts. But his heroics failed to spark the Redbirds as they embarked on a seven-game losing streak. Musial's fifth home run of the season broke a 1–1 tie and helped snap the Cardinal drought on May 10. His best outing of the year, a single, double, his sixth home run, two runs scored, and a pair of RBIs, propelled the Cards to a come-from-behind, 6–5 win over the Phillies the following night. Stan's average was up to .295. "It just takes a little time for me to get going," Stan observed, "but when I start to hit to left field, I feel I'm on my way."

Musial may have been on his way, but the Cardinals weren't. With the season barely a month old, St. Louis pennant chances were effectively ended: at 10–13, St. Louis was mired in fifth place, eleven games behind the phenomenal Brooklyn Dodgers, winners of twenty-one of their first twenty-three outings. On May 22, the Cardinals lost the opener of a twin bill at Crosley Field. Dick Bartell, coaching third base for Cincinnati, had taunted St. Louis manager Eddie Stanky during the game, and when Stanky reached the clubhouse to find a sandwich spread laid out for his players, he threw a temper fit of major-league proportions and broke every condiment jar he could spot. Owner Gussie Busch got wind of the tantrum and even though he was fond of the fiery Cardinal skipper, began making plans to replace him.

Five days later, perhaps sensing something in the wind, Stanky announced, "I intend to manage St. Louis for a good many years," but his comment, "I thought it was agreed that this was a young club, that it might take two weeks, two months or longer for it to hit its best stride," had a definite whining quality about it. Gussie Busch was unavailable for comment, but Rochester manager Harry "The Hat" Walker was missing and club officials were maintaining a stony silence as to the reason why. The hammer dropped the following afternoon. Stanky was asked to remain in the Cardinal organization, but was relieved of his managerial duties in favor of the talkative Walker. In the first game under their new skipper, the Redbirds were defeated by Cincinnati, 5–1, but Musial's three-run homer capped a six-run fourth the next evening and gave Walker his first win, a 7–2 victory over the Reds.

Clearly this was a team going nowhere. By early June, the Cardinals, with fourteen losses in their last nineteen games, were struggling to stay out of the National League cellar and showing all the signs of a club just going through the motions. But Musial's average continued to rise. By June 25, Stan was up to .313 and just four safeties shy of career hit number 2,500. On June 29, against Cincinnati, Musial's first-inning single gave the Cardinals their first run of the day. With a man on base in the sixth, Musial slammed his fifteenth home run of the year and number 307 of his career, a two-run shot which tied the score at four-all. Stan's dramatic blast made him the thirty-seventh man in baseball history to reach the 2,500-hit mark, and the Redbirds made the celebration complete when they went on to post a 9–5 win.

The following afternoon, Musial began his quest for hit number 3,000 when he collected a single and a two-run homer in an 11–7 loss to the Cubs at Wrigley Field. A day later, Stan received the disappointing news that baseball fans had voted Cincinnati's Ted Kluszewski a starting berth at first base in the 1955 All-Star Game, outpolling Musial by 150,000 votes. By the time he reached the mid-summer break, Stan was batting .298, but had sixty-five RBIs on only ninety-three hits. His most significant home run of the season would come on July 12 in the All-Star Game at Milwaukee County Stadium.

The American League players held their usual pre-game meeting to analyze National League hitters. When they reached the name of Stan Musial, everyone had a theory to try. Pitch him low and outside, said one player. Fastballs, up and in, said another. Yankee catcher Yogi Berra chuckled. "You guys are trying to stop Musial in fifteen minutes," said Yogi, "when the National League ain't stopped him in fifteen years."

Manager Leo Durocher put Musial into the game as early as good taste would allow, pinch-hitting Stan for Del Ennis in the fourth inning, by which time the American League had a 4–0 lead. Musial struck out, then went to left field for the balance of the contest, the twelfth time Stan had performed in an All-Star Game, breaking the old mark held by Mel Ott and Joe DiMaggio. "The only trouble with all this," Musial quipped after the game, "is that it gives the other guys a perfect right to put the word 'old' in front of whatever else they're calling you. And now you feel that they mean it. They start with 'old man' and go on from there. You can argue about the name, but you can't argue about the 'old' part of it."

By the time the Cardinal superstar batted in the last half of the ninth, the senior circuit had fought back to tie the the score at five-all. Representing the winning run, Musial tapped out to second base, sending the game into extra innings. "You know, Yogi," said Stan when he came to the plate in the twelfth, "I'm getting pretty tired." "So am I," replied Berra. "It's these extra innings, tough on a guy catching every day."

Musial stepped into the batter's box and Boston Red Sox reliever Frank Sullivan sent in his first delivery of the twelfth, a letter-high fast ball on the outside corner. Stan met the pitch squarely and sent it over the right-field screen to give the National Leaguers a stunning 6–5 victory. (Musial's home run was his fourth in All-Star competition, breaking a tie with Ralph Kiner and Ted Williams.) "Funny thing," said Stan in the clubhouse after the game, "I was going for the bundle the two previous times up. This time, as leadoff man, I was just trying to get on base. I just met the ball. But when I connected, I knew it was over the fence."

When the Cardinals resumed play in the second half of the season, Stan fell into a prolonged slump during which his batting average fell below .300. Musial had now played in 569 consecutive games and Harry Walker was beginning to come under criticism for not resting the Cardinal superstar more often. On August 9, Stan's twenty-fourth home run of the year, a two-run shot against the Braves, gave him 999 career extra-base hits, one shy of joining the elite circle of eight other ballplayers who had reached the one-thousand plateau. All eight—Babe Ruth (1,356), Lou Gehrig (1,190), Ty Cobb (1,139), Tris Speaker (1,133), Jimmie Foxx (1,117), Mel Ott (1,071), Rogers Hornsby (1,011), and Honus Wagner (1,004)—were in baseball's Hall of Fame, an honor which now seemed a sure bet for the Cardinal superstar as well. The following evening, Musial wasted no time reaching his latest milestone when he doubled off Milwaukee hurler Lew Burdette in the first.

Stan's one-thousandth extra-base hit was one of the few highlights on the year for a youthful Cardinal team that had fallen fourteen games under .500 and twenty games behind the Dodgers. Two weeks later, St. Louis was mathematically eliminated from the pennant race. For the ninth straight year, Stan Musial would be going back home for an early winter.

The next day, Musial's consecutive game playing streak was jeopardized when he was struck on the right hand by a Johnny Podres fastball. X-rays of the hand showed no breaks or fractures, and Stan played in his 594th consecutive game the following evening, making a token appearance before he was lifted for a pinch-hitter in the second. Musial's string was cheapened even further on August 31. He played a half inning against the Pirates, and was pulled in favor of Pete Whisenant when it came his turn to bat in the bottom of the first. The swelling had abated enough for Stan to play a full game the next evening.

Five days later, just as the hand was beginning to heal, Musial was struck on the right elbow by an errant pitch from Philadelphia hurler Ron Mrozinski and was taken to Jewish Hospital for X-rays, which proved negative. Both his hand and elbow hurting, Stan belted home run number twenty-eight the next day, a two-run shot in the third which provided the margin of difference as the Cards took a 4–3 decision from the Phillies. Musial's average was now up to .313, but he trailed Richie Ashburn by twenty-four points. With only fourteen games remaining, it looked as if he was going to run short of time in his quest for a seventh batting title. The consecutive game streak, however, was still alive at 606. On September 16, Stan's streak was jeopardized for the third time in nineteen days when he was forced to leave the game after pulling a muscle in his right leg, beating out an infield hit in the first. Hobbling, Musial finished out the year at .319, nineteen points behind Ashburn.

The 1955 Cardinals had set a National League record for futility by surrendering 185 home runs to the opposition. Never in the pennant race, St. Louis finished thirty and a half games behind the Dodgers. The club's 68–86 record was its worst since 1924 and the seventh-place finish was the lowest since 1919. The team scored a full run per game less than in 1954, despite hitting a franchise-record 155 home runs, and the club's batting average plummeted from .281 to .261. Reflecting the Redbirds' strange offense, Musial fell below one hundred runs scored for the first time since his rookie season. Indeed, with the consecutive game streak beginning to wear on him, Stan's numbers fell across the board.

A week after the season ended, the Cardinal front office signed Frank Lane to a three-year contract as the club's general manager. Lane had spent the last seven years as general manager of the Chicago White Sox. Six days later, with Busch's consent, he made his first of many moves by hiring former pitcher Fred Hutchinson to a two-year pact as the Redbirds' manager. In his own mind, Lane already had Musial on the trading block.

◇14◇

Trader Frank

He was always the nice boy he is now. He never sasses anybody. Ask his teachers. But he has changed. His head is still the same, it's got no bigger. But now he speaks a whole lot better than he did.

MARY MUSIAL, STAN'S MOTHER

F rank Lane wasn't nicknamed "Trader Frank" for nothing. From December 1955 through the end of the 1956 season, Lane would engineer nearly a dozen trades involving over forty ballplayers, not including other men who were bought, sold, or signed in single transactions. This was Frank Lane's version of rebuilding, moving players around like checkers, often with little or no regard to whether the move helped the club. Cardinal fans were bewildered at the outburst of activity. The adage "You can't tell a player without a scorecard" was never more true in St. Louis than during the 1956 season. Lane could have been forgiven his excesses if it weren't for the fact that those players traded away hit or pitched better than the players he obtained.

One ballplayer who supposedly had been designated as untouchable was Stan Musial. Stan hit a solid .348 in the Grapefruit League, and the Cardinals looked like they might have a pennant contender when the club posted a league-best 21–11 record before traveling north for the 1956 opener at Cincinnati. Hitless when he batted in the ninth with two out and roommate Red Schoendienst on first, Musial drove a Joe Nuxhall fastball deep into the right-field stands for a two-run homer and what proved to be the winning runs.

By May 9, the Cardinals were leading the league with a 13–6 record. Most general managers might have taken a moment to rest on their laurels, but not Frank Lane. In the next two weeks, he would do his utmost to demoralize the team with a whirlwind series of moves. On May 11, Lane grabbed headlines by purchasing thirty-three-year-old third baseman Grady Hatton from the Red Sox and dealing hurlers Harvey Haddix, Stu Miller, and Ben Flowers to the Phillies for pitchers Herm Wehmeier and former Redbird Murry Dickson. In making the latter deal, Lane traded three men whose average age was twenty-seven for a pair of hurlers whose average age was thirty-four. "I waited almost a full month after the season opened to tamper with the ball club," said Lane. "As everybody knows, I like to deal, but I don't swap players just to be swapping them. Every one of the deals we made, and I say 'we' because Fred Hutchinson and I consulted along with the coaches on every one of them, had a purpose behind it."

But Lane's justifications for the moves seemed lame. The acquisition of Wehmeier, for instance, defied logic: with a lifetime 0–14 record against St. Louis, the right-hander should have been the last man in baseball Lane wanted to see wearing a Cardinal uniform.

The Cards were idle on May 14, but Lane was in the headlines again when he swapped infielder Sol Hemus to the Phillies for infielder Bobby Morgan. Two days later, Lane sent shortstop Alex Grammas and fly-catcher Joe Frazier to the Reds for outfielder Chuck Harmon and on May 17, the Cardinal general manager dealt 1954 Rookie of the Year Bill Virdon to the Pirates for pitcher Dick Littlefield and outfielder Bobby Del Greco. Only eight men remained from the club that had opened the previous season.

Musial was hitting a lowly .253 and had collected just two hits in his last twenty-five at-bats and none in his last nine. On May 20, Stan was hit on the left wrist by a Johnny Antonelli fastball in the seventh inning of the opening game of a doubleheader against the Giants. Trainer Bob Bauman applied ice packs to the wrist and Musial returned to play the full nine innings in the nightcap. Less than a week later, Stan was hit by a pitch again. With the Redbirds holding a comfortable 8–0 lead against Cincinnati, reliever Hal Jeffcoat plunked the Cardinal superstar on the back. Musial, who would be hit by a pitch eight times in 1955, more often than any other National League player, showed his displeasure when he went out of his way to break up a double play with a hard slide into suprised second baseman Johnny Temple. "I didn't want to cut him," Stan told reporters after the game, "but I wanted to jar him good." His ire aroused, Musial was a perfect four-for-four in the contest and regained the .300 mark for the first time in nearly a month. "I'm sick and tired of having these guys throw at Musial," fumed Frank Lane. "Musial is one of the most even-tempered athletes that I know and he wouldn't hurt a fly."

With just nine days remaining until the trading deadline, Lane wondered aloud why his recent moves hadn't been better received in St. Louis. "I never heard of fans who were so loyal to players," he said in an interview with *The Sporting News*. "Why, I really think they would rather finish seventh with names they know than try to get up a few pegs with new faces."

Coupled with a story that Philadelphia ace Robin Roberts was on the trading block, St. Louisans were now holding their breath that Lane had another deal working. Cardinal fans were right on the money: the Redbird GM was doing his best to swing a Musial-for-Roberts deal. Stan's business partner, Biggie Garagnani, got wind of the possible trade from J.G. Taylor Spink, the publisher of *The Sporting News,* and passed word along to the brewery that Musial wouldn't report to Philadelphia. "He'll quit and I'll bet you on it," said Biggie. "You'll have no Phillies deal and no Musial either. Just a lot of embarrassment."

Lane might have engineered the trade, but August Busch put his foot down, squarely in the middle of Trader Frank's back. On June 11, Lane announced that "Mr. Busch and I are one hundred percent in agreement that Musial will not be traded," adding that "we've never offered Musial to anyone," and Stan was "not available for trade, period."

With just a few hours left before the trading deadline, Lane dealt Musial's road roommate, second baseman Red Schoendienst, to the Giants. Along with Schoendienst went catcher Bill Sarni, outfielder Jackie Brandt, pitcher Dick Littlefield, and infielder Bob Stephenson in exchange for shortstop Alvin Dark, catcher Ray Katt, pitcher Don Liddle, and outfielder-first baseman Whitey Lockman. Schoendienst was in the middle of moving into a new house with his wife Mary and was caught completely off-guard by the trade. "In baseball," said Red, "you feel sometime that you're going to get traded. But it was a shock to me. That was the biggest disappointment I've ever had. I had come up through the organization years ago. I was established here in St. Louis. I wanted to finish my career here, but baseball is baseball."

On the bus ride to Pittsburgh, most of the Cardinal players had little comment on the trade. The usually loquacious Musial was uncharacteristi-cally tight-lipped, refusing to say anything to reporters. The Redbirds lost decisively the next evening at Forbes Field, 12–1. Despondent over losing his best friend on the club, Stan was hitless in three at-bats, his average falling to .299. It was not until a week later that Musial broke his silence on the Schoendienst trade. "Of course, I hated to see Red go," said Stan in what most members of the press felt was a kind attempt to follow the party line and support Frank Lane, "but I can see how the deal is going to help us." When asked to comment on a report out of New York that he was thinking of retiring, Musial snapped, "When I get ready to quit, I'll make the announcement in St. Louis, not in New York."

Wracked by dissension over Lane's many deals, the Cardinals slumped to fifth place, eight games behind the Braves, by the All-Star break. Musial was mired in a six-for-thirty slump, but received the greatest honor of his playing career when *The Sporting News,* which had just completed a poll of managers, scouts, club owners, writers, broadcasters, umpires, and ten-year players, bestowed upon him its first Player Of The Decade Award. When informed of the accolade, Stan said humbly, "I don't know of any-thing except selection to the Hall of Fame that could please me so much."

Joe DiMaggio, Ted Williams, and Bob Feller finished second, third, and fourth, respectively, in the voting. The award, a $400 grandfather clock, was presented to Musial at a luncheon at the Touchdown Club in Washing-ton, D.C., a day later. Stan was his usual essay in modesty. "Everybody knows I can't pitch like Bob Feller," said Musial. "Ted Williams can hit better than I can and Joe DiMaggio always was a better defensive outfielder. All I can say is that I've been lucky throughout my career and I guess I'm still lucky."

With a three-for-five performance and two glittering stops in the field, Cardinal third baseman Ken Boyer was the star performer for the National League at Washington's Griffith Stadium the next day as the senior circuit rolled up a five-run lead en route to a 7–3 victory. But it was Stan Musial the fans would always remember. In the bottom of the sixth, Ted Williams hit a long home run into right-center off Braves hurler Warren Spahn. At the top of the seventh, as Musial was taking his position in the batter's box, the field announcer was trumpeting over the intercom that "Ted Williams's home run was his fourth in All-Star competition and tied Stan Musial . . . ." But before the announcer could finish the sentence, Stan blasted the first pitch from Boston right-hander Mel Brewer into the stands. "Sorry," apolo-gized the pressbox announcer, "Mr. Musial has just untied the record."

Years later, sportswriter Bob Burnes remembered the moment clearly.

"I found myself standing on top of the work bench in the press box cheering," said Burnes. "And the thing was, I looked around and there were a lot of other guys doing the same thing. And this was the effect Stan had on you. This guy was so great in every way that everybody in our business wanted him to do good."

The next day, Wednesday, July 11, Stan was paid another tribute when Pennsylvania Congressman John P. Saylor, speaking to the House of Representatives, said, in part, "A word of tribute to Stan 'the Man' belongs in the *Congressional Record,* not alone because he is one of the greatest baseball players of all times; rather because while achieving sports immortality he has remained the quiet, modest, humble, dignified, religious, refined and sympathetic person that he was in the days of his boyhood in a small town of western Pennsylvania."

Stan was on a hot streak for several weeks following the All-Star break, but on August 22, he suffered through the lowest point of his professional career when he was hitless in four trips to the plate, including two strikeouts. Worse yet, Stan made two damaging errors, booting a ground ball at first and throwing away a sure double-play ball later in the game which earned the Cardinals a 5–3 loss to the Dodgers. For the first time in his major-league career, Musial heard raspberries and boos in his home park. A day later, after the Redbirds had swept a doubleheader from the Pirates, during which Stan was cheered raucously each time he batted, the ten employees of the Rio Syrup Company in St. Louis took out a display ad in the St. Louis *Globe-Democrat* which read:

A PUBLIC APOLOGY
TO STAN MUSIAL

For the thousands of us who were shame-faced by the thoughtlessness of a few spectators at Wednesday's game, please accept our apologies. We are certain that even now those who took part in the demonstration regret their actions. For to you, Stan Musial, we owe our gratitude for giving us many years of fine sportsmanship and superb play. St. Louis and the nation will always acclaim you as the Greatest Player of Our Era. We look forward to seeing "the Man—the Best Man," for years to come.

Sincerely,
TEN OF YOUR MILLIONS OF ADMIRERS

Stu Tomber, president of the company, said, "Some of us had been at the game and others had listened to it over the radio and we were pretty unhappy about the rude treatment of Stan. We wanted to let him know that people in St. Louis don't think that way."

Musial, gracious as ever, responded, "I never could get mad about anything in baseball, you know that," he told reporters. "But it's a nice gesture on the part of those fans. I appreciate it."

Such was the popularity of Stan Musial. Musial being booed was such headline news that two weeks later, *Time* magazine highlighted the unprecedented incident in its sport section:

> St. Louis had never heard the sad sound before. Last week, after watching First Baseman Stan ("The Man") Musial go hitless in four times at bat, after watching him make two errors and boot away a game with the Dodgers, 5–3, Busch Field bleacherites finally blew up. They booed the best Cardinal of them all. Even St. Louis' hard-case fans were not that angry at Stan. But watching The Man fumble like a Pittsburgh infielder trying for a double play was the final indignity. After many a loyal but losing season Redbird fans are fed up . . . It hurts so much that the fans are impatient even with their old friend and favorite, Musial.

In early September, the Redbirds were mathematically eliminated from the pennant race. But if the Cardinals weren't good enough to win the pennant, they could still play the role of spoiler, which they did in a three-game set against the Braves at Busch Stadium. Milwaukee had held the National League top spot nearly every day of the 1956 season, but although Braves manager Fred Haney wound up pouring five pitchers into the opening contest of the series, the Redbirds pulled out a 5–4 victory which sliced Milwaukee's margin over the Dodgers to a half game. The next day, Musial doubled in the twelfth and came home with the winning run a moment later as the Redbirds eked out another one-run victory over the Braves. Coupled with Brooklyn's doubleheader sweep of the Pirates, the loss knocked Milwaukee out of first place and cost them the pennant. The Braves beat St. Louis the next afternoon, but it was all for nought as the Dodgers downed Pittsburgh to win the title by a game.

Although St. Louis hurlers had shaved a half run off the team ERA and the club had jumped from seventh place to fourth, the extent of the Cardinals' improvement was better measured by the fact that they had won just eight more games than the year before. Musial had slumped to .310, fourth in the league, but the lowest mark of his career and the third straight year in which his average had fallen. Stan slugged twenty-seven homers and led all National League batters with 109 RBIs, finished second in the league in doubles (33), fourth in hits (184), and fifth in total bases (310). Musial had already collected three hundred total bases in eleven previous seasons, a major-league record, and his career total of 4,730 was exceeded only by Ty Cobb (5,863), Babe Ruth (5,793), Tris Speaker (5,105), Lou Gehrig (5,059), and the lone National Leaguer on the list, Mel Ott (5,041).

Nearing thirty-six years old, the Cardinal superstar had played almost eight hundred consecutive games. He was beginning to slow down. No one expected him to enjoy the sort of year he would have in 1957.

◆ ◆ ◆

Cardinal owner August Busch, Jr. had put Lane on notice: "I expect the Cardinals to come close to winning a pennant in 1957 and 1958 is going to have to be a sure thing or Frank Lane will be out on his rump." In November 1956, Frank Lane swapped infielder Bobby Morgan and out-fielder Rip Repulski for Del Ennis, a good hitting outfielder who was held in disfavor in Philadelphia because of his nonchalant attitude. (Musial would later credit the insertion of Ennis into the number-four spot in the batting order for his own fine year at the plate.)

In January, Musial was guest of honor at a fund-raising dinner given by the St. Louis branch of the Denver American Cancer Hospital. The highlight of the dinner came when Gussie Busch proudly announced that Stan's uniform number 6 was to be retired, making Musial the first Cardinal so honored. Busch told the attendees he believed Stan could win another silver bat, the symbol of the batting championship, but at thirty-six years old, Musial was doubtful. A month later, Stan signed his sixteenth Cardinal contract, foregoing his usual $5,000 attendance clause and taking, in effect, his first salary cut.

Stan batted a blistering .434 in the Grapefruit League, then opened the regular season with a perfect four-for-four as he paced the Cards to a 13–4 win over Cincinnati. But Musial injured his lower back swinging the bat his last time up, and would have seen his consecutive game streak end at 775, forty-seven shy of Gus Suhr's National League mark, if it hadn't rained the next day. Team trainer Bob Bauman sprayed Musial's back with ethyl chloride, taped him up, used an ultra-sonic device, and gave Stan whirlpool treatments, yet told the press, "The way it looked, I'd say he's doubtful. Still, knowing The Man and his intense desire to play, I reserve judgment."

After thirty-eight games, the Redbirds had evened their record at .500. But they entered the month of June looking very little like a pennant contender. Just when the Cardinals seemed poised to drop out of sight in the National League, as they had for most of the decade, the club got blazing hot, reeling off seven straight victories. On June 11, Musial became baseball's most durable player since Lou Gehrig when he appeared in his

822nd consecutive game, tying the National League record Chicago catcher Gus Suhr had set from September 11, 1931, through June 5, 1937. Musial hadn't missed a game since the last day of the 1951 season and didn't foresee sitting out until the dog days of summer. "The first hundred or so are the easiest," said Stan.

A day later, as the Cards posted a 4–0 win over Philadelphia at Connie Mack Stadium, Musial, batting .385 for the year, captured sole possession of the National League endurance record. After the contest, Musial was handed a telegram from Gus Suhr that said, "Congratulations on breaking the National League record for consecutive games played. Rooting for you to get 3000 hits." Cardinal general manager Frank Lane wheeled out a huge cake with the inscription "Iron Man Stan," and Musial posed for photographs with seven-year-old Benny Hooper, who had just recently been rescued after spending twenty-three hours at the bottom of a well at his home in Manorville, New York. The Cardinals, meanwhile, had moved into a tie for third place, a game behind the league-leading Cincinnati Reds.

The St. Louis winning streak was snapped at eight the following day when the Phillies blasted Vinegar Bend Mizell and reliever Herm Wehmeier, 8–1. Musial doubled twice in a 2–1 loss to the Dodgers the next evening, tying Jimmie Foxx at 1,117 for the fifth position on the all-time extra-base hit list, then lashed his thirteenth home run of the season the following day. The blow enabled him to pass Foxx and set his sights on American League Hall of Famer Tris Speaker, fourteen extra-base hits away. On June 16, the Redbirds swept a doubleheader from the Dodgers and edged into second place, a game and a half behind the Braves. Two days later, Musial's fifteenth homer of the year extended his hitting streak to nineteen games as the Cards moved to within a half game of league-leading Milwaukee. The following day, Stan ran his string to an even twenty with a first-inning double as St. Louis took over sole possession of first place. Stan's hitting streak was snapped at twenty on June 21 when he was blanked in two trips to the plate in a 2–0 victory over Brooklyn, the Cardinals' fifteenth win in their last nineteen outings.

After the series finale with Brooklyn, Musial flew to Washington, D.C., to appear before a House judiciary subcommittee which was looking into antitrust aspects of professional sports, particularly baseball's reserve clause. Stan's plane developed engine trouble and was forced to land at Louisville, Kentucky, at three o'clock in the morning of June 25, delaying Musial's arrival for another four hours. Following a brief tour of the nation's capitol conducted by Missouri Senator Stuart Symington, Musial spoke before the subcommittee and representative Emanuel Celler, who several times referred to the Cardinal superstar as Mr. Feller. (Bob Feller was due to testify later in the day.) Cardinal general manager Frank Lane, annoyed that his star first baseman had been taken, even temporarily, from the club, snapped, "It's good to realize that the country is in such good shape that Congress can take time out to investigate baesball."

Stan was the cover boy on that week's *Newsweek* magazine, which featured Roger Kahn's flattering article entitled "Musial: Why Birds Fly High." Kahn, confronting the same problem sportswriters everywhere had always faced when talking about Musial, said, in part:

> Because he is somewhat reticent and more talked about than quoted, Musial has appeared to be relatively colorless. He does not sound off on the shortcomings of mankind as Ted Williams and Jackie Robinson have done. He has never been in a fight on a ball field. He has never second-guessed a manager. Except for an incident in the minor leagues eighteen years ago, he has never been ejected from a game.

St. Louis closed out the first half of the season with a 46–31 record and a two-and-a-half-game lead over the second-place Milwaukee Braves. Cincinnati fans had stuffed ballot boxes and elected hometown ballplayers for all eight of the National League's All-Star starting positions, but baseball Commissioner Ford Frick compensated for the sham by naming Musial, New York center fielder Willie Mays, and Milwaukee right fielder Hank Aaron to the roster. The city of St. Louis was host to the mid-summer classic on July 9, 1957, and a packed house of nearly thirty-one thousand fans turned out to see the American League down the senior circuit, 6–5. Musial, the only Cardinal in the lineup, collected a double in three official trips to the plate, then walked and scored in the ninth inning as the Nationals mounted a three-run rally which fell just short.

The Cardinals opened the second half of the season on an ominous note by losing four of their first five games, but the club seemed to have righted itself by July 18 in a contest at Ebbets Field. Trailing by two, St. Louis scored seven times in the top of the ninth to take a 9–4 lead, but the Dodgers, on Gil Hodges' grand-slam home run, fought back to tie in the bottom of the frame. Brooklyn scored one in the bottom of the eleventh and pulled out a 10–9 victory in a contest Frank Lane characterized as "pitiful, tragic, and disastrous." The Cardinals were now a game behind Milwaukee.

A day later, Musial paced the Redbirds to a 9–4 win over the Pirates with a three-for-five performance that gave him two more career milestones. Batting .344, Stan's first-inning triple gave him 1,137 extra-base hits, leaving him two behind Ty Cobb, fifty-three behind Lou Gehrig, and 219 long blows behind "Babe Ruth's unattainable 1,356 record," as the St. Louis *Globe-Democrat* characterized it. Musial's third safety of the game was number 2,900 of his career. Musial also extended his consecutive-game record to 861, but manager Fred Hutchinson warned reporters the Cardinal first baseman would play both ends of the upcoming doubleheader only "if it's cool and Stan doesn't feel too tired."

Musial was in the lineup for the opening game of the twin bill the next day, but true to his word, Hutchinson rested Stan in the nightcap. Fate intervened when the game was suspended in the top of the ninth and scheduled to be played to a conclusion on August 27. Questioned about the streak, the reluctant Iron Man admitted he didn't care if he kept the record or not. "I've reached the point where playing two nine-inning games in one day takes too much out of me," said Stan. "I'm sluggish, slow and tired, and of little use to the club."

On July 22, Musial was on hand for the ceremonies inducting Sam Crawford and former Yankee manager Joe McCarthy into baseball's Hall of Fame at Cooperstown, New York. Stan posed for photos with Ty Cobb, toured the museum, and viewed the bat with which he hit five home runs in a doubleheader against the Giants three years earlier. Frank Frisch, a Hall of Famer himself, paid tribute to the Cardinal superstar by insisting the five-year rule for induction be waived when Musial retired. "I'd like to see Stan get in early," argued Frisch. "Why make him wait five years when you know as well as I do that he'll get in?"

Musial closed out July with a .329 batting average and brushed off suggestions that he needed more rest, saying, "I don't feel tired. I'm in a little slump, that's all." On August 1, Stan boosted his average seven points with a perfect four-for-four, including two home runs, in an 8–0 victory over the Giants. The second round-tripper, which earned Stan the league lead in RBIs, gave him 1,140 career extra-base hits, enabling him to pass Ty Cobb for second place. The next night, Stan tripled and scored in the first, doubled and scored the tying run in the seventh, then doubled home the winning run in a ten-inning victory over the Phillies that gave the Cards their eighth straight win and sole possession of first place. And then the Redbirds' momentum ground abruptly to a halt.

After splitting a doubleheader with the Phillies, St. Louis embarked on a disastrous nine-game losing streak, the club's longest drought in a decade. Worse yet, the Braves picked the same moment to win ten in a row. It wasn't until August 16 that the Redbirds won again. Paced by Musial's two hits, which enabled him to take over the league lead in batting, the Redbirds snapped their losing streak with a 6–2 win at Milwaukee. A day later, Stan slammed his twenty-sixth homer of the year, a two-run shot in the tenth that gave the Cards a dramatic 8–6 win in the opening game of a twin bill with the Braves. The round-tripper allowed Musial to pass Rogers Hornsby and Jake Beckley on the all-time hits list. The Cardinal legend reached another milestone in the nightcap when he singled in the third inning, giving him five thousand career total bases, an accomplishment equalled by only five other ballplayers, Ty Cobb, Babe Ruth, Tris Speaker, Lou Gehrig, and Mel Ott. Cardinal publicity director Jim Toomey called for the ball. "I'd like to keep this one for myself," Musial said proudly.

On August 23, the Redbirds were leading Philadelphia, 6–2, when, with Wally Moon breaking for second on a hit-and-run play, Musial tried to hit behind the runner by swinging at a high, outside curveball. The unnatural motion yanked Stan's left arm out of its joint, fractured a bone in his shoulder socket, and tore muscles over his collarbone. "I felt something snap," said Musial. "If I had tried to hit straight away, nothing probably would have happened. I knew something ripped in my shoulder when I swung."

Stan took his position at first base, but was unable to throw the ball and had to leave the game. "I've counted him out several times before and he's fooled me," said Cardinal trainer Bob Bauman, "but this time I'm afraid he's hurt." Bauman expected Musial would be out of the lineup for a week to ten days. The next morning, Stan received a cortisone injection from Dr. Paul Colonna of the University of Pennsylvania Medical School, who announced that Stan would be ready to play "in a few days." Musial's consecutive-game streak officially came to an end at 895 games that evening when the Redbirds lost a 3–2 squeaker to the Phils with Joe Cunningham at first base.

A year later, in a *Saturday Evening Post* article, Musial would say, "For some reason I didn't particularly care about that record. It was something that just came about. It wasn't a record that had anything to do with the game, like hitting or fielding or throwing or running. Having it end may have been a blessing in disguise. Everybody wanted me to continue it, and naturally I wanted to keep it going in a way, but there were some years, take 'Fifty-six, when I felt like I was getting run down a little by playing all those games. If I could've taken a game off here and there, it probably would've helped me to hit better, and helped the club, too."

Without Musial, who in August hit more homers and drove in more runs than any other three Cardinal players combined, Redbird pennant hopes looked slim indeed. Two days later, Bob Bauman said Stan might return to the lineup that night against the Pirates. "I know Stan wants very much to play," said Bauman, "but we won't know until he takes batting practice if he can or not."

He couldn't. Manager Fred Hutchinson inserted Musial into the lineup as a pinch-runner as the Cards completed their suspended game of July 21 with the Pirates. (Had Stan not appeared in the contest, his consecutive-game string would have ended at 862.) Cardinal team physician Dr. I.C. Middleman treated Stan on August 30 with a novocaine injection and gave Musial the encouraging news that his back injury would have no permanent disabling effect. Two days later, after a bruise had developed under his left shoulder, Stan declined to take batting practice. "I think a little layoff from swinging may help," said Musial, who was improving slowly. By September 4, Stan had missed twelve games, more playing time than he had lost over the past ten years. Middleman was now talking in terms of Musial returning in an "indeterminate" time. Four days later, Stan returned to the lineup.

With their superstar on the sideline, the Cardinal attack had often been reduced to a whisper as the Redbirds split fourteen games. Musial's return inspired the Redbirds, who closed to within two and a half games of Milwaukee by September 14. But that was as close as the team would come to winning the 1957 pennant.

Since returning to the lineup, Musial had collected eleven hits in twenty at-bats and was leading the league with a .348 average. When the Cardinals arrived at Milwaukee's County Stadium for a three-game series beginning September 23, it was do or die: one loss would eliminate the Redbirds from contention. The opening game went eleven innings before Henry Aaron blasted a two-run homer which gave the Braves a 4–2 win and clinched the 1957 National League pennant. Musial was three-for-four with a pair of doubles, the first giving him thirteen seasons of three hundred or more total bases. Another Henry Aaron home run, this one the first grand-slam of his career, propelled the Braves to a 6–1 victory the next day. Cardinal manager Fred Hutchinson told Musial, "You're my Most Valuable Player candidate, Stan. Take off the last three days while I look at some kids. Those other guys couldn't catch you in the batting race if they tried all winter."

At almost thirty-seven years of age, Musial finished the year with a .351 average, capturing his seventh and last National League batting title. Gussie Busch's optimistic January prediction had been fulfilled. Since returning from his shoulder injury, Stan had concentrated on just meeting the ball and had collected an amazing sixteen hits in thirty-one at-bats for a .516 average. For the year, Musial had blasted twenty-nine home runs, finished second among all National League batters in slugging average (.612) and doubles (38), third in RBIs (102), and sixth in total bases (307). The final honor of the year for Stan came when he was named National League Player of the Year by *The Sporting News*.

A month after the season ended, general manager Frank Lane, miffed at not being allowed to trade popular third baseman Ken Boyer to the Pirates, resigned to take the same post with the Cleveland Indians. Cardinal fans all over the country breathed a sigh of relief at Lane's departure and again when his replacement, Bing Devine, turned his back on the Pittsburgh deal. Devine's first move came on December 5 when he sent pitchers Willard Schmidt, Ted Wieand, and Marty Kutyna to Cincinnati for outfielders Joe Taylor and Curt Flood. The trade was a complete washout for the Reds, but Curt Flood would anchor center field at Busch Stadium for the next twelve seasons, win seven Gold Glove awards, and help lead the Redbirds to three pennants in the 1960s. Flood was the first piece in the puzzle which would bring the Cardinals a National League pennant in 1964, their first in eighteen years.

Devine's next order of business was to sign Musial.

◇15◇

The Three Thousand Club

---

*Everybody in St. Louis, every kid in
St. Louis, wanted to be Stan Musial.
He was the best.*

MIKE SHANNON

O ver the winter, Cardinal general
manager Bing Devine offhandedly asked Musial what sort of contract he
was looking for in 1958. Stan had a simple request: he wanted to be the
highest-salaried player in the history of the National League. Pittsburgh
slugger Ralph Kiner had drawn $90,000, so Devine and Musial informally
settled on a pact for a thousand over that. But when the contract talks
became official, Devine called Stan into his office and said, "Mr. Busch
wants you not only to become the highest-salaried player in National League
history, but the first to receive $100,000."

Musial might have been the first ballplayer in the history of the game
to get more money than he asked for at contract time. On January 29,
1958, with August Busch in attendance at the brewery's plush offices, the
Cardinal superstar, still insisting he would have settled for less, achieved
his goal of signing the most lucrative pact in National League history.

With the National League's premier hitter safely in the fold, the
Cardinals limped through a 16–17 spring training and dropped their home

opener to the Cubs, 4–0. Musial, in his quest for hit number three thousand, singled once in five trips to the plate and struck out twice. Stan was just forty-three hits shy of his goal, a target *The Saturday Evening Post* reckoned Musial would hit by June. "I'm going out to get them in a hurry," quipped Stan, "because, who knows, I might get hit by a cab."

Musial doubled and blasted his first home run of the season the next night, bringing him to 5,046 total bases in his career, a new National League record eclipsing the old one held by Mel Ott, but the Redbirds again lost to the Cubs. Two more losses to Chicago followed before the Redbirds snapped their unenviable string on April 20 when, paced by Musial's two home runs and four RBIs, St. Louis defeated Chicago, 9–4.

Stan was, indeed, in a hurry to get to three thousand. When California fans in the baseball-hungry crowd at Seals Stadium finally got a look at the long-time Cardinal superstar on April 22, Musial did not disappoint. Stan smashed an opposite-field double and a pair of singles for his fifth multiple-hit in a row as the Cards rolled to a 7–5 win over the Giants, now of San Francisco. Three more hits a day later gave Musial seventeen safeties in thirty-four at-bats and an even .500 batting average. Stan seemed unstoppable when he batted safely in his eleventh straight game on April 27 and looked positively superhuman when he was a perfect four-for-four the next evening, boosting his average to a whopping .551.

Musial was hot as a firecracker, but the Cardinals were fizzling. With a 3–10 record, St. Louis had fallen into the National League cellar. The Redbirds extended their losing streak to seven games while Musial, with his twelfth multiple-hit game of the season, closed to within seven hits of three thousand. "As long as Stan Musial holds up," said Bing Devine, "we've still got a chance to finish in the first division."

Stan wanted to collect the record safety before the home folks, but had just three games remaining to do so. Musial was blanked the next evening, leaving just a Sunday May 11 doubleheader against the Cubs to achieve his goal at Busch Stadium. Stan did his best, collecting four singles and a two-run homer for the twin bill, but fell short of the magic number by two. That evening, Musial and his business partner Biggie Garagnani closed their restaurant and threw a star-studded private party in anticipation of his three thousandth hit. Among the three hundred attendees were Missouri Governor James T. Blair, St. Louis Mayor Raymond Tucker, and National League President Warren Giles. "This was to have been a three thousand dinner," cracked Cardinal publicity director Jim Toomey, "but we all settled for 2,998." Stan conceded, "In my younger days, I always tried to get six hits in a doubleheader. Today, I would have liked to have gotten seven, but I was more than happy to settle for five."

Accompanied by several of their close friends, Stan and Lillian left the dinner party shortly before midnight to catch the train to Chicago for a two-game series. Musial doubled his first time up the next afternoon, leaving him just one hit shy of three thousand, then drew a base on balls and grounded out his next three times at bat as the Redbirds downed the Cubs. "I hope we win tomorrow," he confided to coach Terry Moore, "but I get four walks."

Manager Fred Hutchinson planned on benching Stan to save the historic safety for the first game of a home stand at Busch Stadium beginning on May 14. "I'm not going to snow you," Hutchinson told the press. "I could tell you tomorrow that Stan wasn't playing because he had a bellyache, but, hell, I'm just not going to use him unless I need him. It means more to the fans back home than it does here. After all, only five thousand people showed up today. And besides, I know Stan wants to get it at home, before his friends." The decision to bench baseball's leading hitter, even for a day, was not without controversy. Commissioner Ford Frick, when contacted in New York, dodged the question entirely by saying, "It's a National League issue." National League President Warren Giles pulled the covers even further over his head; reached in Chicago, he was "unavailable for comment."

On Tuesday, May 13, Musial left his suite at the Chicago Knickerbocker Hotel and taxied to Wrigley Field. He spoke with reporters, had his picture taken a dozen times, and suited up. Just as Hutchinson had predicted, there were fewer than six thousand fans in the stands. Musial was sunning himself in the bullpen and the Cards trailed, 3–1, entering the sixth when Gene Green doubled off Moe Drabowsky and Hutchinson reluctantly called on his superstar to pinch-hit. Chicago field announcer Pat Pieper called out loud and clear, "Attention . . . Number Six . . . Stan Mus-i-al . . . batting for Sam Jones."

Drabowsky took the count to two-and-two before painting the outside corner with a perfect curveball. Caught off-balance by the pitch, Stan nonetheless awkwardly drove the ball into left for an opposite-field RBI double. Up in the announcer's box, Cardinal broadcaster Harry Caray, perhaps the most excited observer in the ballpark, shouted into his microphone, "Here's the pitch . . . Line drive! Into left field! Hit number three thousand! A run has scored! Musial around first, on his way to second with a double. Holy cow! He came through!"

The thirty-seven-year-old Musial had collected hit number three thousand in his sixteenth season, the earliest any ballplayer had attained the milestone. (Ty Cobb, although three years younger than Stan when he collected number three thousand, had taken seventeen seasons.) Musial became only the eighth man in major-league history to reach the elite club, following Cap Anson, Honus Wagner, Nap Lajoie, Cobb, Tris Speaker, Eddie Collins, and Paul Waner.

Third-base umpire Frank Dascoli, one of Stan's biggest admirers among the National League arbiters, retrieved the ball and happily presented it to the Cardinal legend. Fred Hutchinson came out to replace Musial and said, "Congratulations, Stan. I'm sorry. I know you wanted to do it in St. Louis, but I needed you today." Musial's teammates swarmed around him and after a prolonged standing ovation, Stan left the game, replaced by pinch-runner Frank Barnes. Exiting the field, he spotted his wife in a front box by the Cardinal dugout and trotted over to give her a kiss. After the contest, one of the photographers asked, "Stan, do you know that blonde who kissed you out there?" "I'd better," answered Musial. "That's my wife."

The Redbirds scored three more times in the inning to post a 5–3 victory, their sixth in succession. When the final out was announced, Musial jumped up and shouted, "Great! This makes it perfect." There wasn't enough room in the clubhouse for everyone, so Stan returned to the playing field for dozens of photo opportunities.

The Cardinals took the bus to the Illinois Central Depot and trained to St. Louis, an experience Musial would remember as one of the highlights of his major-league career. A steward brought out a huge cake with the number "3000" in red frosting, and Harry Caray topped off the moment by presenting Musial with a pair of diamond cuff links. Stan bought winning pitcher Sam Jones a bottle of champagne. By the time everyone finished dinner, the train was stopping at Clinton, Illinois, where a crowd of about fifty people was waiting. "We want Musial! We want Musial!" chanted the fans, who broke into raucous cheers when Stan appeared to sign autographs and shake hands. An hour later, at Springfield, over a hundred people sang "For He's A Jolly Good Fellow." When the train left the state capital, Musial went to the parlor car, sat down, and promptly fell asleep. "Doesn't he ever show any nerve?" said *Life* magazine writer W.C. Heinz to Lillian. "Never," replied Lil. "You know, we have three children and sometimes if they do something wrong and he raises his voice just a little they stand there with their mouths open, as if to say, 'Look at Daddy. What's the matter with Daddy?'"

Back at St. Louis, a crowd had begun to form at 9:30 that evening. By 11:15, when the train arrived from Chicago, nearly a thousand people were jammed into Union Station. Stan was led through a throng of cheering fans to a platform where he gave a brief speech. "I never realized," Musial said, "that batting a little ball around could cause so much commotion. I know now how [aviator Charles] Lindbergh must have felt when he returned to St. Louis." A voice in the crowd shouted out, "What did he hit?"

After leaving the station, Stan and Lillian went to the restaurant to unwind. At three in the morning, following one of the biggest days of his life and the most important milestone of his major-league career, he finally fell into bed.

Before the game at Busch Stadium the next evening, Musial was praised by Warren Giles, Gussie Busch, and Bing Devine in ceremonies hosted by broadcaster Harry Caray. Giles called Stan an "inspiration to our youth," and added, "I am proud to represent a league which boasts of you as one of its players. We are grateful for the immeasurable contribution you have made to the prestige of a great league. On behalf of the National League, I salute you." In addition to the obligatory floral tribute bearing the number 3000, Stan received dozens of congratulatory telegrams from baseball dignitaries, former teammates, active and retired ballplayers, and dozens of friends and acquaintances. Asked if all the names on the telegrams were familiar, he replied, "Oh, some of them are, especially those from here and from Pittsburgh. But there are so many that I know I've never met. It sort of shakes you up to realize that what I did means so much to so many people."

The fans at Busch Stadium whistled, applauded, and stamped their feet when Musial slammed a home run, hit number 3,001, in his first at-bat.

Four days later, between games of a doubleheader with the Dodgers, Stan was given the Lou Gehrig Memorial Award of Phi Delta Theta fraternity by Chicago *Tribune* sports editor Wilfrid Smith, a member of the fraternity's national committee. Musial was the third recipient of the honor, presented annually to the major-league player who, on and off the ball field, most exemplified the character of the late Lou Gehrig, a 1925 graduate of Columbia University and member of the fraternity. "I certainly appreciate getting this award," said Musial, "for Gehrig was one of my idols. And I'm happy that I'm in such select company as [the two previous winners] Alvin Dark of the Cardinals and Pee Wee Reese of the Dodgers."

On May 22, an article appeared in the St. Louis *Globe-Democrat* that spoke volumes about Stan Musial's character. "When the Cardinals were in town this spring, Stan came out to see us as he always does," said Musial's close friend and former manager Dickie Kerr. Kerr told how Stan had insisted that Dickie buy himself a birthday present, a house. "He had mentioned a house before," said Kerr, "but we'd never taken it seriously. This time, he told us to get busy. So we did." At the very pinnacle of his fame and acclaim, Stan had not forgotten Kerr and his wife Pep, who had taken the Musials into their home when Lillian was expecting her first child in 1940. Stan and Lil had named the boy in honor of Kerr, and Dick Musial, now eighteen, was preparing to enter Notre Dame in September. Stan was embarrassed when questioned by reporters about the gift.

Between games of the Sunday, June 8, doubleheader with the Phillies, Stan was "officially" inducted into baseball's three-thousand-hit club. Age and illness, respectively, kept Ty Cobb and Napoleon Lajoie from attending, but Tris Speaker and Paul Waner were on hand for the ceremonies. Speaker, a member of the Hall of Fame since 1937, said, "I want to thank all of you wonderful people attending today's ceremony and I want you to know that it gives me great pleasure to be with our newest member of the three-thousand-hit club. I don't know who gave Stan the name of The Man, but he couldn't have made a wiser selection." Waner, Musial's boyhood idol, got a big laugh from the crowd when he said, "I hope that Musial continues to get more hits and sets more records, but there's one record of mine that I wouldn't like to see him break: they got me out sixty-three-hundred times." National League President Warren Giles presented Stan with the John A. "Bud" Hillerich Award, a silver bat emblematic of the 1957 batting title, and quipped, "This is getting to be a habit, and I hope you win it one more time at least." Missouri Governor James T. Blair gave Stan a license plate stamped with the number 3000 and Cardinal executive vice president Dick Meyer presented a silver bowl to Stan's mother. Musial was given a silver bowl and a plaque from his teammates which read:

> To Stanley Frank Musial, an emblem of esteem from his teammates. An outstanding artist in his profession, possessor of many baseball records; gentleman in every sense of the word; adored and worshipped by countless thousands; perfect answer to a manager's prayer. To this, we, the Cardinals, attest with our signatures.

The Cardinals, winners of twenty of their last twenty-eight outings, had closed to within five games of the league-leading Milwaukee Braves when Musial embarked on an oh-for-nineteen string which sent his batting average plummeting to .379. On June 24, Musial was honored in Pittsburgh by the Circus Saints and Sinners, an organization of businessmen and professionals, for his three thousandth hit. In his speech, Stan recalled that he nearly signed with Pittsburgh and said, "I might have made it three Pirates in the three-thousand hit club, along with Paul Waner and Honus

Wagner." Umpire Frank Dascoli brought down the house with a story about Philadelphia hitter Willie "Puddin' Head" Jones, who once argued a called strike. "Why are you always complaining?" asked Dascoli. "Musial never complains." "Of course not," replied Jones. "Musial can hit. I can't."

Both Dascoli and fellow arbiter Augie Donatelli disavowed the widely held theory that Stan and his American League counterpart, Ted Williams, got the benefit of the marginal pitch from umpires because of their sharp vision and superstar status. "Stan still has to worry about that close pitch," said Donatelli, as if anyone believed him.

The Cardinals headed into the All-Star break with a 37–35 record, two and a half games behind Milwaukee. On July 8 at Baltimore's Memorial Stadium, Musial made his fifteenth appearance and what proved to be his last start (playing first base) in baseball's annual All-Star game. Stan scored a run and was one-for-four as the American League pulled out a 4–3 win.

On July 28, the Cardinal front office announced that the Redbirds would be making a post-season trip to Japan, pending the approval of baseball Commissioner Ford Frick. Yetsuo Higa, representing the Japanese newspaper sponsoring the trip, acknowledged the selection of the Cardinals was due mainly to Musial. "No one in Japan knows the Cardinals," said Higa, "but everyone knows Stan Musial. That is one of the reasons I came to St. Louis to talk to the club." Higa added that Musial could almost single-handedly ruin Japanese ball: "All Japanese will try to copy his stance and never hit the ball again."

An eight-game losing streak in late July and early August dropped the Cardinals back into the cellar again and Musial, mired in the midst of a two-for-thirty-two drought, dipped to .335 on the year. But the Redbirds snapped their losing streak with a victory over the Dodgers on August 4, while Stan began a four-game hitting tear which propelled him past Richie Ashburn into the lead for the National League batting championship with a .346 average.

Stan held his lead over Ashburn throughout August, but the withering St. Louis summer began to work on Musial. By the first of September, Stan had dropped to .341 and was tied again with Ashburn. Forty-eight hours later, Musial pulled a leg muscle running out an infield hit and was forced to the bench, his batting average frozen at .340. The same day, Ashburn belted out three hits to boost his mark to .342 and take over the league lead in hitting. On Monday, September 8, Musial returned to the lineup and hedged on his prediction that a .350 batting average would take the National League batting crown. "I think .345 should do it now," said Stan. "If I can get my hit a game, I'll be all right."

Blanked in three trips to the plate that evening, Stan failed to get his hit. The leg still bothering him, he sat out the next nine games, not returning to the lineup until September 20. Oh-for-four that evening, Musial's average slipped to .335, three points behind Ashburn and five points behind the league's leading hitter, Willie Mays. By this time, the Cardinals had undergone a change in management. On September 17, August Busch had dismissed Fred Hutchinson and his entire coaching staff, retaining only Stan Hack, whom he named interim manager.

With just three game remaining, Stan's hopes for a National League record-tying eighth batting championship were fading fast, but he wasn't going to go down without a fight. On September 26, in head-to-head competition with Mays, Stan singled twice in four trips to the plate while the San Francisco outfielder was hitless in three at-bats. At Pittsburgh, Richie Ashburn collected two hits in four tries and at .3448, led both Mays (.3441) and Musial (.337). The following day, Stan could do no better than a double in five at-bats. Nothing short of a five-for-five performance in the final game of the season would give him the batting championship. That was too much to ask of anyone, even a thirty-seven-year-old baseball legend. On September 28, as the Cards closed out the 1958 season with a 7–2 loss to the Giants, Stan rapped a single and double in four trips to the plate, finishing the year at .337, thirteen points behind Ashburn. The Cardinals ended the season in sixth place with a 72–82 record, twenty games behind the Braves. The next day, former Cardinal infielder Sol Hemus was given the St. Louis managerial post. The ascension of Hemus would mark the darkest days of Musial's career.

Stan had finished the year with 472 at-bats, just five more than he had collected in his rookie season, thirty-five doubles (third best in the National League), and a .528 slugging average. Musial had homered just once over the last two and a half months of the season, and his seventeen round-trippers were his lowest total since 1946. Worse yet, in thirty fewer at-bats, Stan had driven in forty less runs than the year before. By his own admission, he was completely worn out by year's end.

When the post-season trip to Japan had been announced, Musial was opposed to the trip, but the Japanese had made it clear: if Stan didn't come, they didn't want the Cardinals. So a week after the season ended, Musial and Lillian, six months pregnant, flew to Hawaii and joined the team in time for a one-game trip to Seoul, South Korea, the first time an American club had ever appeared there. Years later, Musial would remember the trip as "one unending whirl of parades, ball games, receptions, conducted tours, cocktail parties, dinners and entertainment. From the prime minister to the countless kids we saw playing ball every day on their way to school, the Japanese were gracious, kind and courteous."

The Japanese fielded an all-star team pooled by players from top clubs of the Central and Pacific Japanese Leagues to meet the Cardinals. When the Redbirds left Tokyo for San Francisco on November 17, they had played to over four hundred thousand fans and won fourteen of the sixteen games. Musial, the top drawing card, had hit over .300 and collected two home runs. Yetsuo Higa, the organizer of the trip, paid the Cardinals a tribute when they left. "Of all the major-league teams that have come to Japan," said Higa, "the Cardinals hustled the most, taught the Japanese more about baseball, and made the best impression on the Japanese fans, on and off the field. Above all they have done, the Cardinals have set a precedent that all American baseball clubs should follow when they come to Japan in the future: go all the way, or don't go at all."

That could have been Musial's own motto.

Benched

---

*I remember one game at St. Louis. I threw a
forkball down and away and Musial hit it on
the right-field roof. And I think I'd been
twenty-one innings without giving up a run
and we lost the ball game on that, a good
pitch. After the game I'm sitting at my locker
and Murtaugh—he had this dry sense of
humor—he comes in and slaps me on the
back and says, "Relief pitcher, my ass!"*

ELROY FACE

In December 1958, the Musials spent
a week visiting Dickie and Pep Kerr in Houston. Lillian and Pep talked
about the upcoming birth of Lil's fourth child while Stan and Dickie went
hunting. Musial was as successful with a gun as he usually was at the plate,
bagging a twenty-pound turkey, a ten-point buck, and the state limit on
duck and quail. In February, a month before spring training was scheduled
to open, the Musials' fourth child, Jeanie, was born.

And then Stan made the worst decision of his career.

Because of the recent arrival to the household, Musial, about ten pounds overweight, was given permission to report late to Florida. Stan decided to conserve his energy for the season by playing and running less in the spring exhibitions in Florida. As a result, he was in less than peak physical condition when the season began. Because Musial wasn't hitting, the Cardinals had their worst spring training in years, winning just eight of twenty-five games. When manager Sol Hemus opened the season with Stan in left field, a position he hadn't played regularly since 1956, it nearly proved to be a disaster. On opening night, Stan misjudged a fly ball and slammed into the left field wall as the Giants squeaked past the Cardinals, 6–5. The next evening, Musial drove in both St. Louis runs in a 5–2 loss, but crashed into the wall again and bruised himself badly. Hemus shifted first baseman Bill White to left and put Stan back on first, but the defensive realignment failed to help the Redbirds, who dropped their third straight game to San Francisco.

The Cards snapped their three-game losing streak the following night with a 6–2 win over the Dodgers and Musial, oh-for-four for the second straight evening and one-for-fifteen on the year, saw his average drop to .067. Even though he was sluggish in the early going, Stan was still wily enough to spoil a pair of no-hitters. On April 16, he came off the bench in the seventh inning to spoil Jack Sanford's bid with a pinch single, the only safety the Redbirds would muster off the San Francisco right-hander. Three days later, his opposite-field double off Glen Hobbie left the Chicago hurler with a one-hit shutout. It took until May 3, twenty games into the season, for Musial to post his first three-hit game of the year and until May 6 for him to club his first home run. The next night, Stan's four-hundred-foot homer in the bottom of the ninth lifted St. Louis to a 4–3 win over the Cubs and gave Musial the singular distinction of being the first ballplayer in major-league history to collect four hundred home runs and three thousand hits. On May 10, Stan received his first indication of how he was going to be handled by his new manager: even though a right-hander was on the mound for the Cubs, Hemus benched him.

Barely a month into the season, the Redbirds had fallen to last place in the National League. With ten wins in their first thirty games, the worst record in baseball, St. Louis trailed the league-leading Braves by eight and a half games. At .244, Musial was off to his worst start since 1947, when he had suffered through his year-long bout with appendicitis. Stan was in and out of the lineup for the next two weeks and was hitting .230 when on June 2, in a 3–0 loss to Pittsburgh at Forbes Field, he collected the 650th double of his career, moving to within a single two-bagger of Honus

Wagner's National League record. Two days later, still in front of his home-state friends, the Cardinal legend tied the mark.

The next day, Stan was benched again. It would take two weeks for him to break Wagner's record.

On June 8, a smiling Musial was photographed in the dugout with Hemus. Stan reacted publicly to what the Cardinal manager had termed a "rest" when he told reporters that 1959 might be his last season unless he could get back in the groove at the plate. When asked why he looked so happy posing with Hemus, Musial replied grimly, "I always smile when I'm having my picture taken."

Stan didn't earn another start until June 13 when the Redbirds faced Cincinnati at Busch Stadium. Ignominiously dropped to the sixth slot in the lineup—the Cardinal superstar had batted third or fourth during most of his career—Musial turned the situation around and made Hemus look bad, clubbing a two-run homer and a bases-loaded single that paced the Redbirds to a 7–0 win over the Phillies. Stan's average stood at .253 when the Redbirds faced Pittsburgh in a doubleheader at Busch Stadium. In the opening game, Stan collected a pair of doubles, numbers 652 and 653 of his career, to break Honus Wagner's National League record. Ahead stood only Ty Cobb, with 724.

On June 26, Musial struck a blow for old folks everywhere when he blasted two home runs in a 7–6 loss to the Reds at Busch. But despite his heroics, Stan was back on the bench the next afternoon when the Redbirds faced Cincinnati southpaw Jim O'Toole. Two days later, Milwaukee manager Fred Haney named Musial to the All-Star squad, the sixteenth such honor for the Cardinal superstar. That afternoon, at Wrigley Field, Stan was involved in what was easily the strangest play of his career. In the fourth inning of a game against the Cubs, Musial walked on a 3–1 pitch from Chicago right-hander Bob Anderson. Ball four caromed past catcher Sammy Taylor and bounced off the home plate screen. While Taylor and Anderson were arguing that the pitch had ticked off Stan's bat for a foul ball, Musial took off for second base. The Chicago batboy picked up the ball and tossed it to the field announcer, but third baseman Al Dark intercepted the throw and fired a strike to shortstop Ernie Banks, who tagged the sliding Musial. Back at home plate, umpire Vic Delmore, thinking the first ball was out of play, had given a new one to Anderson. Anderson turned back to the mound, saw Stan on his way to second, and unleashed a wild throw into center field. After a ten-minute debate, Delmore ruled Musial had been tagged with the original ball and was out. The Cardinals protested the game, but withdrew the gripe when they won, 4–1.

The Redbirds reached the first All-Star break in sixth place, eight games back and five games under .500. Breaking with tradition, baseball moguls had introduced a two-game format in order to raise more revenue for the pension plan. On July 6, the evening before the contest, the Pittsburgh chapter of the Baseball Writers Association honored the two most distinguished active veterans of the game, Musial and Ted Williams, with a banquet attended by some twelve hundred people, including Vice President Richard Nixon, who was scheduled to throw out the first pitch. Stan's mother was at Forbes Field the next day and like any other fan, giddily asked for Williams' autograph. "You're my favorite player," gushed Mary Musial as she watched the Red Sox slugger scribble his name in her autograph book. Williams couldn't wait to get to the batting cage to tell Musial the story. When the game began, Stan popped out in a pinch-hitting appearance in front of thirty-five thousand fans, most from his home state.

By mid-July, Musial had raised his average to .273 when, without fanfare or announcement, Hemus inexplicably sent him back to the bench until July 23. Even though the Cardinal skipper was "resting" Stan more than ever, he began to fall back during the hot summer months. On August 3, in the second All-Star Game, Musial pinch-hit and drew a walk at the Los Angeles Coliseum as the American League downed the Nationals, 5–3. When the Redbirds resumed the final leg of the season, the club was still languishing in seventh place, seven games under .500 and ten and a half lengths behind the league-leading Giants. Musial, with one hit in his last eighteen at-bats, was down to .260.

Back in St. Louis two weeks later, general manager Bing Devine assured Musial the Cardinal organization wanted him to return in 1960. Stan agreed that he'd like to play at least one more year and Devine called a press conference later in the day to make the announcement. "I feel good," Musial insisted. "I just got off to a poor start and never got over it. I began pressing. I'm confident I'll do better next year. I feel that this just has been a bad year, not one in which old age caught up with me. It's a mechanical rather than physical problem. If I were full of aches and pains and if pitchers were getting the fastball by me because I'd slowed up, well, then I'd know it was time to quit." Stan was reminded by a reporter that he'd said once if he couldn't hit .300, he would retire. "That was when batting .300 was easy," Musial snapped, uncharacteristically. "I know I can't be this bad next season."

Devine cautioned Stan that Hemus and the front office wanted to look at their young talent for the remaining six weeks of the season. With seventy-four hits in 284 at-bats, Stan was hitting .261 at the time of the announcement. After the decision was made public, Hemus took him out of the lineup for the rest of the year, excluding pinch-hitting appearances and an occasional spot start.

Musial came off the bench five times over the next eight days and was unsuccessful in each appearance as a pinch-batter. On August 21, *The Sporting News* quoted an "unidentified but reliable source" as saying a coolness had developed between the Cardinal superstar and manager Sol Hemus. Then came the rumor that Stan was to be traded for New York Yankees catcher Yogi Berra. Musial called the report "so silly, I don't want to comment," and Cardinal general manager Bing Devine termed the rumor "ridiculous." Hemus handled the awkward predicament with humor: "I'm not going to his restaurant anymore. I'll probably get a tough steak."

The Cardinal manager attempted to ease the situation by announcing Musial would play first base in the Sunday, August 23, contest against the Reds, Stan's first start since August 11. Musial was one-for-five in the contest, then languished on the bench again until August 29 when he looked like the superstar of old with a homer, double, and single as the Redbirds triumphed over Cincinnati. Stan's average had fallen to .251 when he collected the 3,200th hit of his career, a two-run homer in an 11–4 victory over the Cubs on September 21. But Musial finished the season on a high note, rapping a single and his fourteenth home run of the year in a 14–8 win over the Cubs.

The Cardinals won one game less in 1959 than the year before and dropped a rank in the standings, from sixth to seventh, the club's lowest finish since 1919. It had been a long season for a team that never got to the .500 level or rose higher than fifth place in the standings.

Older and heavier, Musial had slipped to .255, the first time he had failed to reach the coveted .300 plateau, and had the worst season of his career. Starting in ninety-two games and appearing in twenty-three others as a pinch-batter, Stan collected just eighty-seven hits in 341 trips to the plate, of which a mere twenty-nine were for extra bases. Musial finished the season with career lows in every offensive category except home runs and his meager total of fourteen round-trippers was the lowest since 1944, back before he became a home run hitter. Things could only get better in 1960.

◆ ◆ ◆

Musial didn't return to the Cardinal fold in 1960 because he needed the money. The restaurant was doing well—construction had begun on a new location on Oakland Avenue—and Stan had even taken a pay cut to $75,000. Income was not an issue with the Cardinal veteran. Pride was.

Musial was still burning with the desire to play baseball and more importantly, to prove the 1959 season was not his swan song.

Stan put himself in the hands of Walter Eberhardt, the director of physical education at St. Louis University, and underwent a rigorous regimen of muscle-toning exercises. "It's old men like me who need this the most," said Musial. When spring training came, Stan played more often and worked out harder, unlike the year before. Musial responded with the bat and the Redbirds won the Grapefruit League title. Opening Day, Tuesday, April 12, found the Cardinals playing the Giants at their new digs, Candlestick Park. Vice President Richard M. Nixon was on hand to dedicate the new stadium as "the best baseball park in America," but he got an argument from at least one Cardinal, who described the hitting background as "brutal." Former San Francisco outfielder Hank Sauer, now a Giants' coach, disagreed, saying, "It's about time they did something for the pitchers for a change," to which Stan quipped in response, "Yeah, he can feel that way now that he's no longer playing."

Musial was blanked in three trips to the plate and the Redbirds opened the season with five straight losses. With his leading slugger, Ken Boyer, off to a slow start, manager Sol Hemus changed his batting order, shifting Stan from third to fifth to give Boyer a chance to see more fastballs. Not since July of 1958 had the Cardinals stood at the .500 point, but they achieved that goal in spectacular fashion on April 29 when they blasted Chicago pitching for eighteen hits and a crushing 16–6 victory. It was only a momentary reprieve for the St. Louis fans. The Redbirds embarked on an extended losing streak, and on May 6, Sol Hemus reacted by benching Musial, hitting .268. Publicly, Stan accepted the move, but those close to him knew he was hurt and bewildered. Hemus' move failed to help. The Cardinals dropped eight of their next nine games, a streak which culminated when Chicago right-hander Don Cardwell no-hit St. Louis on May 15. In Musial's only appearance of the contest, he pinch-hit and struck out. "I was swinging at sound," said Stan. "When I got up there, he was throwing BBs."

By now, Hemus had lost all confidence in Musial, believing the veteran was washed up. It seemed as if every time Stan was successful at the plate, the Redbirds lost, and every time he didn't hit, the club won. To Hemus, Musial's hits were meaningless and his failures loomed large. With the score tied at three-all the day following Cardwell's no-hitter, the Cardinal skipper sent Stan up to pinch-hit with men on second and third in the ninth. Philadelphia manager Gene Mauch ordered an intentional pass, but the move backfired when pinch-hitter Carl Sawatski lofted a sacrifice fly to give the Redbirds a 4–3 lead in a game they eventually won. Delighted with his strategy, Hemus boasted that he figured Sawatski would have been more likely to hit the fly ball than Musial, a comment which earned him criticism from St. Louis sportswriters Bob Burnes of the *Globe-Democrat* and Bob Broeg of the *Post-Dispatch*. Both writers pointed out that Stan had been wasted as a pinch-hitter in losing situations, started against left-handers, and on at least one occasion, benched against a right-handed pitcher. To Burnes and Broeg, it appeared as if the Cardinal front office was trying to humiliate Musial into retiring, a decision Stan was not prepared to make.

On Saturday, May 28, Stan was asked to Gussie Busch's estate, Grant's Farm, where he met with Busch, Cardinal executive vice president Dick Meyer, Bing Devine, and Sol Hemus, who broke the news to the Redbird superstar that he was going with a youth movement. Musial, batting .247, would be benched indefinitely. "Whatever you want is all right with me," said Stan, ever the professional, "though I think I can still help the ball club." In a press conference announcing the move, Devine denied the articles by Bob Burnes and Bob Broeg had motivated the decision. "The situation had been leading up to a point where we had to make a move," said Devine. "This change was prompted by the desirability and need of playing a set lineup over a longer stretch than Musial has been playing. The articles coincided with the club thinking." Questioned by reporters, Musial was wishful. "I think I'll be back in the lineup soon."

The Cardinal youth movement was hammered that afternoon for fifteen hits as the Giants posted an easy 8–0 victory. Musial, pinch-hitting in the sixth, was called out on strikes. Over the next twelve days, Stan pinch-hit four times and was unsuccessful in each appearance, proving decisively that thirty-nine-year-old superstars aren't at their best coming off the bench in pinch-hitting appearances.

On June 11, his average down to .235, Musial appeared in a Cardinal victory for the first time in two weeks, pinch-hitting and lining out as the Redbirds downed Pittsburgh. For the first time, the newspapers were reporting that the Cardinal superstar was thinking about retiring. Prior to the contest, St. Louis *Post-Dispatch* sportswriter Bob Broeg suggested to Pittsburgh manager Danny Murtaugh that Stan might be interested in playing first base for the Pirates. Murtaugh was stunned that the Cardinal front office would even entertain the idea of trading its all-time best ballplayer. Broeg hastily consulted with Musial and was somewhat surprised himself when Stan said yes, he might like a move back to his home state. When the rumors appeared in print, Sol Hemus quickly responded, "Stan's always been a Cardinal and I personally feel he'll wind up a Cardinal." Perhaps in jest, perhaps not, Musial replied, "You know the old expression: you finish in your home town."

Still acting as a non-official intermediary, Broeg spoke to Murtaugh again. Knowing his front office would never approve giving up a young player—Musial, after all, was almost forty years old—Murtaugh wondered if the Redbirds might give Stan his unconditional release. But Musial, conscious that St. Louis management and the Cardinal fans had always treated him well, let the deal fall through because he refused to ask the Cards to let him go. In making his decision, Stan missed the opportunity to play in the last World Series of his career.

When Musial pinch-hit on June 19, it marked his first appearance in nine games. A succession of Cardinal ballplayers had been installed in left field, but none had done the job. Since benching Stan, Hemus' "new look" Redbirds had posted a 14–12 record and risen to fourth place, but the club still trailed the Pirates by nine and a half games. On June 24, Stan was returned to the starting lineup for the first time since May 26. Batting .238 and more than a little rusty from his time on the bench, Musial threw out a runner at the plate during the contest and collected a single in four at-bats as the Cards lost to the Phillies, 4–3. Stan began to show signs of getting back in the groove almost immediately, but it took him until July 8 before he clubbed a home run, his first in six weeks. Hemus was pleased with his brainstorm to return the best hitter in the history of the National League to the lineup. Since returning, Musial had collected twenty-one hits in fifty at-bats for a robust .420 average, and he left for the All-Star game with an even .300 mark. "Stan's popping the ball again," said the Cardinal skipper, showing a flair for understatement, while admitting that sending Musial to the bench had been a mistake: "Musial has delivered the most key hits the last few weeks that I've seen any player get in years."

In the first All-Star Game of 1960, Stan stroked a pinch single as the National League posted a 5–3 win over the Americans. The hit was Musial's eighteenth in All-Star competition, his thirty-fifth total base, and his fifty-sixth at-bat, all records for the mid-summer classic. The second All-Star Game was held two days later. In his first appearance at Yankee Stadium since 1943, Stan became the only player in history to collect two All-Star pinch hits in one year when he slammed a home run into the third deck of the right-field bleachers off former teammate Gerry Staley in the seventh inning. Yankee scout Mayo Smith told Musial that the home run had moved him so much, he cried. Teammate Ken Boyer added a two-run clout of his own in the ninth as the National League coasted to a 6–0 win. "How does an old guy like me keep this up?" Musial quipped to reporters.

When the Cards resumed the second half of the season, Stan's hot bat helped pace the club to a .500 record and a share of third place. By August 11, when the Redbirds opened a five-game series at Forbes Field, the club had won thirty of its last forty-one outings. St. Louis was in second place, but still trailed Pittsburgh by five games. Musial's twelfth-inning, two-run homer snapped the Pirates' seven-game winning streak and gave the Redbirds a 3–2 win in the opening game of the series. Even though the Pirate pennant drive had been momentarily derailed, the partisan crowd gave Stan a standing ovation as he circled the bases. St. Louis won the second game handily, 9–2, as Musial delivered the key blow, a two-run single in a four-run seventh. The Redbirds were poised to move back into pennant contention. But former Cardinal Harvey Haddix captured a 4–1 decision the next night and the turning point of the season came when St. Louis lost both ends of a Sunday doubleheader. The Redbirds left town six games back.

The jittery Cardinals ran their losing streak to six games and by the time the Pirates arrived in St. Louis on August 26, St. Louis had dropped eight and a half games back. Musial, the old warhorse, broke a 1–1 tie with a two-run homer to propel the Redbirds to a 3–1 victory in the opening contest. The following evening, Stan raised his average to .296 with a single and his fourteenth round-tripper of the season, a solo shot with two down in the bottom of the ninth that gave the Cards a dramatic 5–4 win. The Redbirds completed their sweep of the series the next day with another 5–4 victory. Musial then fell into a horrendous slump in which he collected just three hits over his next thirty-one at-bats, his average falling to .274.

In a press conference on September 15, Stan announced his decision to return for the 1961 season. "This has been the toughest decision of my life," said Musial. Until the announcement came, most of Stan's friends had felt he would call it a career at the end of the 1960 campaign. "That was the way I felt about it all along, too," said Musial, smiling faintly, "until the last couple of weeks. Actually, I will be playing for the Cardinals next year for only one reason. The Cardinals asked me to reconsider any decision I had made about retiring. They felt that I could be of some help to the ball club in 1961. That, so help me, is the only reason I am coming back. In my whole career with the Cardinals, I have always tried to do what was best for the ball club."

Musial conceded he would like to play in one more World Series and insisted neither his salary nor the prospect of collecting more records figured in his decision. "I have all the records any man could ever want. One or two more aren't going to make any difference. This past season in particular, I played with no idea of shooting at any record. All I did was play each game as it came up. When somebody would tell me that I had reached a particular milestone or had passed somebody's record or set one, I was completely surprised. I'd like the total bases record, but I'm not worried about it."

Bing Devine praised Hemus for his careful handling of Musial. Hemus, vilified by Cardinal fans everywhere since benching the superstar back in May, defended himself against his detractors when he replied, "My only obligation is to twenty-five players on the club."

The next evening, Musial was honored in pre-game ceremonies at Busch Stadium by the National Council of the Boy Scouts. Dr. Delmer E. Wilson, National Director of Personnel, presented a scroll to Stan for his outstanding example as a churchman, community leader, and sportsman, the first time in the fifty-year history of the Boy Scouts that such an award had been made. The scroll read, "Because the example Stan has set throughout life parallels the Boy Scout Oath and Law, the Boy Scouts of America, in this year 1960 celebrating the fiftieth anniversary of the founding of Scouting in the United States, salute Stanley F. Musial for his many benefactions to youth."

Musial celebrated the presentation of the giant-size scroll with his seventeenth home run of the year, but the Cardinals spoiled the evening by losing to San Francisco. Two days later, Stan injured his left elbow and was reduced to pinch-hitting duties for the rest of the year. With Musial riding the bench, the Redbirds were officially eliminated from the pennant race on September 25. On the same day, Boston Red Sox owner Tom Yawkey announced that Stan's American League counterpart, forty-two-year-old Ted Williams, was retiring as an active player.

The Cardinals closed out the season at 86–68, in third place, nine games behind the Pirates. There was hope for the future. Ernie Broglio had become the first twenty-game winner on the club since 1953 and reliever Lindy McDaniel had posted twelve victories and saved twenty-six games. From a .300 average at the All-Star break, Musial had tailed off to .275, twenty points higher than the .255 he had posted in 1959. Stan had hit seventeen home runs and collected sixty-three RBIs, nineteen more than the year before. Just two months shy of his fortieth birthday, Stan said, "Other players have stayed on at that age. And I feel I can, too."

◆ ◆ ◆

Many of his friends had urged him to quit after 1960, but Stan still believed he had one more good year left in him. So a forty-year-old Musial was in left field on Opening Night, huffing and puffing as he legged out a triple in a ten-inning 2–1 win over the Braves. But after the first week, Stan was hitting just .235, with four hits in seventeen trips to the plate. The Cardinals, so full of hope before the season, were devastated by injuries to shortstop Daryl Spencer, first baseman Bill White, second baseman Julian Javier, third baseman Ken Boyer, and pitchers Larry Jackson and Lindy McDaniel. Ironically, Musial, the oldest man on the club, was one of the most able-bodied.

Despite the occasional good game, Stan's average had fallen to .220 when Sol Hemus benched him for good on April 26. By May 5, after several unsuccessful pinch-hitting appearances, Stan's average was down to .205. Hemus revealed his latest plan to reporters: Musial would play long stretches, then have long rest periods. The Cardinal skipper insisted that Stan was out of the lineup only because of the cold weather and the necessity of looking at the young outfielders before cutdown time. "Musial will be back in the very near future," said Hemus. "Platooning is out for Stan, at least for the time being. I don't think you get the most out of him that way."

Musial didn't make another start until May 7 when he was blanked in three at-bats in a victory over the Cubs, his average slipping to a lowly .191. In the Redbirds' next game, Musial had already singled and doubled when he drew a leadoff walk in the eighth, representing the tying run. Hemus inserted pitcher Ray Sadecki as a pinch-runner and the Cardinal hurler advanced to second as Daryl Spencer also drew a base on balls. When Joe Cunningham attempted to bunt, Sadecki wandered too far from the bag and was picked off by Cincinnati catcher Bob Schmidt, a base-running blunder which brought quite a lot of heat down on Hemus. It seems unlikely Musial would have made the same mistake.

Stan's batting average slowly began to rise. By May 18, following a three-for-four performance in a 4–3 loss to the Pirates, he was hitting .262. Three days later, Musial singled for career hit number 3,311, tying him with Eddie Collins for fourth place on the all-time list. On May 22, Stan slammed a ninth-inning home run which gave the Redbirds a win over Chicago and snapped a St. Louis six-game losing streak. The round-tripper broke the tie with Collins and moved Musial into fifth place on the all-time major-league runs scored list, having crossed the plate 1,819 times in his career. A day later, with two hits off San Francisco hurler Jack Sanford, Stan raised his average to .282. "Musial almost took my head off in the second inning [with a single through the pitcher's box]," said Sanford. "He always has hit me. He'll probably be able to hit me when he's in his rocking chair."

On May 28, Stan rapped a pair of singles and slammed his fourth homer of the year, raising his average to .312, tops on the club and the first time on the year he had crested the .300 plateau. But, inexplicably, Hemus benched the Cardinal superstar the next evening when Pittsburgh southpaw Harvey Haddix took the mound against St. Louis, as though Musial, after almost two decades in the major leagues, had forgotten how to hit left-handers.

Playing with an abscessed tooth on June 7, Musial singled twice and blasted two two-run homers as the Redbirds downed Chicago and moved to within a victory of .500. Stan's four-for-four performance left him ninety-nine safeties shy of Honus Wagner's National record of 3,430 hits. Two weeks later, Musial proved a pet theory of his that a hitter can concentrate better when he isn't feeling well. Bothered by a nagging cold and a pulled leg muscle, Stan slammed a three-run homer to give the Cards a 3–0 lead over the Giants. In the seventh, with the sacks jammed and the Redbirds leading by one, Stan crushed a Stu Miller fastball for the ninth grand-slam home run of his career, giving the Birds a 10–5 victory over San Francisco. Musial's eighth and ninth round-trippers of the year tied the highest single-game RBI total of his career, seven, and gave him 2,340 extra-base hits, replacing Lou Gehrig in second place on the all-time list. But when a rookie southpaw started for the Giants the next evening, Musial found himself back on the bench.

Stan reached another career milestone three days later when he batted for the ten thousandth time. Home plate umpire Al Barlick took Musial by surprise when he proffered his hand in congratulations to the Cardinal superstar for his accomplishment. Remembering the non-fraternization rule, Stan hesitated. Barlick smiled warmly and said, "Aw, you're not worried about all the fans, are you? The heck with that now."

"So I shook hands with him," said Stan. "I think that's the first time an umpire has ever shaken hands with me during a game."

Nearly halfway through the season, Stan led all Cardinal regulars in home runs, was second among all regulars in batting average, and trailed only Ken Boyer in runs batted in, thirty-six to thirty-five. Boyer had come to the plate eighty-five times more often.

On July 5, with the Cardinals at 33–41, Anheuser-Busch released the fiery Sol Hemus and replaced him with minor-league pilot Johnny Keane, the eighth St. Louis manager since 1950. The Redbirds skidded to the All-Star break with a 36–43 record, in sixth place, fifteen and a half games behind the Cincinnati Reds. In the first All-Star Game, played July 11 at Candlestick Park in San Francisco and won by the National League in ten innings, Musial pinch-hit for Cincinnati pitcher Bob Purkey and flied out to left field. Stan continued to hover around the .300 mark while the Redbirds fell below .500 again. On July 31, Musial was given a lengthy standing ovation when he came to the plate in the fifth inning of 1961's second All-Star Game to pinch-hit for Philadelphia hurler Art Mahaffey. Swinging for Fenway's Green Monster, the tantalizingly close left-field wall, Stan struck out. Stan left for New York immediately following the contest to be honored by *Sport* magazine as the outstanding athlete of the last fifteen years.

But the hot summer was beginning to take its toll on Stan the Man. By early August, Musial had collected just two hits in his last twenty-six trips to the plate and had fallen below .300 again. September 17 was Stan Musial Day at Forbes Field, Pittsburgh. On hand for the ceremonies were John Bunardzya, the sports editor of *The Valley Independent* of Donora; Donora Mayor Albert Delsandro; and Dr. Michael "Ki" Duda, president of the California (PA) State Teachers College and Stan's former high school coach. In front of dozens of friends and members of his family, Musial slammed the 443rd home run of his career, making it a perfect day as he paced the Redbirds to a 3–0 win over the Bucs.

While the nation's attention was riveted on Roger Maris's pursuit of Babe Ruth's home run record, the 1961 baseball season entered its final two weeks. Helen Kloz, the librarian from Donora who had urged Musial to sign his first baseball contract over two decades earlier, was in the stands one evening as the Cards played the Phillies. "This is probably the last time I'll see you play, Stan," she said. "Won't you hit a home run for me?" Musial was batting .285 at the time, but forty-year-old ballplayers rarely hit home runs on request. Stan was less than optimistic about his chances to make Miss Kloz's wish come true. With the wind blowing in, Musial was lucky enough to get hold of a John Buzhardt fastball and drive it into the right-field stands, bringing a smile to the face of the woman who, perhaps more than anyone else, was responsible for his career. The round-tripper held a great deal of sentimental value for the Cardinal legend.

Two weeks later, Musial closed out the season with two hits against the Cubs. Stan had finished the year with a .288 average, thirteen points better than 1960, had driven in seventy runs with just 107 hits, and collected fifteen home runs. (Musial would go on to hit forty-six home runs after his fortieth birthday, the most of anyone in the history of the National League.)

Under their patient new skipper, Johnny Keane, the Cardinals had quietly posted a 47–33 record to finish the season at 80–74. In the final weeks of the year, Keane called Musial aside and said, "Stan, I want you back, not to play less next year, but to play more. I've watched you and I'm convinced that you could have played more. What do you think?" Relieved to be out from under the heavy-handed direction of Sol Hemus, Musial welcomed the challenge. "Good," said Keane. "Get yourself in the best possible shape. If next year is going to be your last one, make it one to be remembered."

There wasn't a Cardinal fan on the planet who could have predicted what happened next.

◇**17**◇

Comeback

Along with great skill, he is distinguished by
something simple and old-fashioned called
character. Nobody ever had to lecture him,
as New York's Mayor Jimmy Walker
once lectured Babe Ruth, on his
obligation to "the kids."

LIFE MAGAZINE, AUGUST 10, 1962

Forty-one-year-old Stan Musial was the relic of the National League. But in spring training, he worked hard and showed the youngsters who wanted his job that he still knew a thing or two about hitting when he batted .339. When the Cards headed north after an 18–8 record in the Grapefruit League, KMOX, the Redbirds' flagship radio station, ran a half-page advertisement in both major St. Louis newspapers, announcing the station would again be broadcasting the games in 1962. The ad featured a giant photograph of Musial and referred to Stan as the symbol of the team. Manager Johnny Keane announced that Musial was one of the key members of the squad and would be starting the opening game. "We're looking for Stan to play at least one hundred games," said the Cardinal skipper, "and do about what he did last year."

Center fielder Curt Flood was going to be flanked by Musial in right and thirty-nine-year-old Minnie Minoso in left. "We expect to keep Curt Flood in great condition all summer," quipped Stan.

The Cardinals opened the 1962 season on April 11 with a crushing 11–4 victory over the New York Mets in the first game in the history of that franchise. Musial, disproving the adage that baseball is a young man's game, was three-for-three and scored the 1,859th run of his career in the contest, tying the National League record held by Mel Ott. A day later, Stan broke Ott's record in a fifteen-inning victory over the Cubs. On April 15, in a 9–4 win over the Mets, Musial, the youngster with a twenty-one-year career behind him, drove in three runs with a pair of singles and tied Babe Ruth for second place on the all-time total bases list. It seemed every time Stan stepped on the field, he was setting a record of some kind.

The season was just six games old, but the Cardinals were undefeated and Musial was batting an astounding .458, with eleven hits in twenty-four at-bats. St. Louis fans, giddy with optimism, had their bubble burst a day later when the Redbirds were swept in a twin bill by the Cubs. Stan singled in four trips to the plate in the opening contest, a hit which enabled him to pass Babe Ruth for second place on the all-time list for total bases. The only ballplayer ahead of him was Ty Cobb, with 5,863. Musial was a safe bet to overtake the Georgia Peach before year's end.

By May 1, Stan was batting .396, second-best in the league to teammate Curt Flood's .435. Keane was using Musial carefully, allowing the superstar to husband his strength for the upcoming hot summer months. Stan was trying hard to justify his skipper's confidence. On Sunday, May 7, the Cards were trailing Cincinnati by a run and had the bases loaded in the top of the ninth. Musial faced reliever Dave Sisler, a journeyman hurler who, in former years, would have been duck soup for the Cardinal veteran. But Stan got under Sisler's delivery a bit too much and popped a foul fly to the catcher for the second out of the inning. Ken Boyer then hit a long fly ball that, one out earlier, would have tied the score. The loss hanging heavily on his mind, Musial dragged himself into the Crosley Field clubhouse, knowing he wouldn't play again until Tuesday night. Just then, Keane slapped him on the back and said, "You're playing the second game, Stan, and you'll get four hits."

Musial didn't quite fulfill Keane's prediction, but he did get three hits, the final one a three-run homer in the ninth that gave the Redbirds a 3–0 victory. By appearing in both ends of the doubleheader, Musial eclipsed Pittsburgh shortstop Honus Wagner's National League mark for most games (2,787), and was just six hits shy of reaching the Flying Dutchman's league record 3,430 hits. "Somehow it doesn't seem to be making me as nervous as when I was getting close to three thousand hits," said Stan, speaking to reporters after the twin bill. "Maybe it will be different the closer I get."

With his usual modesty, Stan took a moment to reflect on his distinguished career in the game he loved so much. "Baseball still is a lot of fun to me. That is what counts. As long as I can do a good job, as long as I can help the ball club, I want to play. I still get a kick out of it. Getting close to Wagner's record reminds me of the time when I had just won my first batting title [1943]. At one of those affairs in the winter, Wagner came over to my home town. I always appreciated it that he thought enough to bother to come. He told me that he had won seven or eight batting titles and he hoped I'd be able to match him. I never thought then that I'd be up there so close to his records."

Tuesday evening came and Musial, with a double and home run number 449 of his career, seemed to be in a hurry to reach Wagner's record. Stan collected a pair of singles the next night, boosting his average to .394, best in the National League, and was now just one hit shy of tying the record Wagner had set forty-five years earlier. All systems were go for the eager Musial, who promptly fell into an oh-for-thirteen slump, losing fifty points off his batting average. "I have about five hundred feet of film on Stan Musial shooting for the hit record," complained Cardinal catching coach Hal Smith, "and I don't have a thing to show for it yet." Smith wasn't the only ballplayer perched on the top step of the dugout waiting for this moment of history, armed with his trusty 8mm box. In addition to the amateurs, professional cameramen from all corners of the nation used every possible vantage point, hoping to catch the big hit for posterity.

Wednesday, May 16, Candlestick Park. With one out in the sixth, Musial stepped up and lashed a Juan Marichal fastball into right-center field for a single, hit number 3,430. The safety tied Wagner's National League mark and gave Stan an even forty records for his career. After nearly 2,800 major-league ball games, the Cardinal veteran was now just one safety shy of establishing a new National League record for hits, thirty RBIs from Mel Ott's record for runs batted in (1,860), and forty total bases from Ty Cobb's record (5,863). In the clubhouse after the game, Stan was relieved the chase was over. "I guess I was trying to pull the ball last week," he said, "and hoping to hit a home run. But this time, I just tried to hit to left field."

In the crowd at Candlestick Park that day was Jim Tobin, the pitcher off whom Musial had gotten his first hit two decades earlier. "What are you looking for, another hit?" joshed Tobin after Stan had located him in the stands.

If Musial thought he had left his slump behind after gathering in the record-tying hit, he was wrong. Hitless in his next eight at-bats, Stan came to the plate two days later to face the Dodgers' premier reliever, Ron Perranoski. Musial reached for an outside pitch and laced a single into right field. The crowd of almost forty-five thousand gave the Cardinal legend a standing ovation when he reached first base. Not realizing how badly he had wanted the record, Stan felt his legs go limp. After his history-making hit, Musial stood on first base, waiting for a pinch-runner, while the crowd roared its approval of the greatest National League hitter of all time. At long last, Don Landrum trotted out to take Stan's place on the bag and the Cardinal superstar scampered off the field and into the St. Louis dugout shouting, "I got it! I got it!" at the top of his lungs. "I kept you waiting," said manager Johnny Keane, "because the fans were giving you such a big hand that I didn't want to spoil their fun." Back in St. Louis, Lillian had fallen asleep and had missed her husband's big moment. "I guess I'm too old for this game," said Lil. "It's for young people, like Stan."

Musial admitted after the contest, "I never worked so hard as I did for the last two," and during a post-game interview with Cardinal announcer Harry Caray, ordered "drinks for the house" at his restaurant back in St. Louis. Johnny Keane, commenting on Stan's usual placid manner, told reporters, "This is the first time I've ever seen Stan show emotion in all the years I've been with the club."

Musial's record-breaking hit garnered him coverage in both *Time* and *Newsweek* magazines. In an article entitled, "A Saint with Money," featured in the sport section of the May 25 issue, *Time* magazine said:

> Musial, his reflexes still sharp and his aging muscles still limber, keeps right on playing for the Cards with a young man's speed. And each time he uncoils from his familiar, knock-kneed batting crouch to hammer a single over second, he rewrites baseball's record book. Even today, says Los Angeles Dodger Coach Leo Durocher, "there is only one way to pitch to Musial—under the plate." Stan Musial seems pleasantly out of place—living proof that nice guys do not necessarily finish last. Nobody has ever seen him sulk or throw a tantrum. Unlike Ruth, he never punched a cop. Unlike Cobb, he has never attacked a crippled heckler in the stands. Unlike Wagner, he has never stuffed a ball into a base runner's teeth.

Three days later, *Newsweek* featured a reflective Musial in its sports section. Stan said he had no delusions about the quality of his play at age forty-one. "The big difference now," he said nostalgically, "is that there are no more big days, no more four-for-fours. Most of the time, I'm out for a pinch-runner or another fielder."

Despite Musial's achievements, the Cardinals were struggling. By the end of May, the Redbirds had sunk to fourth place and trailed the Giants by six games. Stan skipped the game of May 29 to fly back to St. Louis for the graduation of daughter Gerry from Villa Duchesne. On Sunday, June 3, Musial and Lillian attended graduation exercises for son Dick at Notre Dame in South Bend, Indiana. Stan found the shoe on the other foot the next day when he received an honorary Doctor of Humanities degree from Monmouth (Illinois) College.

The Redbirds reeled off a seven-game winning streak at home and closed to within six games of first place. Musial, with twelve hits in his last twenty-seven at-bats, had belted the ball around for a .440 clip at Busch Stadium and was hitting .340, fourth best in the league. On June 22, Stan tied Ty Cobb's major-league record for total bases with a home run off Philadelphia's Paul Brown, a pitcher young enough to be his son. Musial batted again in the inning and rapped a two-run single off reliever Dallas Green to capture the mark all for himself. The crowd of twenty-seven thousand gave Stan a standing ovation when the record was announced. Trainer Bob Bauman retrieved the ball from umpire Stan Landes for Stan's already bulging trophy case. When Musial spoke to reporters at the end of the day, he confessed he had been under the impression Babe Ruth had held the previous record for total bases. "For some reason, this is one record I never paid much attention to. I can't understand it, because my friends tell me this is a record which will be talked about for a long time. That's an awful lot of total bases." Stan added, "I'm glad I finally broke a record in my own state."

Musial now led all National League hitters with a .345 average, but manager Johnny Keane was fearful that Stan might not get enough plate appearances to qualify for his eighth batting championship. "I don't think it's possible," said Keane, "to get him in that many games and give him enough rest to keep strong." (Under the rules, Musial needed 3.1 appearances for each game. Sixty-nine contests into the season, he was averaging only 2.84.) Over the next two weeks, Stan's average fell to .324, seventh best in the league. On July 7, Musial's 453rd career home run gave St. Louis a 3–2 win over the Mets. The next afternoon, the Cardinal superstar had one of the biggest days of his lifetime as he tuned up for the All-Star Game.

After first baseman Bill White clubbed a solo home run off New York starting pitcher Jay Hook in the first, Musial made it a back-to-back effort with his tenth round-tripper of the year. In the fourth, Stan touched Hook for his second home run of the day, a two-run shot which gave the Cardinals a 6–0 lead. In the seventh, off reliever Willard Hunter, Musial blasted his third homer of the day and his fourth in as many at-bats. As Stan stepped on home plate, he turned toward the Cardinal dugout and smiled at Lillian, sitting above the dugout, remembering how his wife had missed the other three-homer performances. Musial's fourth consecutive round-tripper tied a major-league record held by twelve other players. The last National Leaguer to perform the Herculean feat had been Ralph Kiner back in 1947 and the most recent American League player to do so was Mickey Mantle, just four days earlier. Stan had an opportunity to become the first ballplayer to hit five in a row when he came to the plate in the eighth. Trying too hard, he struck out swinging. At that, the ball eluded catcher Chris Cannizzaro and Musial reached first base safely. The Redbirds went on to win the game handily, 15–1, and long after the contest was over, Musial stood patiently and signed autographs for a group of Little Leaguers who couldn't seem to stop shouting, "We want Stan! We want Stan!"

Musial reached the All-Star Game batting .333, his lifetime average. On July 10, at D.C. Stadium in Washington, D.C., President John F. Kennedy emerged from the American League dugout to take his place in the presidential box. Summoned to the stands by a Kennedy aide, Stan shook hands with the President and reminded him of the time, two years earlier, when they had first met in Milwaukee. Kennedy had said on that occasion, "They tell me you're too old to play ball and I'm too young to run for president. I have a hunch we'll both fool 'em."

Musial added, "I think we're both doing a good job," earning a laugh from the President.

Stan was on the bench when the game began, but got his chance to hit in the sixth inning of a scoreless tie when he was sent up to bat for pitcher Juan Marichal. Minnesota's Camilo Pascual got two quick strikes on the Cardinal legend, then tried to slip a curveball past on the inside corner. Musial stepped back and rocketed the ball into right field for a single, his third pinch hit in All-Star competition and what proved to be his final safety of the mid-summer classic. Kennedy and the rest of the American League partisan crowd gave Stan a standing ovation as he left the game in favor of pinch-runner Maury Wills. The Nationals went on to score two runs in the inning, en route to a 3–1 victory, the senior circuit's fourth straight win. Musial now held All-Star records for most games played (22), base hits (20), total bases (40), and at-bats (60). "I had played in a lot of All-Star games before," explained Stan, "but playing here in the nation's capital and before the President of the United States somehow gave me a warm feeling. I don't know how to explain it, but it felt good." When told by a reporter that the President had cheered him, Musial beamed and said, "The President is my buddy."

Later that day, Stan, Lillian, and daughter Janet visited the White House where they were presented an autographed picture of Musial and Kennedy shaking hands before the All-Star Game, then given a tour of the President's residence.

On Sunday, July 14, in the second game of a doubleheader with Pittsburgh at Forbes Field, Musial broke Honus Wagner's National League record for at-bats when he came to the plate for the 10,428th time in his career. The next day, Stan boosted his batting average to .348, second-best in the National League, with a perfect three-for-three against the Bucs. A week later, just a few hours after former Dodger Jackie Robinson became the first black man to enter baseball's Hall of Fame, Musial's double against Los Angeles tied Mel Ott for the National League lead in runs batted in, with 1,860. But Stan's delight turned to embarrassment a moment later when he was picked off second base by Stan Williams. Musial added a single later in the contest, giving him two-for-three on the evening and the league's best batting average, then became the National League's all-time leader in RBIs the next night with a two-run homer.

With seventeen hits in his last thirty-three at-bats, Stan's average stood at .351. But with the season two-thirds gone, he still needed an additional 210 plate appearances to qualify for the batting title. "I don't think I'll have enough times at bat," said Musial, who admitted, "Actually, I haven't been thinking about that. I'm not concerned about those things any more." When told that Stan might not qualify, Los Angeles center fielder Willie Davis, who trailed Musial by three points, said "I hope not."

In 1962's second All-Star Game, held on July 30 at Wrigley Field, Stan pinch-hit and grounded out in the third, then went into the game playing left field. On the evening, he was hitless in two at-bats. Musial began the last leg of the 1962 season with four straight multiple-hit games and boosted his league-leading average to its highest point of the year, .359, before falling into a one-for-seventeen slump. With 346 trips to the plate, Stan was on a pace to finish with 476 appearances, twenty-six short of qualifying for the batting title. Johnny Keane had handled Musial's playing time carefully to this point, but now, knowing how much an eighth batting championship would mean to Stan, especially at his age, Keane decided Musial would begin playing a little more often.

On August 13, with the Redbirds languishing in fifth place, thirteen and a half games behind the Dodgers, team owner Gussie Busch sounded off. Busch exonerated manager Johnny Keane, but threatened a major shakeup in the front office which might include Bing Devine, chief of player procurement Wally Shannon, and troubleshooter Eddie Stanky. "As far as I'm concerned," railed Busch, "I'm almost at the point where I'd trade just about everybody." Everybody, that is, but the three players he designated as untouchable: Musial, center fielder Curt Flood, and pitcher Bob Gibson, who was blossoming into one of the game's best pitchers. Gibson, asked for his reaction to the Cardinal owner's tirade, thought for a moment and admitted, "I guess we have been disappointing, at that. Maybe he ought to sell the club." Standing within earshot, Musial cracked, "I'll buy it."

Busch's pep talk had little effect on the Redbirds, who took ten innings to lose to the Colts the next evening, and even less on the Cardinals' oldest veteran, who was hitless in his third straight game, his average falling to .339.

Hitting or not, Stan was an enormously popular ballplayer. On August 18, he was given a special night by the Mets at New York's Polo Grounds, the first such honor for a visiting player in the eighty-year history of the park. Musial had insisted that he wanted no expensive gifts and the New York front office suggested a Stan Musial scholarship fund at Columbia College, Lou Gehrig's alma mater. *Naked City* television actor Horace McMahon, one of Stan's close friends, said the fund expected to realize eight thousand dollars. Musial's wife Lillian and daughters Jeanie, Janet, and Gerry were on hand for the pre-game ceremonies along with dozens of other guests. Stan received a telegram from President Kennedy which read:

> Congratulations on two decades of achievement in the major leagues. In 1942, you batted .315 and now twenty years later you are batting .337. You make us all believe that life really begins at forty.
> With warmest regards, John F. Kennedy.

In addition to the President's telegram, Musial's gifts included a portable typewriter from New York baseball writers, a mounted photostat of *The New York Times* for his birthdate, November 21, 1920, a year's supply of coffee from restaurateur Toots Shor, a shotgun, a home machine shop, golf clubs, sport shirts, a framed portrait, and a fishing rod from Ted Williams. New York manager Casey Stengel gave Musial a plaque on behalf of the club which read:

> The New York fans, through the Mets, salute the greatest ball player of his generation for over two decades. Stan Musial of the St. Louis Cardinals has enhanced the prestige of the National League both on and off the field.

"And if those fellas in St. Louis decide they don't want you," added Casey, "we want you with the Mets. You'd be a great asset to our organization."

While Musial's youngest daughter, Jeanie, danced on home plate, Stan clung nervously to the microphone and shook with emotion when he spoke to the New York fans. "I especially want to thank the Mets," said Musial, "for bringing National League baseball back to New York so that I could play here once more." The Cardinals made it a perfect day when they swept the doubleheader. With the Redbirds well ahead in the nightcap and the fans chanting, "We want Musial! We want Musial!" more loudly with every passing moment, Keane sent Stan up to pinch-hit. Jittery at the reception accorded an opposition player, New York reliever Bob Moorhead walked the Cardinal veteran on four pitches. Musial received his third standing ovation of the day when he left the game in favor of a pinch-runner. The following evening, fans at the Polo Grounds booed when the Cardinal starting lineup was announced and Musial wasn't in it.

On September 1, the Cards posted a 10–5 win over the Mets, the high point of the contest coming when Stan laced a double to right field for the 3,515th hit of his career. That tied him with Tris Speaker for the number two slot on the all-time major-league list. Ahead of Musial stood Ty Cobb who, at 4,191 hits, was untouchable. The following night, Stan lined a pinch single to pass Speaker.

On September 7, manager Johnny Keane was rehired for the 1963 season and the Redbirds celebrated their skipper's new contract by crushing Milwaukee, 7–1. But the long season began to slow Stan down. Musial fell into another slump, during which he collected just four hits in twenty-seven at-bats. Stan was now hitting .327, sixteen points behind Tommy Davis and Cincinnati's Frank Robinson, who were tied for the league lead in batting. On September 27, Musial enjoyed the last five-for-five day of his career, boosting his average to .333. When the Cards arrived at Los Angeles for a three-game series beginning on September 28, the Redbirds had a chance to play spoiler in the pennant race. The Dodgers needed just one victory to clinch at least a tie for the pennant. But they never got that win.

On the last Friday of the season, St. Louis downed Los Angeles in ten innings while Musial, two-for-five, raised his average to .334. On Saturday evening, Ernie Broglio shut out the Dodgers, 2–0, and on the last day of the season, Curt Simmons blanked Los Angeles, 1–0, to force a playoff between San Francisco and Los Angeles. The Giants won the playoff and went on to lose to the Yankees in the World Series, four games to three.

The Cardinals had improved their record to 84–78, but dropped from fifth place to sixth in the standings. Musial had refused to act his age, clubbing nineteen home runs and collecting eighty-two RBIs, his highest total since 1957. Never a particularly effective pinch-hitter, Stan had compiled an incredible .615 average off the bench, stroking eight hits in thirteen at-bats and drawing six bases on balls. And even though he had closed out the season with just one hit in his last eight trips to the plate, Musial had qualified for the batting crown with 505 plate appearances. Stan's .330 mark, third-best in the league, was the highest in modern day major-league baseball history for anyone his age, eclipsed only by Cap Anson of the 1894–95–96 Chicago White Stockings.

A month after the season ended, Branch Rickey returned to the Cardinals as a special consultant on player personnel, exactly twenty years to the day after he left the organization. The eighty-year-old Mahatma had been in virtual retirement since stepping down as the Pirates general manager in 1955, and almost immediately embarrassed general manager Bing Devine and field manager Johnny Keane by publicly stating his belief that Musial should have retired at the end of the season.

Asked for his opinion, Gussie Busch replied gruffly, "Since when do you ask a .330 hitter to retire?"

◇18◇

Once More,
with Feeling

---

*Stan Musial is an undramatic man. He has
an uncluttered mind. He is not obsessed with
the ego problems that infest Ted Williams;
he has none of the depressive fears that grip
Willie Mays; he cannot showboat like Willie
Davis; he has none of the fitful violence of Al
Dark or Gene Mauch.*

WRITER ARNOLD HANO

Stan Musial was forty-two years old. It didn't seem possible.

One generation of fans had watched this youngster from his first days in the majors, comparing him to the greats of yesteryear, the Cobbs, Speakers, Wagners. Another generation, about the same age as Stan, had reached its own mid-life point right along with him. And there was that third generation, the children, who grew up idolizing and imitating him. This last group was in their twenties now, some graduating college and looking for jobs, others still yearning for a life like his. And each generation could remember

189

Musial running the bases, chasing down fly balls, lining doubles off the right-field screen at Sportsman's Park.

But the Stan Musial who arrived at spring training in 1963 wasn't that Musial of yesterday. In baseball age, he was an old man. On the field, he often looked like an old man: no longer fleet of foot on the basepaths or in the outfield, frequently fooled by the slider, having trouble hitting the fastball. If the 1962 season felt like old times to Musial, 1963 would be nothing but hard work.

Three consecutive successful spring training seasons had failed to produce a pennant for the Cardinals, and when the Redbirds left St. Petersburg in early April with a 15–14 record, St. Louis fans hoped the mediocre showing might be a good harbinger. Musial had posted a respectable .280 batting average in the Grapefruit League and was eager, despite the introduction of a new and expanded strike zone, to begin what would prove to be his last major-league season. "I've been trying to lay off that high pitch all my life," groused Baltimore slugger Jim Gentile, "and now it's a strike." Stan had a different view of the new rule. "If the pitch looks good to me," said Musial, "I swing at it. I don't need an umpire to tell me whether the pitch is a ball or a strike."

On the final Opening Day of his career, Musial played left field and was one-for-three as Ernie Broglio shut out the New York Mets. Lefty Ray Washburn blanked the Mets a day later and Curt Simmons ran the Redbirds scoreless string to twenty-seven innings with a 7–0 whitewash in the home opener at Busch Stadium. But the bubble burst two days later when the Phillies swept a doubleheader from St. Louis. A week later, with ten wins in their first fifteen games, the Cardinals took over the National League lead.

But Musial, batting just .237, was having problems. Age had eroded his considerable playing skills.

Stan took a private hitting drill at Busch Stadium, but didn't get a chance to try out his new batting eye until May 2 when his seventh-inning bases-loaded double drove home three teammates and gave Ray Washburn a 4–3 win over the Cubs. The two-bagger boosted Stan's extra-base hit collection to 1,356 and tied him with Babe Ruth for the number one position on the all-time list. The RBI gave Musial 1,901 for his career, fourth behind Jimmie Foxx (1,921), Ty Cobb (1,961), Lou Gehrig (1,991), and Ruth (2,209).

Two days later, Stan suffered a personal loss when his longtime pal Dickie Kerr passed away in Houston at sixty-nine years of age. "Baseball has lost a real friend," said Musial. He and Lillian flew to Texas to attend the funeral.

Before the home folks at Busch Stadium on May 8, Stan captured the major-league record for extra-base hits with a fourth-inning solo home run off Bob Miller in an 11–5 loss to the Dodgers. *Time* mentioned the hit in the magazine's sport section, adding that "Stan the Man is not quite ready for the rocking chair." The defeat was the fifth in the last six outings for the Cardinals, who had dropped to fourth place, two games behind the league-leading Giants.

By the end of May, Musial had raised his batting average to .277. Stan opened June with a trio of singles and two RBIs in a victory over the Giants, but he broke a blood vessel behind his right knee running out his last base hit. Musial was in the lineup the next afternoon, but felt something pop in the knee and was forced to leave the contest for a pinch-runner. Stan insisted on playing the next scheduled game, but hobbled about the diamond and failed to hit the ball out of the infield in four attempts. Musial sat out the next two games, then returned to the lineup on June 8 when Ernie Broglio two-hit everybody's favorite doormat, the Mets. The following day, Stan committed a two-base error which led to a pair of unearned runs as New York defeated St. Louis in the first game of a twin bill, 8–7. Musial left the contest in the sixth inning for a diathermy treatment. The Cards salvaged the nightcap, but fell to second place, a half game behind the Dodgers. A day later, Stan was on the bench again when the Redbirds took over sole possession of the National League top spot with a 3–1 win over the Pirates. In late June and early July, St. Louis suffered through an eight-game losing streak which left the club with a 46–38 record at the All-Star break, four and a half games behind the Dodgers.

On July 9, Musial made his twenty-fourth All-Star appearance. Had baseball officials known this would be Stan's swan song in the mid-summer classic, some ceremony would have been forthcoming. Stan pinch-hit against Detroit's Jim Bunning in the fifth and hit the ball on the nose, but lined out to Al Kaline in right field. The Nationals won the game, 5–3, with former Cardinal pitcher Larry Jackson posting the victory.

Musial was one-for-four in both ends of a doubleheader split with the Braves when the Redbirds resumed play in the second half of the season, then went seven straight games without a hit, including three strikeouts in four pinch-hit appearances. Reluctantly, Johnny Keane benched the Cardinal legend. Stan didn't return to the lineup until July 25, when his RBI double handed fellow senior citizen Warren Spahn a 3–1 defeat.

When Musial offhandedly told a writer that he hated to think 1963 would mark his last All-Star appearance, he realized he hadn't come to a firm decision about whether or not to return in 1964. On July 26, Stan was invited to breakfast with Cardinal general manager Bing Devine, who wanted to know what his plans were. Musial had given the future careful thought. "After this year," he said, "I'll have had it." Devine, the first to witness the end of an era, asked Stan how he wanted to handle his decision. Musial replied that he wanted to make the announcement to his teammates at the annual Cardinal team picnic on August 12.

A day later, the Academy of Sports Editors, a group of one hundred editors from the largest newspapers in the country, voted Stan the seventh spot on their all-time top ten list of ballplayers, preceded, respectively, by Ty Cobb (93), Babe Ruth (90), Rogers Hornsby (52), Honus Wagner (41), Joe DiMaggio (35), and Walter Johnson (34), and followed by Christy Mathewson (26), Tris Speaker (23), and Ted Williams (15). (Percentage of votes received are shown in parentheses.) Musial was named on twenty-eight percent of the ballots.

Stan didn't return to the starting lineup until August 1, when the Cards downed Cincinnati and moved into a tie for second place, four and a half games behind the Dodgers. A little over a week later, at the annual Cardinal team picnic held at Gussie Busch's estate, Grant's Farm, a smiling and tearful Stan Musial shocked the baseball world when he announced that he would be retiring at the end of the season. "Even when I signed this winter, I had the feeling that this would be my last year," conceded Stan, who added, "I just think I've had enough."

"It's a sad day for baseball, the Cardinals, and St. Louis," noted Devine, echoing the sentiments of baseball fans everywhere. There were many tributes to Musial that day, all of them delivered quietly, some delivered with voices choked with emotion. Traveling secretary Leo Ward confessed he had the best job in baseball, "traveling with the Cardinals and watching Musial hit." Team captain Ken Boyer called Stan "an inspiration, the leader who's won for us," and turning to Musial, added, "My congratulations to the greatest player who ever put on a uniform." Johnny Keane agreed: "My greatest thrill has been putting on the same uniform worn by Stan Musial." But perhaps Lillian Musial put it best when she stammered through her tears, "I hate to see it end. It's been so much fun."

Stan's greatest hope now was that he could go out on a winner, and Cardinal chances brightened somewhat when they swept a three-game series from the Giants a few days later. On Sunday, August 18, it was announced that Musial would be honored following the season with the Dr. Robert F. Hyland Award for meritorious service at a special retirement dinner given by the St. Louis chapter of the Baseball Writers Association. The dinner would kick off a fund-raising effort to erect a statue of the

Cardinal superstar at the site of the proposed new downtown stadium. NBC sportscaster Joe Garagiola had already agreed to emcee the dinner.

Two days later, the Cardinals set out for the West Coast and what proved to be a disastrous road trip. In his final visit to Los Angeles, Musial was honored by the Los Angeles County Board of Supervisors and the Viking Social Club, but the Dodgers spoiled the celebration by taking two out of three. Two losses at Houston dropped the Redbirds into a second-place tie, six games out. Musial was named an honorary mayor at San Francisco, but the kudos failed to impress the Giants, who took two of three at Candlestick Park. Stan was mired in a five-game drought during which his average fell to .245, but opened September with a double against the Pirates, giving him 724 two-baggers for his career and a tie with Ty Cobb for second place on the all-time list.

In the early hours of September 11, Stan's daughter-in-law, Mrs. Dick Musial, gave birth to a son, Jeffrey Stanton Musial, at Fort Riley, Kansas, where twenty-three-year-old Dick was stationed as an Army lieutenant. Musial passed out cigars that evening in the clubhouse and celebrated becoming a grandfather by blasting a two-run homer in his first at-bat off Chicago hurler Glen Hobbie. That was all the offense Bob Gibson needed as the Cardinal righthander shut out the Cubs, 8–0. A day later, the Redbirds kept the heat on Los Angeles with their sixth successive victory and fifteenth in the last sixteen outings.

In the opener of a four-game series with Milwaukee at Busch Stadium, Stan collected the 725th and final double of his career, giving him second place on the all-time list, sixty-eight two-baggers behind Tris Speaker. A 3–2 win over Milwaukee the next evening pulled the Cards to within two and a half games of the Dodgers, and St. Louis closed the margin to a single length on Sunday, September 15, when they swept a doubleheader from the Braves. "I've never been with a club this hot," said Musial, showing a flair for understatement. Winners of ten in a row and nineteen of their last twenty, the Cardinals were poised to take first place away from Los Angeles, arriving at Busch Stadium for a three-game series.

A pennant race never ended so quickly.

The Dodgers took a 1–0 lead in the opening game when Maury Wills doubled in the sixth, stole third, and scored when Curt Flood misjudged Tommy Davis's fly ball for an RBI single. It was the first time in ten games that the Cardinals had trailed an opponent. Musial slammed his twelfth home run of the season, and the last of his career, to pull St. Louis into a 1–1 tie in the bottom of the seventh, but the Dodgers scored twice in the ninth and clipped the Cardinal wings, 3–1. "We hate to lose the first game," said Cardinal manager Johnny Keane, "but I'm not pessimistic. I feel I've still got my best pitching coming up and we can take the next two."

The best pitching to which Keane referred was lefty Curt Simmons, 15–7 on the season and a shutout winner in each of his last three starts. But Simmons was outduelled the next evening by a better left-hander, Sandy Koufax, who scattered four hits and blanked the Cards, 4–0. Musial spoiled his no-hitter with a seventh-inning single. On September 18, Bob Gibson was handed an early 5–1 lead, but the Dodgers rallied to send the game into extra innings. Fumbles on successive plays by the Cards' usually brilliant second baseman, Julian Javier, gave Los Angeles an unearned run and a 6–5 victory in thirteen innings. The Dodgers had refused to succumb to the pressure, and left town with a four-game lead and nine contests remaining in the season.

St. Louis extended its losing streak to five with a doubleheader loss to the Reds. Los Angeles was now assured a tie for the pennant. Between games of the twin bill, Stan was given a matched set of rocking chairs, a five-tiered cake, and told that Xavier University was establishing a Stan Musial baseball scholarship. Just prior to the contest, Musial was photographed with arbiters Frank Walsh, Paul Pryor, Ken Burkhardt, and Frank Secory, in what was believed to be the first time an umpiring crew ever posed for a shot with an active player. "This is one picture I really want," said Secory.

On Tuesday, September 25, the Dodgers clinched the 1963 National League title while the Cards were losing to the Cubs at Wrigley Field, the club's sixth straight loss. The next day, Stan was presented with an automatic shotgun, a $100 savings bond for his grandson from the Chicago Baseball Writers, and a silver bowl from television station WGN. "All I wanted to do was retire," said Musial to reporters. "Since I announced my retirement in August, I have had three seasons, it seems, crammed into a few weeks. If I had known we would have made the pennant bid we did and what was going to happen on my final swing around the league, I never would have announced my retirement when I did."

Before he left Chicago, Stan received the news that he had been named a vice president of the Cardinal organization by the board of directors. A day later, in yet another tribute to Musial, the popular St. Louis department store Famous-Barr took out a full-page advertisement in the St. Louis *Globe-Democrat*. The ad featured a picture of a smiling Musial and said:

> The Man! Born 11–21–20; man of the hour 9–29–63. The secret of his success? Stan Musial has never given less than 100 per cent of him-

self . . . to his game, to his fans, to his city. Truly, the measure of this man has been accurately gauged in the nickname by which he is affectionately known to millions. Famous-Barr proudly joins all of St. Louis in saluting Stan Musial as he starts a new game . . . and expects, with all St. Louis, to applaud more new records to come from The Man.

Stan was given the day off on Friday, September 27, to attend St. Louis' biggest social event of the year, the Veiled Prophet Ball. Daughter Geraldine was one of the maids of honor. The Cardinals lost to the Reds on Saturday, and then the big day arrived.

On Sunday morning, September 29, Musial had breakfast with his family and actor and friend Horace McMahon, then posed for photographs with Lillian in front of his white Cadillac on which was his personalized license plate, "3000." On the way to the ballpark for the last time as an active player, Stan was accompanied by McMahon; author Arnold Hano; a photographer from *Look* magazine; and *Life* magazine writer W.C. Heinz. When Musial arrived at the ballpark and opened the clubhouse door, he was mobbed by reporters and photographers. First off was a television director who asked him if he'd go back out and make another entrance, this one for the cameras. "You know something?" said Stan. "You guys are wearing me out. All I want to do is retire."

While Musial slowly dressed in his uniform jersey, pitcher Sam Jones, a notorious prankster, sprayed sneezing powder at the members of the press, who rubbed their eyes and blew their noses. Jones disappeared. Musial grabbed his glove, and when he emerged from the dugout into the sunlight, early attendees at the park shouted encouragement to him and applauded his every move. Stan took batting practice, signed a few baseballs for some of the Cincinnati players, then returned to the clubhouse where he sought some much-needed privacy in Johnny Keane's office. Stan was still making last-minute changes to his farewell speech. When he finished his notes, he returned to the clubhouse. "I've changed my mind," he shouted playfully to reporters. "I'm not going to retire."

Musial and his family were chauffeured around the perimeter of the ballpark, the centerpiece of a three-car motorcade. In the Cardinal dugout, trainer Bob Bauman wept unashamedly. He was not alone. When the hour-long, pre-game ceremonies began, Stan strode uncertainly to the center of the diamond with the rest of the baseball celebrities while the Reds and Cardinals stood at right angles to each other. Stan sat with Lillian and their four-year-old daughter Jean. Behind him sat son Dick and daughters Geraldine and Janet. The roar of the crowd was deafening while overhead not one, but two, airplanes flew, bearing streamers which read, "We Salute The Man." The bleacher scoreboard said simply, "Dear Stan, Thanks for the Memories."

Two Cub Scouts presented Musial with a neckerchief. Teammate Ken Boyer, on behalf of the players, gave Stan a ring with the number 6 set in diamonds. Musial fought back tears when Johnny Keane said that while it was true Stan was playing his last game with the Cardinals, the Cardinals were playing their last game with Musial. "I try to picture the clubhouse after the game," said Keane, his voice faltering. Stan began to cry quietly. Sportscaster Harry Caray, his voice also choked with emotion, asked Musial to "hit one more out on Grand Avenue." American League President Joe Cronin presented the Cardinal legend with a plaque as an "expression of the American League's esteem," and Sid Keener, director of baseball's Hall of Fame, declared, "I hope I will occupy a seat at Cooperstown when Stan joins other baseball immortals in the Hall of Fame." St. Louis Chamber of Commerce president Aloys Kaufman presented Stan with a miniature of the bronze statue of Musial which would be erected in front of the new downtown stadium. Cardinal President August A. Busch, Jr. remarked that "We wish you could go on forever," adding that Stan's number 6 would never appear on a Cardinal uniform again. "Nobody could do justice to it," said Busch. "The only other place it will appear is in the Hall of Fame."

Baseball Commissioner Ford Frick stepped to the microphone and indicating Stan, said, "Here stands baseball's happy warrior. Here stands baseball's perfect knight." A Dixieland band played "Auld Lang Syne," and then it was Musial's turn to speak. "This is a day I'll always remember," Stan began, his familiar, high-pitched voice echoing through the stilled stadium. "This is a day of both great joy and sorrow, the sorrow which always comes when we have to say farewell. My heart is filled with thanks for so many who made these twenty-two years possible. I want to thank my wife and children for their strong support for a part-time husband and father. I want to thank God for giving me the talent I have and the good health I've been blessed with."

Musial paused to collect himself, but when he continued, his voice failed. "I hate to say good-bye. So until we meet again, I want to thank you very much."

Stan's initial trip to the plate was halted after the first pitch so the baseball could be given to Hall of Fame director Sid Keener. Facing Cincinnati right-hander Jim Maloney, Musial took a fastball on the outside corner for a called strike, then fouled off a fastball in on his hands. Maloney's next pitch was a slow curve on the outside corner. Stan watched the pitch sail by. Umpire Al Barlick's right arm went up, signalling a called strike three. Musial trotted back to the dugout, where trainer Bob Bauman uncharacteristically chastised him. "You weren't bearing down up there." Surprised, Stan smiled and said, "You're right, boss. If only I could concentrate like the Musial of old, not an old Musial."

In the fourth, on a one-and-one count, Stan got the Cardinals' first hit, a ground single past second baseman Pete Rose, the man who would eventually pass his own National League hit record. In the sixth, with Curt Flood on second, Musial fouled off a high fastball, watched a curve bounce in the dirt, and took a fastball off the corner. The next pitch was a sharp curve which dropped low and inside. Let Cardinal broadcaster Harry Caray tell the story: "Take a good look, fans, take a good look. This might be the last time at bat in the major leagues. Remember the stance and the swing. The pitch to Musial . . . A hot shot on the ground into right field! A base hit! Here's Flood around third! Here's the—no throw! The Cardinals lead, one to nothing. Listen to the crowd. Listen to the crowd."

The single was hit number 3,630 and the last in the major leagues for Musial. After what seemed like an eternity of applause, the Cardinal legend trotted off the field in favor of pinch-runner Gary Kolb. Up in the press box, reporters stood and applauded. Some openly wept. Musial posed for photographers in the dugout and returned to the clubhouse to change clothes. "You know, that's the way I came in," Stan said, referring to his major-league debut in 1941. "Two base hits. And that's the way I leave."

The Reds tied the score with two out in the ninth, but in the fourteenth, Jerry Buchek and Curt Flood singled and Dal Maxvill's blooper to right won the ball game for St. Louis, 3–2, the same score as Musial's major-league debut. Not surprisingly, neither Maxvill, with his game-winning hit, nor Flood, with two hundred hits on the season, was the "Star of the Game." Harry Caray had only once choice for his post-game interview: Stan Musial.

◆ ◆ ◆

When Musial left the field, he held some fifty major-league and National League records. He topped the major leagues in extra-base hits (1,377), total bases (6,134), and most years led in doubles (8), and held National League marks in most games played (3,026), hits (3,630), doubles (725), at-bats (10,972), runs scored (1,949), runs batted in (1,951), highest fielding average for a left fielder (.938), and most years leading in hits (6), triples (5), and runs scored (5). Musial was second in the National League in bases on balls (1,599) and home runs—Stan had the most career homers (475) of anyone who never led his league in homers—third in slugging percentage (.559), and the first ballplayer in the history of the major leagues to top three thousand hits and four hundred home runs. After attaining the age of forty, Musial had slugged forty-six homers, two more than Ted Williams and a mark which would remain a major-league record until broken by another Boston Red Sox slugger, Carl Yastrzemski. Since Stan's retirement, no one has left the game with a higher batting or slugging average.

The all-time Redbird leader in every conceivable offensive category except batting average and stolen bases, Musial had spent twenty-two years in a Cardinal uniform, tying one-team longevity records set by Mel Ott (1926-47, New York Giants) and Cap Anson (1876-97, Chicago White Stockings). With 1,896 games in the outfield and 1,016 at first base, Stan was the first major-league player to appear in a thousand or more games at two different positions. In the All-Star Game, Musial held the record for most games played (24), at-bats (63), hits (20), runs scored (10), home runs (6), total bases (40), and extra-base hits (8). Never a very successful World Series performer, the only record he held for the Fall Classic was for most assists, two, in a five-game series for a right fielder.

Musial was the youngest player ever to win a Most Valuable Player award, a feat later eclipsed by sixteen days when Johnny Bench won his MVP in 1987. Although Stan won his three MVP awards hands down, he finished a close second in the voting four other times. Musial was named the National League Player of the Year by *The Sporting News* in 1943, 1948, 1951, and 1957, and named the Major League Player of the Year in 1946 and 1951. Stan was selected to the magazine's All-Star Major League Team twelve times.

Fifteen years earlier, New York hurler Sal Maglie, in discussing how to pitch to Musial, had said, "I just throw to him and pray." But perhaps longtime Dodger hurler Carl Erskine said it best. "I just throw him my best stuff," said Erskine, "then run over to back up third base."

◆ ◆ ◆

On Sunday evening, October 20, Stan Musial's retirement dinner was held at the Khorassan Room of the Chase Park Plaza Hotel in St. Louis. Over fifteen hundred celebrities and baseball luminaries were in attendance, too numerous to name, save to say that every major-league club was represented. Missouri Senator Stuart Symington read a telegram from John F. Kennedy, in which the President expressed regret at not being able to attend and sent his "heartfelt admiration" for Stan's "superb professional abilities and personal example." And National League President Warren Giles presented an overwhelmed Musial with a unanimous league resolution, a document which officially recognized the performance of a player for the first time in baseball history.

National League umpire Tom Gorman brought down the house when he said, "It's nice to be invited here," then added with a smile, "It's nice to be invited anywhere." On behalf of the twenty National League arbiters, Gorman presented Stan with an engraved silver tray which read, "To a great ballplayer, gentleman, and sportsman."

Sportscaster Bob Prince, who in 1941, in Stan's home town of Donora, Pennsylvania, emceed the first affair honoring Musial, received the biggest laugh of the night when he quipped, "I think it is ridiculous that we are gathered here tonight to honor a man who made more than seven thousand outs."

At the conclusion of the two-and-a-half-hour event, Musial graciously thanked everyone and concluded his short speech by saying, "If I had known things were going to be this good, I'd have retired five years ago." Baritone Marty Bronson capped the evening by singing "Thanks for the Memory," and the ovation which followed could only be described as thunderous.

The dinner was only the first of many honors to come to Stan Musial in his retirement.

◆ ◆ ◆

"Baseball has lost Stan Musial as an active player when it can least spare him," opened the article in the April 7, 1964 issue of *Look* magazine. In February, Stan had been named director of the nation's Physical Fitness Program by President Lyndon B. Johnson and was preparing to travel about the country extolling the benefits of physical conditioning.

With Musial as their newest vice president, the Cardinals survived a breathtaking pennant race in 1964, capturing the title on the last day of the season. The Redbirds went on to down the Yankees in the World Series in seven games. Playing left field for St. Louis that year was Lou Brock, acquired in mid-season from the Cubs. As Stan said in his autobiography, "If I had been in left field for the Cardinals in 1964, the Redbirds would not have won that long-awaited pennant." With Red Schoendienst at the helm, the Cards dropped into the second division the next two years. Musial became the club's general manager prior to the 1967 season, a year in which St. Louis finished well out in front of the rest of the league and edged the Red Sox in the Fall Classic, four games to three. In June, Stan's longtime business partner, Biggie Garagnani had died. When the season ended,

Musial stepped down as general manager to devote more time to the restaurant and his many business interests.

On August 4, 1968, the Cardinal legend donned his old uniform and took his place in right field for pre-game ceremonies before the St. Louis-Chicago game at the new Busch Stadium. After a standing ovation from forty-seven thousand fans, most of whom were there to see Stan, the Cardinal legend returned to the infield, where such dignitaries as baseball Commissioner William D. Eckert, former Commissioner Ford Frick, and National League President Warren Giles were assembled. "Next year," said Eckert, "I anticipate inducting [into baseball's Hall of Fame] one of the greatest of all players, Stan Musial. I predict the baseball writers will elect him by a landslide vote." Giles concurred, saying, "It's been a privilege to know him, aside from his achievements. His character will be written indelibly in the hearts of the men who know him."

Musial's mother, Mary, was escorted onto the field by Stan's son Dick and this trio was followed by Stan's wife, Lillian, and daughters Geraldine, Janet, and Jeanie. Also clustered around Musial were Dr. Michael Duda, Stan's former baseball coach, and Musial's former basketball coach, Frank Pizzica. Following the game, in ceremonies on the northeast side of the front of Busch Stadium, Washington, D.C., sculptor Carl Mose's eight-foot-tall bronze statue of Musial at bat was dedicated. The St. Louis chapter of the Baseball Writers Association, helped by a $5,000 donation from radio station KMOX and Stan's retirement dinner back in 1963, had raised $40,000 for the statue.

The inscription on the base reads, "Here stands baseball's perfect warrior. Here stands baseball's perfect knight." (Somewhere, without explanation, Frick's "happy warrior" was dropped in favor of the more resonant and grammatically dramatic "perfect warrior.") Speaking at the dedication, Musial, who still dislikes the statue because its depiction of his batting stance is inaccurate, said, in part, "It's truly a great honor. I like to think of this statue as a symbol of sports and sportsmanship and the great freedom of opportunity that this country offers."

His voice breaking, Musial choked for one of the few times in his career when he concluded, "I want to thank the writers from the bottom of my heart, for my mother and the Musial family, for making me a Cardinal forever."

Musial was inducted into the Hall of Fame on July 28, 1969, along with catcher Roy Campanella and pitchers Waite Hoyt and Stan Coveleski. Unbelievably, Stan was not mentioned on twenty-three of the 340 ballots cast by members of the Baseball Writers Association of America, yet he was elected with 93.2 percent of the votes cast and joined Williams, Jackie Robinson, and Bob Feller as the only players to be elected in their first year of eligibility. Stan's records couldn't begin to fit on the plaque, which read:

STANLEY FRANK MUSIAL
"THE MAN"
ST. LOUIS CARDINALS 1941–1963;
HOLDS MANY NATIONAL LEAGUE RECORDS,
AMONG THEM: GAMES PLAYED 3026; AT
BAT 10972 TIMES; 3630 HITS; MOST RUNS
SCORED 1949; MOST RUNS BATTED IN 1951;
TOTAL BASES 6134; LED N.L. IN TOTAL
BASES 6 YEARS, SLUGGING PERCENTAGE
6 YEARS, MOST VALUABLE PLAYER 1943-
1946-1948. NAMED ON 12 ALL STAR TEAMS.
LIFETIME BATTING AVERAGE .331.

Baseball Commissioner Bowie Kuhn said so much had been written about Stan, he found it difficult to find something new to add. "What else do you say about a man who is great all around, who has no weaknesses? Despite all his records, more than fifty of them, he is best known and remembered as a team player. He is one of our greatest ambassadors. He was remarkable for his durability. He was and is The Man." After reading the accomplishments on Stan's plaque in an almost unbearable monotone, Kuhn introduced Musial to the overflow crowd of five thousand which included nineteen of the thirty-seven living members of the Hall.

And then it was Musial's turn to become the 114th member of the Hall of Fame.

Just as Stan was about to step to the microphone, the sun broke through for the first time that day. "Stan brought the sun," said Pat Dean, Dizzy's wife, to Lillian Musial. "He always does."

"I don't mind hitting last in this lineup," began Stan, using a prepared speech so his emotions would not get the better of him. "What better way to make a living than to go out in the fresh air, what there is left of it, anyway, and get paid for playing a boy's game?" Remembering his father's admonition almost three decades earlier on the importance of a college education, Stan added, "For all my good luck, I wish I'd gone to college, and I don't believe I'm being at all disloyal to baseball when I urge young men to get a college education if they can." Stan touched on the many changes in the game since his major-league debut and said, "I've said it before and I mean it. Of all the thrills I experienced, from that first hit off

Jim Tobin to the last two off Jim Maloney my last two times up in 1963, I still say the greatest was in just pulling on the uniform and going out there to compete."

Musial kept his emotions in check until he mentioned his family. "Times were tough when we were young," said Stan with a smile. "The Musials were poor people then, like so many of our friends around Donora, Pennsylvania. But I never felt like I wanted for anything because I had a baseball. My first toy was a baseball. Of course, my mother is here today," Stan said, his high-pitched voice cracking as he indicated Mary Musial, seated in the crowd. Choked with emotion, the Cardinal legend broke down and was barely able to continue. "She's been in my corner all the way."

Composing himself, Stan summed up his career. "I certainly wouldn't have dreamed I'd make thirty-six hundred and thirty hits. Even though I was blessed with durability and a good body, I was extremely lucky to avoid serious injury. I'm eternally grateful for the good years and the health God gave me. Yet, knowing that this is a competitive game as well as a sport, I don't believe He would mind if I expressed a few regrets. I would have liked, for instance, the strong arm I had before it was hurt so that I could have been, all round, as great a player as I tried to be. To me, defense and team effort aren't just words to be expressed emptily between times at bat. But I'm too grateful to complain. I came up in 1941 to play against men who had starred as early as the mid-twenties and I stayed through 1963, playing against men who'll star into the seventies and maybe even until 1980. So I feel qualified, I hope you'll agree, to say that baseball was a great game, baseball is a great game, baseball will be a great game. This is the greatest honor of the many that have been bestowed on me. I hope I gave as much to baseball as it gave to me."

The crowd rose to its feet and with a standing ovation, gave Stan Musial his official place in the Hall of Fame. His place in baseball history had been assured years earlier. But discussing Musial the hitter does not adequately sum up Musial the man. Years later, baseball Commissioner Fay Vincent came as close to anyone when he said, "I think the thing we admire about Stan is that he's been able to lead a life off the field that is every bit as distinguished as his career on the field. He's a fine person. He's somebody that the community can admire and I guess he represents for baseball the kind of person that we would like to admire, to worship, and to honor."

Stan the Man.

Afterword

◆

So how good was he, really?

Any discussion beginning like that begs a few other questions. How high was Musial's batting average? How many home runs did he hit? Did he drive in a lot of runs? Was he a clutch hitter? Did he run the bases well? Was he a team leader? Where would the teams on which he played have finished without him? Were any of his contemporaries better?

There's no doubt that by any standard you care to apply, Stan Musial was the National League's best hitter in the 1940s and well into the next decade until age began to overtake him. For the period during which he played, Musial had only one equal, Boston Red Sox slugger Ted Williams. But look, let's be honest about Stan's ability. In any given year, he didn't hit for average like Ty Cobb, didn't hit home runs with the frequency of Babe Ruth, didn't drive in runs like Lou Gehrig, didn't steal bases as often as Eddie Collins, and didn't have the defensive skills of Tris Speaker.

If you compare single-season performances, Musial's 1948 would be on your long list, but it wouldn't make anybody forget Babe Ruth's 1921 or Ty Cobb's 1911 or Rogers Hornsby's 1924. I will never forget sportscaster Curt Gowdy, an unreconstructed Carl Yastrzemski fan, gushing during a Game of the Week broadcast one Saturday afternoon, "Did anyone ever have a year like Yastrzemski had in 1967?" Yeah, Curt, something like a dozen guys had about fifty years better than that. As James Thurber once said, you could look it up. For performance over a one-year period, it's mighty hard to match some of the numbers the Ruths, Cobbs, and Hornbsys were putting up back in the 1920s.

And if you're comparing perfomance over a sustained period, you could build a pretty good case that the best ballplayer who ever walked on the diamond was Lou Gehrig, the soft-spoken, Hall of Fame first baseman who played for the New York Yankees from 1923–39. From 1927 through 1937, an eleven-year period, Larrupin' Lou terrorized American League pitchers for an average 202 hits, 39 home runs, and 154 RBIs. That's what he *averaged*. Or consider Rogers Hornsby. For the five-year period from 1921

203

through 1925, all he did was compile a .402 batting average. Or how about the Babe, who from 1920 through 1932, averaged 46 home runs a year?

Those numbers are *scary*. They're *superhuman*.

What Musial had was a piece of all the legends of baseball. He was a complete ballplayer, not a one-dimensional performer like Reggie Jackson or Dave Kingman. Stan led the league five times in triples, a hit which is, after all, as much an indicator of speed as it is of power. A smart baserunner, he was fast enough, in an era when they didn't steal bases. (Brooklyn's Jackie Robinson, remembered as a speedster, led the league in stolen bases in 1947 with the meager total of twenty-nine.) Musial wasn't a home run hitter, but he had six seasons in which he hit thirty or more dingers and he led the National League in slugging average an equal number of times. It is remarkable to note that in only one of those thirty-homer years did he lead the league in slugging. And while Willie Mays and Henry Aaron had far more lifetime home runs, their career slugging averages still fell shy of Stan's.

When Musial hung up his uniform, he had more extra-base hits than anyone, more doubles than any other player except Tris Speaker, and more triples than any of his contemporaries. He'd played more games, batted more often, and collected more hits than anybody except Ty Cobb. Only two players in the history of the game had scored more runs, only three had more RBIs, only four had drawn more bases on balls, only five had hit more homers, and only eight had compiled a higher slugging average. Since Musial's retirement, Pete Rose and Henry Aaron have surpassed him in several career marks. But consider this: it took Rose 3,081 more at-bats to collect 21 more doubles, 216 more runs scored, and 626 more hits, and it took Aaron 1,392 more at-bats to collect 100 more extra bases, 141 more hits, 225 more runs scored, and 346 more RBIs.

But more important than Musial's considerable skill with the bat is his contribution to the sport itself. He never came under criticism for poor training habits or lack of pride in his defense. He never balked at being shuttled between the outfield and first base, as he was so often during his career. He was respected by those he played with and those he played against. He never got into trouble with management. He was never fined or suspended. He was a clutch hitter and a team player and a club leader and if it hadn't been for his big bat in the lineup, the Cardinals would have finished in the National League cellar for about ten years straight.

Stan Musial gave to baseball more than baseball gave back to him, a statement he would modestly disavow, but one which is true nonetheless. Unlike Pete Rose and Joe Jackson, Musial's career was untouched by scandal. He wasn't moody and mysterious like Joe DiMaggio and he wasn't ill-tempered and pugnacious like Billy Martin and Rogers Hornsby. Unlike Babe Ruth and Ted Williams, Stan's squeaky-clean reputation off the field has, ironically, only served to diminish his accomplishments as a hitter. But the fans recognized that Stan was the real McCoy. They watched him hit and run the bases and chase fly balls and they knew he gave a hundred percent of himself every moment he was on the field.

Because that is the ultimate truth about Stan Musial: he was born to play baseball.

Playing Record

	Games	BA	SA	AB	H	2B	3B	HR	R	RBI	BB	SO	SB	AB	H	PO	A	E
1941	12	.426	.574	47	20	4	0	1	8	7	2	1		1	0	20	1	0
1942	140	.315	.490	467	147	32	10	10	87	72	62	25	6	2	0	296	6	5
1943	157	**.357**	**.562**	617	**220**	**48**	**20**	13	108	81	72	18	9	2	1	376	15	7
1944	146	.347	**.549**	568	**197**	**51**	14	12	112	94	90	28	7	2	0	353	16	5
1946	156	**.365**	**.587**	624	**228**	**50**	**20**	16	**124**	103	73	31	7	0	0	1166	69	15
1947	149	.312	.504	587	183	30	13	19	113	95	80	24	4	0	0	1360	77	8
1948	155	**.376**	**.702**	611	**230**	**46**	**18**	39	**135**	**131**	79	34	7	0	0	354	11	7
1949	157	.338	.624	612	**207**	41	**13**	36	128	123	107	38	3	0	0	337	11	3
1950	146	**.346**	**.596**	555	192	41	7	28	105	109	87	36	5	1	0	760	39	8
1951	152	**.355**	.614	578	205	30	**12**	32	**124**	108	98	40	4	1	1	816	45	10
1952	154	**.336**	**.538**	578	**194**	**42**	6	21	**105**	91	96	29	7	0	0	502	18	5
1953	157	.337	.609	593	200	**53**	9	30	127	113	**105**	32	3	0	0	294	9	5
1954	153	.330	.607	591	195	41	9	35	**120**	126	103	39	1	0	0	307	15	5
1955	154	.319	.566	562	179	30	5	33	97	108	80	39	5	0	0	1000	94	9
1956	156	.310	.522	594	184	33	6	27	87	**109**	75	39	2	0	0	954	95	8
1957	134	**.351**	.612	502	176	38	3	29	82	102	66	34	1	4	2	1167	99	10
1958	135	.337	.528	472	159	35	2	17	64	62	72	26	0	12	5	1019	100	13
1959	115	.255	.428	341	87	13	2	14	37	44	60	25	0	22	5	624	63	7
1960	116	.275	.486	331	91	17	1	17	49	63	41	34	1	28	4	300	19	3
1961	123	.288	.489	372	107	22	4	15	46	70	52	35	0	19	5	149	9	1
1962	135	.330	.508	433	143	18	1	19	57	82	64	46	3	13	8	164	6	4
1963	124	.255	.404	337	86	10	2	12	34	58	35	43	2	21	4	121	1	4
22 yrs.	3026	.331	.559	10972	3630	725	177	475	1949	1951	1599	696	78	126	35	12439	818	142
WORLD SERIES																		
1942	5	.222	.278	18	4	1	0	0	2	2	4	0	0	0	0	13	0	0
1943	5	.278	.278	18	5	0	0	0	2	0	2	2	0	0	0	7	2	0
1944	6	.304	.522	23	7	2	0	1	2	2	2	0	0	0	0	11	0	1
1946	7	.222	.444	27	6	4	1	0	3	4	4	2	1	0	0	60	2	0
4 yrs.	23	.256	.395	86	22	7	1	1	9	8	12	4	1	0	0	91	4	1

Top ten rankings in all-time offensive records (through 1993):

—Fifth in games played
—Ninth in slugging average
—Fifth in at-bats
—Fourth in hits
—Third in doubles
—Sixth in runs scored
—Fifth in runs batted in
—Ninth in walks

Bibliography

BOOKS

Alexander, Charles. *Our Game: An American Baseball History.* New York: Henry Holt, 1991.

Barber, Red. *1947: When All Hell Broke Loose in Baseball.* New York: Da Capo Press, 1982.

Broeg, Bob. *Stan Musial: "The Man's" Own Story.* New York: Doubleday, 1964.

————. *The Man Stan . . . Musial Then and Now.* St. Louis: The Bethany Press, 1977.

Carter, Craig, ed. *The Complete Baseball Record Book.* St. Louis: The Sporting News, 1985.

Cohen, Richard M., and David S. Neft. *The World Series.* New York: Collier Books, Macmillan, 1986.

Connor, Anthony J. *Voices from Cooperstown.* New York: Collier Books, 1982.

Craft, David and Tom Owens. *Redbirds Revisited.* Chicago: Bonus Books, 1990.

Creamer, Robert W. *Baseball in '41.* New York: Viking Penguin, 1991.

Dickson, Paul. *Baseball's Greatest Quotations.* New York: HarperCollins, 1991.

Durocher, Leo, with Ed Linn. *Nice Guys Finish Last.* New York: Simon & Schuster, 1975.

Goldstein, Richard. *Spartan Seasons: How Baseball Survived the Second World War.* New York: Macmillan, 1980.

Golenbeck, Peter. *Bums: An Oral History of the Brooklyn Dodgers.* New York: G.P. Putnam's Sons, 1984.

Holway, John. *The Sluggers.* Alexandria, Virginia: A Redifinition Book, 1989.

Hynd, Noel. *The Giants of the Polo Grounds.* New York: Doubleday, 1988.

Kaese, Harold. *The Boston Braves.* New York: G.P. Putnam's Sons, 1948.

Langford, Walter M. *Legends of Baseball.* South Bend, IN: Diamond Communications, 1987.

Lenburg, Jeff. *Baseball's All-Star Game: A Game-by-Game Guide.* Jefferson, NC: McFarland & Company, 1986.

Leptich, John and Dave Baranowski. *This Date in St. Louis Cardinals History.* New York: Stein and Day, 1983.

————. *The St. Louis Cardinals: The Story of a Great Baseball Club.* New York: G.P. Putnam's Sons, 1944.

Mead, William B. *Baseball Goes to War.* New York: Farragut Publishing, 1985.

Neft, David S. *The Sports Encyclopedia: Baseball.* New York: St. Martin's Press, 1989.

Okrent, Daniel and Lewine Harris. *The Ultimate Baseball Book.* Boston: Houghton Mifflin, 1984.

Peterson, Robert. *Only The Ball Was White.* New York: McGraw-Hill, 1970.

Polner, Murray. *Branch Rickey.* New York: Signet, 1982.

Rains, Rob. *St. Louis Cardinals: The 100th Anniversary History.* New York: St. Martin's Press, 1992.

Reidenbaugh, Lowell. *The Sporting News Selects Baseball's 25 Greatest Pennant Races.* St. Louis: The Sporting News, 1987.
Ritter, Lawrence and Donald Honig. *The Image of Their Greatness.*
Schoor, Gene. *The Stan Musial Story.* New York: Julian Messner, Inc., 1955.
Seidel, Michael. *Ted Williams: A Baseball Life.* Chicago, Illinois: Contemporary Books, 1991.
Seymour, Harold. *Baseball: The Golden Years.* New York: Oxford University Press, 1971.
Siner, Howard. *Sweet Seasons: Baseball's Top Teams Since 1920.* New York: Pharos Books, 1988.
Slaughter, Enos with Kevin Reid. *Country Hardball.* Greensboro, NC: Tudor Publishers, 1991.
Stockton, J. Roy. *The Gashouse Gang and a Couple of Other Guys.* New York: A.S. Barnes, 1945.
Thorn, John and Pete Palmer. *Total Baseball.* New York: Warner Books, 1989.
Tiemann, Robert. *Cardinal Classics.* St. Louis: Baseball Histories, Inc., 1982.
Vricella, Mario. *The St. Louis Cardinals—The First Century.* New York: Vantage Press, 1992.
Westcott, Rich. *Diamond Greats.* Westport, Connecticut: Meckler Books, 1988.
Wilber, Cynthia J. *For The Love of the Game.* New York: William Morrow, 1992.
Williams, Ted with John Underwood. *My Turn at Bat.* New York: Fireside Books, 1988.
Baseball: A Doubleheader Collection of Facts, Feats, and Firsts. Compiled by The Sporting News. New York: Galahad Books, 1992.
The Baseball Encyclopedia: The Complete and Official Record of Major League Baseball. Eighth edition. New York: Macmillan, 1990.
The Cardinals: The Complete Record of Redbird Baseball. New York: Collier Books, 1983.

PERIODICALS

Broeg, Bob. "Remembrance of Summers Past." *Baseball Historical Review of the Society for American Baseball Research;* 1982.
Cohane, Tim. "The Changing Days of Stan Musial. *Look;* April 7, 1964.
———. "Stan Musial's Last Day." *Life;* October 11, 1963.
Mead, Alden. "The Cardinals in the Forties." *Baseball Research Journal: Twenty-First Historical and Statistical Review of the Society for American Baseball Research;* 1992.
Murden, Robert A. "Who Rate As Baseball's Most Complete Sluggers." *Baseball Research Journal: Fifteenth Annual Historical and Statistical Review of the Society for American Baseball Research;* 1986.
Musial, Stan as told to Bob Broeg. "The Man Behind The Man." *Look;* April 7, 1964.
Paxton, Harry T. "A Visit with Stan Musial." *Saturday Evening Post;* April 19, 1958.
Shutt, Timothy Baker. "When Baseball Came Home from The War." *Sports History.* Leesburg, Virginia; July, 1987.
Stockton, J. Roy. "Rookie of the Year." *Saturday Evening Post;* September 12, 1942.
"Old Pros Take on Trimming." *Life;* March 21, 1960.
"That Kind of Man." *Newsweek;* August 26, 1963.
"That Man." *Time;* September 5, 1949.

Index

Note: All entries except those that identify other people are in reference to Stan Musial and his life.